The person charging this book is
responsible for its return to the
**Learning Resources Center (LRC)**
**Richland Community College**
**One College Park**
Decatur, IL 62521-8512
on or before the latest date
stamped below.

To renew, call
**Circulation Department of the**
**LRC, 875-7211, Ext. 303**

| Due Date | Due Date |
|----------|----------|
|          |          |

# ON THE PICKET LINE

# On the Picket Line

Strategies of Working-Class
Women during the Depression

**MARY E. TRIECE**

UNIVERSITY OF ILLINOIS PRESS
URBANA AND CHICAGO

⊚ This book is printed on acid-free paper.

Library of Congress Cataloging-in-Publication Data

Triece, Mary Eleanor, 1967–

On the picket line : strategies of working-class women during the Depression / Mary E. Triece.

p.   cm.

Includes bibliographical references and index.

ISBN-13: 978-0-252-03151-9 (cloth : alk. paper)

ISBN-10: 0-252-03151-2 (cloth : alk. paper)

ISBN-13: 978-0-252-07391-5 (pbk. : alk. paper)

ISBN-10: 0-252-07391-6 (pbk. : alk. paper)

1. Working-class women—United States—History—20th century.

2. Protest movements—United States—History.

3. Social conflict—United States—History—20th century.

4. Depressions—1929—United States.

5. Communism—United States.

I. Title.

HD6058.T75     2007

331.4 79297309043—dc22     2006022622

# Contents

# Acknowledgments

There are many people to thank for providing inspiration, optimism, mentoring, and technical assistance that enabled me to see this book to completion. Some of these individuals I know personally; others I have only read about in the archival materials I studied. I must first acknowledge the women whose writings and speeches provided rich resources that enabled me to understand what it was like to be a working-class mother, laborer, or activist during the 1930s. The ingenuity, bravery, and militance of these individuals stand as an example for women and men to follow as we continue the struggle for equality of class, race, and gender.

Additionally, family members, friends, and colleagues have provided invaluable support at each stage of this project. First and foremost, I thank Mark, Dashiell, and Lillian Tidrick for their friendship and love, which both sustained me and provided balance in my life as I became immersed in my work. Others, whose support I could not have done without, include William and Eleanor Triece and Marla Tidrick. Thanks go also to my colleagues at the University of Akron, who continue to lend an ear and offer ideas as we discuss issues pertaining to communication, struggle, and social justice. A special thanks to those colleagues, both in the School of Communication and across the University of Akron campus, who have worked so hard to unionize our faculty. Their dedication to the cause of workers' rights inspired me as I wrote this book. I am also thankful to have received funding for this project as part of the University of Akron's Summer Faculty Fellowship in 2003. Although a number of years have passed since I worked closely with them, my mentors at the University of Texas at Austin—Dana Cloud, Roderick Hart, and John Rodden—continue to influence my research and writing.

There are also many people to thank who had a direct hand in the shaping of this book. Thank you so much to Kerry Callahan, acquisitions editor at the University of Illinois Press, for taking an interest in this project and nurturing it as it went through the review and revision process. The readers of the manuscript for the Press provided suggestions that were not only useful but essential to the creation of a strong manuscript. The archivists in several institutions who helped to locate photos for inclusion in the book were always helpful, quick, and very kind in answering all of my questions. Thank you to Elizabeth Clemens at the Walter P. Reuther Library, Wayne State University; Karen Kukil in the Sophia Smith Collection, Smith College; and Barbara Morley and Valerie Fusco at the Kheel Center, Cornell University. A very special thank you to Mark Rosenzweig at the Reference Center for Marxist Studies, New York City, for granting permission to publish from the Elizabeth Gurley Flynn Papers. And thank you to Ellen Shea at the Schlesinger Library, Radcliffe Institute for Advanced Study, for granting permission to quote from the Leonora O'Reilly Papers and to Karen Kukil at the Smith Collection, Smith College, for permission to quote from the Ella Reeve Bloor Papers. Thank you also to the librarians at the University of Akron's Bierce Library, especially John Ball and Mae Schreiber, for their expertise and kindness.

As we collectively struggle for communities that value humanity above all else, may we strive to be as outspoken and creative as the women whose lives mark the pages of this book.

# ON THE PICKET LINE

# Introduction: Paradox and Social Change in the 1930s

"The woman's place at the time of a strike is not at home, but on the picket line. What can the women do at home, anyway, when there is nothing to cook, no food to serve; their place is on the picket line" ("Women Auxiliaries Aid" 1931). Mary Smith made this statement as a delegate at the 1931 Pittsburgh District Conference of the Women's Auxiliaries of the National Miners' Union. She and thousands of other working-class wives knew all too well the extent to which economic issues impacted the quality of life in the home. Workplace and home front were not distinct or unrelated realms; for the working poor and for the unemployed, home was not "a haven in a heartless world" (Lasch 1977, xvii) but an extension of the unforgiving terrain of the mines, factories, and farms where husbands, wives, and often their children spent most of their waking hours.

Yet, according to the doctrine of separate spheres, which gained widespread acceptance in the early 1800s with the entrenchment of industrial capitalism (see Barrett and McIntosh 1991; Coltrane 1996; Coontz 1988; Matthaei 1982; Zaretsky 1976), the home represented a locus of tranquility in the midst of industrial turbulence. Prevailing beliefs that women were innately benevolent and virtuous (see Welter 1966) dictated that women's place was in the home, where their moral suasion would properly guide children and comfort husbands after a hard day's work at the office or factory. Despite the prevalence of separate-spheres rhetoric—found in popular magazines and newspapers and spoken from pulpits and public platforms—the lives of Mary Smith and her comrades gave lie to the images of domestic bliss; and Smith and her comrades gave voice to this lie.

This book is about the struggles of Mary Smith and thousands like her who spoke publicly in their roles as mothers, workers, and wives of unemployed men during the Depression era. In a period of scarce jobs and inadequate wages, these women forged a community-based activism that linked domestic concerns with the sphere of production, breathing new life and a new understanding of solidarity into the 1930s labor movement.[1]

The time period under study, roughly 1930–39, was one of widespread economic uncertainty, and it often conjures images of the down-and-out man, unemployed, standing in a breadline. Less often studied are the more than three million unemployed women, many of whom were sleeping on park benches and standing in breadlines alongside men.[2] But women didn't just stand in breadlines; they organized bread *strikes*—along with meat and rent strikes, sit-ins for shoes, and walkouts for fair wages. *On the Picket Line* uncovers the voices of women who were working poor, unemployed, and/or African American, particularly those active in the Communist Party USA, in order to examine how these individuals confronted the tensions specific to their position in the socioeconomic system, which arose when material need necessitated a violation of norms delineating "men's jobs" in the workplace and "woman's place" in the home.

At a broader level, this book examines what we might term a reality gap, the space between prevailing, widely accepted ideologies (such as the doctrine of separate spheres) and the reality of people's day-to-day existence. Reality gaps give rise to contradictions or paradoxes that, it will be shown, provide an opening for social critique and change. This book focuses less on the dominant ideologies themselves, though such investigations remain important in communication studies.[3] Instead, the following chapters outline the ideological backdrop of the day and then focus more intently on the strategies radical Left women employed in order to counteract or challenge the prevailing belief systems that constrained their lives. Women's challenges arose out of and were shaped by the daily reality of their lives, that is, the conditions they faced in their homes as wives and mothers, their experiences at the market as consumers, and the double shift many endured as workers in both the paid labor force and the domestic realm. These realities did not accord with prevailing notions of "womanhood," "domestic life," and "family values," but rather they gave rise to a host of contradictions or paradoxes that women often exploited in order to challenge the dominant socioeconomic system.

The rhetorical scholar Carol Mattingly notes that feminist efforts to broaden the traditional canon of rhetoric are still relatively recent and that more time is needed to "recover, evaluate, and make meaning" of women's contributions to the rhetorical tradition (2002, 99). In this spirit, *On the Picket Line* sets the contributions of radical women of the Depression era alongside those of the suffragists; antislavery, labor, and early woman's movement agitators; Progressive era reformers; and present-day female activists who have found their rightful place within the rhetorical canon.[4] Examining both the rhetoric and creative tactics these women employed, this book asks, How did working-class women in a well-known leftist organization, the Communist Party USA, manage the paradoxes arising from gender and class discrimination during a tumultuous period in U.S. history? Studies of the labor movement of the 1930s tend to overlook the specific contributions of women while literature on women of the 1930s tends to overlook their roles as laborers. Rabinowitz notes "even many women's historians have accepted the characterization of the 1930s as irrelevant to feminist issues because of the predominance of class struggle, and so for the most part they have ignored women's struggles during the period" (1991, 4). The following chapters fill the gap in U.S. labor and women's history by giving voice to the Mary Smiths of the 1930s whose struggles in the workplace and the home remain relevant for us in the twenty-first century.

## Emergent Discourses and Agency

In *Rhetoric and Marxism,* James Aune establishes what he believes to be a "central unresolved problem in Marxism," namely, the "relationship between structure and struggle" (1994, 13). That is, he asks what is the "relationship between the structures that determine and limit social action and the possibilities for human action and choice that exist within those structures?" (13). Aune's work raises important questions concerning rhetoric, social change, and left politics, which have been explored elsewhere (Triece 2001, 1–29, 177–236). Continued exploration of these complex issues is warranted by the present-day crisis created by global capitalism and hyperimperialism that is undermining basic human rights and creating an ever-widening gap between rich and poor.

One place to begin theorizing the relationship between structure and struggle is the work of the Marxist scholar Raymond Williams and his discussion of "dominant, residual, and emergent" discourses (1977, 121–27). These concepts enable us to understand the relationship between economics and culture as dynamic and unfixed, yet delimited by entrenched but not inalterable structures and systems. Williams's concepts account for the "complex interrelations between movements and tendencies both within and beyond a specific and effective dominance" (121) and thus may shed light on what Aune terms the relationship between structure and struggle.

Dominant discourses are the hegemonic discourses, beliefs, and practices that delineate the common sense of a culture. Perhaps of more interest are the residual and emergent discourses and the ways they interact with dominant discourses. Residual beliefs are those that have been "formed in the past, but [are] still active in the cultural process, not only and often not at all as an element of the past, but as an effective element of the present" (Williams 1977, 122). The "cult of True Womanhood" (see Welter 1966), a mid-nineteenth-century ideology that dictated women be domestic, submissive, pious, and pure, exemplifies a residual discourse that took root with the emergence of industrial capitalism in the mid-1800s but held sway in various degrees throughout the twentieth century. The contours of True Womanhood did not remain the same between the mid-1800s and the 1930s but rather changed as the ideology was incorporated into the dominant discourses—and the economic needs—of subsequent decades. For instance, as the growth and spread of factory production necessitated the entrance of women and girls into the paid labor force as a pool of relatively inexpensive labor, an ideology termed Practical True Womanhood (Triece 1999) emerged, which contained traces of True Womanhood but was better suited to the evolving economic needs and worldviews of the early 1900s. The cult of True Womanhood and the doctrine of separate spheres are two residual discourses that were particularly resonant in the context of Depression era cultural backlash and which influenced the lives of working-class women in profound ways.

Emergent discourses are those that pose a challenge to the dominant. They represent "new meanings and values, new practices, new relationships and kinds of relationships" (Williams 1977, 123). Williams's elaboration of dominant, residual, and emergent discourses is significant for the way it underscores the dynamic relationship between culture and economics. In so doing, it provides room for agency or struggle, while retaining the relevance of the determining factors of various structures. Determination should not be understood as totalizing, fixed, or permanently setting bounds. Rather, as Engels ([1890] 1978) established and as subsequent Marxist scholars (Hall 1996; Williams 1977) have explained, determination is more usefully viewed as the ways that objective conditions set limits on the ideological. Engels observed, "We make our history ourselves, but, in the first place, under very definite assumptions and conditions" ([1890] 1978, 761). Furthermore, determination may be viewed not only in its "negative" sense—as setting limits—but also in a "positive" sense, as the "exertion of pressures . . . against the limits" (Williams 1977, 87). In this view, determination implies a will to accomplish some-- thing ("I am determined to earn higher wages"). This twin understanding of determination opens the way to a clearer understanding of the relationship between structures and struggle. According to Williams, society is "never only the 'dead husk' which limits social and individual fulfillment. It is always also a constitutive process with very powerful pressures which are both expressed in political, economic, and cultural formations and, to take the full weight of 'constitutive,' are internalized and become 'individual wills'" (87).

*On the Picket Line* examines oppositional emergent discourses posed by radical Left women as a challenge to the existing social order. The following analysis explores the ways that working-class women resisted incorporation and sustained a steady fight for their counterhegemonic ideas through specific rhetorical strategies and extra-discursive actions. As I will demonstrate in the following chapters, paradoxes arising out of what was earlier termed the "reality gap" open up a significant wedge through which emergent discourses can surface.

In the following study, extra-verbal context necessarily figures significantly in the analysis. In order to understand the ways that paradox (both its formation and challenges to it) arises out of a reality gap, one must have an idea of the reality or rhetorical situation from which it emerges. As Hall pointed out, "Material circumstances are the net of constraints, the 'conditions of existence' for practical thought and calculation about society" (1996, 44). In the present study, material circumstances or the "structures" mentioned earlier are intended to refer to a reality existing outside of, but understood through, language. This is not to imply that language is a transparent mechanism that describes or reflects an outside reality in a straightforward or unproblematic way. To the contrary, messages that describe the world vary widely according to a host of variables including the historical and immediate contexts, the rhetor, and the audience, to name a few. Communication scholars must explore competing messages that vie for recognition and legitimation in public settings for the ways that social relations and experiences are explained and/or justified.

Within this conceptual framework of language and reality, a key element of the material world is understood to be the economic system by which a society feeds, clothes, and reproduces itself. Further, the relationship between language and the material or extra-verbal world is dialectical (each influences the other), but not indeterminate. Economic forces are most influential in the last instance. Thus, undergirding this study of rhetoric, paradox, and social change is the straightforward observation that the living conditions of working-class women in the 1930s, particularly as they were shaped by industrial and corporate capitalism, profoundly influenced the form the women's arguments took as they challenged the socioeconomic system. Note I use the phrase "profoundly influenced," pointing again to the central—but not determinant—impact that an extra-discursive reality has on one's understandings or expressions of that world. Political interests, then, are not (only) discursive constructions "conceive[d] and define[d]" through political language (G. Jones 1983, 22), but are influenced by one's "socially determined standpoint" (Eagleton 1991, 51), which often decides things as basic as who has enough food to eat and who has not.[5] To speak of an extra-discursive reality that influences or impacts a group's communication and struggles for social change is to acknowledge that not everything can be reduced to language and that, furthermore, language is not material in the same way that machinery and food are material. One cannot eat a menu, as John Clarke (1991) reminds us.[6]

As I explain in the following chapters, women often employed what I call "extra-discursive" tactics that employed physicality—bodily presence or absence—in order to challenge material processes and relations, for example, piece rates and speedups, that influenced whether they ate or starved. Events such as strikes, sit-ins, flying squadrons, and boycotts included but went beyond words to rely on physical presence or absence for their success. Understood as examples of "coercive persuasion" (see Simons 1972), these actions were effective to the extent they forced the hand of employers, owners, and landlords who worried about the impact of a work stoppage or customer loss on the bottom line. Given the uneven playing field inherent in a system in which only a few own the means necessary for creating basic goods and services, extra-discursive tactics were often the most effective option, if not at times the only one, for working-class women and men.

Lloyd Bitzer's (1968) concept of the "rhetorical situation" provides another way to understand the significance of the extra-verbal context surrounding any rhetorical act. Bitzer defined the "rhetorical situation" as a "complex of persons, events, objects, and relations presenting an actual or potential exigence which can be completely or partially removed if discourse, introduced into the situation, can so constrain human decision or action as to bring about the significant modification of the exigence" (6). The "situation controls the rhetorical response," or put differently, "discourse is rhetorical insofar as it functions, (or seeks to function) as a fitting response to a situation which needs and invites it" (6).[7] A speaker's response to a particular situation is shaped by the "exigence" (the change needed, obstacle to be overcome, or "thing which is other than it should be"), the audience or individuals capable of enacting the needed change, and the various constraints "made up of persons, events, objects, and relations which are parts of the situation because they have the power to constrain decision and action needed to modify the exigence" (8). As we shall see in the following chapters, working-class women's rhetorical as well as extra-discursive tactics represented fitting responses given the exigences, audience, and constraints they faced.

## Women in the Communist Party

Chapter 1 previews the contradictions working-class women faced in their roles as mothers, housewives, and workers in an era of economic decline and

New Deal legislation. It may be useful to examine these contradictions and their functions through the concept of paradox.

Chesebro identifies "semantic paradoxes," which "are created whenever the connotations associated with a word are inconsistent with the denotations of the word" (1984, 166). He continues, "[S]emantic paradoxes exist, then, whenever the value associated with the word used to label an object is contradicted by the physical existence, physical characteristics, and/or physical functions of the object" (166). The paradoxes faced by working-class women of the 1930s can be similarly seen as arising when hegemonic ideologies contradict material reality. Prevailing discourses concerning women, work, home, and motherhood relied on particular images and associations in order to maintain rigid sex roles and sex-typed jobs and to ensure unpaid domestic labor in the home, all of which sustained capitalist and patriarchal relations (see Barrett and McIntosh 1991; Coltrane 1996; Coontz 1988; Matthaei 1982; Zaretsky 1976). Tensions arose when women's actions, that is, their physical presence in the workplace or on the public platform, contradicted prevailing notions of "woman," "worker," and "public speaker." Women—associated with domesticity, submissiveness, nurturance, and passivity—assumed jobs in the paid labor force where "breadwinner" connoted a "male" head of household, and they advocated for social justice in the public arena where "manliness" was an indispensable attribute.[8]

Paradox can function as a type of social logic, a way of ordering and understanding the world in such a way as to create order where unrest may have previously existed (Chesebro 1984). This understanding of paradox encourages us to examine its hegemonic functions, or the ways that a paradoxical worldview can reinforce the status quo and undermine social change by constructing a rationale around contradictory circumstances so as to thwart critical discussion and confrontation of those contradictions. Within the framework of the rhetorical situation, which necessitates a full understanding of the socioeconomic and historical context of a speaking situation, paradox represents an important rhetorical constraint to be examined as it shaped women's responses to their surroundings.

Studies have explored the Depression era in terms of the period's impact on families, the implementation of Roosevelt's New Deal, the increase in union activities, the development of the Congress of Industrial Organizations (CIO), and the growth of the Communist Party. Among all of these works, little has been done to understand women's reactions to the discourses, policies, and structures that affected their lives. Using the artifacts of women involved in the CP during the 1930s, we can discover the ways that these activists confronted and reinterpreted the paradoxes or contradictions surrounding womanhood and work.

One contradiction women faced was that pertaining to the relationship between production and reproduction, or workplace and domestic issues. The popular ideology of separate spheres maintained that the two realms were separate or uninfluenced by the other. Yet, as Mary Smith's observation at the beginning of this chapter revealed, conditions in the factory, mine, or mill had a direct bearing on life at home, and as individuals held responsible for the quality of home life, women knew that connection better than most. In the 1930s, the Communist Party played a central role in countless strikes and demonstrations on behalf of the country's workers, particularly those in heavy-industry jobs such as auto and steel. The CP devoted considerably less attention to the unique needs and concerns of women, particularly in their roles as mothers and homemakers.[9] Chapter 2 explores the ways that CP women relied on the rhetorical strategy of perspective by incongruity to demystify the so-called sanctity of the family and to politicize conditions that had heretofore been considered personal.

Part and parcel of the doctrine of separate spheres was a gender ideology prescribing women's proper place as the home. A second contradiction central to working-class women's lives is that which arose when material necessity called on women to step outside the confines of the home. In the 1930s, the wage cuts and layoffs of male workers made income earned by wives that much more critical to family survival. Despite this reality, demands on women to take their "proper" place in the home as family caretaker and consoler became even more strident during a decade when jobs were scarce and despair widespread (Coiner 1995, 39). Chapter 3 sheds light on how these activists negotiated work and gender relations through a justificatory rhetoric that created a new context for understanding women's work in the paid labor force by emphasizing women's need and right to work.

Finally, working-class women faced a third contradiction that stemmed from constraints unique to the audiences they were most often trying to persuade. The "problem of audience"—particularly salient for speakers addressing young, uneducated, poor working girls and women in the early 1900s (see Campbell 1973; Triece 2003)—persisted throughout the 1930s as expectations that women be submissive, dependent, and demure shaped self-images and continued to pose obstacles for speakers attempting to rouse an audience to act on its own behalf. Studying the rhetoric of working-class women activists of the 1930s provides a window into the ways they created identification with their listeners while reconstituting them into the strong-willed, independent activists necessary for a broad-based labor movement consisting of men and women and concerned with the interconnected needs of home and workplace (the topic of chapter 4). Taken together, perspective by incongruity, justificatory rhetoric, and reconstitution provided the means for upending the paradoxical discourses that constrained women's abilities to live decent and humane lives.

The following chapters represent an important contribution to studies of rhetoric and the history of the Left. Though scholars have continued to round out the traditional canon of rhetoric with inclusion of women's voices, many issues still call for sustained attention. For instance, influences of class and economic constraint remain understudied in the field of rhetoric, yet these issues and the ways they intersect with gender inequality are particularly relevant when recovering the voices of working-class female activists. On the Picket Line also contributes to recent scholarly attempts to "re-envision" or "reinvent" prevailing understandings of the 1930s (see Mullen and Linkon 1996; Rabinowitz 1991; Staub 1994). A majority of these important studies focuses on radical women fiction writers of the 1930s. The following chapters add to our understanding of women's influence on the 1930s cultural and political landscape by focusing on the public speeches and writings of women who struggled first-hand with the issues of which they spoke and who had a hand in economic and political reform that improved the lives of men and women alike.

The writings and speeches of women active in the Communist Party USA in the 1930s represent previously untapped sources for exploring the three tensions described above. Ella Reeve Bloor, Elizabeth Gurley Flynn, Grace Hutchins, Ann Burlak, Clara Lemlich Shavelson, and Margaret Cowl, to name a few, were influential CP activists who devoted their activist careers to addressing the unique concerns of working-class women. Yet scholars have yet to explore fully their oratory contributions. Ella Reeve Bloor, known as "Mother" Bloor, had an activist career of over fifty years, taking up suffrage, union organizing, and socialism before joining the CP when it first organized in 1919. Elizabeth Gurley Flynn gained activist experience as a young agitator in the Industrial Workers of the World (IWW). She eventually joined the CP in 1937 and quickly rose to leadership positions on the Women's Commission and the CP National Committee. Grace Hutchins published an incisive study of women's work in capitalism, Women Who Work (1934a), addressing the fact of women's "double yoke," or the twin burdens of unpaid domestic work and work in the paid labor force. Ann Burlak gained prominence for organizing textile workers and was adept at involving wives, daughters, and mothers in strikes of male-dominated industries such as steel and mining (Ware 1982, 46, 130). Clara Lemlich Shavelson, a full-time housewife and mother, was a primary force behind the successful housewives' movement, which organized thousands of women in bread, meat, and milk strikes. Margaret Cowl wrote extensively on women of the working class, particularly in CP publications such as the *Communist* and *Party Organizer*. She made speaking tours, served on the Women's Commission and the CP's Central Committee (see Shaffer 1979), and was editor, in the mid-1930s, of the *Working Woman*, a CP periodical geared specifically to "working women, farm women, and working class housewives." This magazine, which carried commentary from Bloor, Hutchins, and countless "ordinary" women struggling through the Depression, provides another fruitful source for examining the voices of working-class women whose contributions to the labor movement have remained largely unrecognized.

*On the Picket Line* examines the ways that working-class women, including influential CP activists, negotiated and often confronted the contradictions and complexities that arose when boundaries delineating "woman's work" were thrown into question during a time of great economic disruption and change. The following chapters explore the rhetorical strategies women employed to address tensions in workplace production and domestic well-being, and the material and ideological factors that constrained women and their abilities to speak on their own behalf as workers and housewives. Investigating these activists' arguments in the context of the broader labor movement, we find the influence of foremothers who employed similar strategies in earlier labor struggles as well as that of the CP, an organization that both shaped and was shaped by the discourse of these women. In other words, we should understand messages of labor struggle not as static or ahistorical, but as existing in a dynamic relationship with other messages that influence, instigate, or otherwise shape arguments under study.

The following chapters highlight the extent to which radical Left women of the 1930s challenged, rather than passively accepted, the economic and cultural structures that oppressed them. As such, this book takes issue with the contention that working-class women and their advocates took a primarily defensive posture and remained content with what little they could get from New Deal legislation (Scharf 1980, 136–37). In the midst of intellectual, reformist, and even male-dominated CP discourses highlighting the impact of the economic collapse on the average working *man,* working-class women of the party raised their voices and called attention to their needs as female workers, mothers, and wives. Despite the lack of a tangible feminist network from which to draw resources, support, or models of agitation, these women articulated arguments that can be identified as "feminist" (though they did not apply the label to themselves). Their rhetorical strategies represent important contributions to feminist and rhetorical theory insofar as they deconstructed oppressive gender ideologies and offered materialist critiques of unpaid labor in the home and sex-typed labor in the workplace. Additionally and equally important, radical women of the 1930s engaged some of the most creative tactics imaginable that materially challenged workplace discriminations and resulted in gains for male and female workers alike.

ONE

# Establishing the Context

---

"All the statements made by President Roosevelt, by General Johnson, Administrator of the NRA, and by other spokesmen of the administration, about 'shortening hours,' 'increasing employment and wages' for the working class, are merely empty phrases, while the main purpose, 'business recovery,' really spells increased profits for the employing class" (Hutchins 1934a, 108). Grace Hutchins, CP activist and author of *Women Who Work*, was straightforward in stating her views on New Deal legislation that was passed with the alleged intent of putting the nation's fifteen million unemployed back to work. The New Deal was Franklin D. Roosevelt's sweeping plan for recovery after the stockmarket crash of October 1929 led to one of the most intense depressions the United States has ever faced. A cornerstone of the New Deal was the National Industrial Recovery Act (NIRA), which was managed by the National Recovery Administration (NRA).

## Working-Class Women and the New Deal

The NIRA legislation set up codes that regulated wages and hours in industries engaged in interstate commerce. As initially passed, a number of the codes stipulated unequal pay for female workers. After protests from women's organizations, including the National Woman's Party, the National Federation of Business and Professional Women's Clubs, and the Women's Trade Union League, the legislation was revised so that 75 percent of the 493 codes provided equal pay for equal work (Foner 1980, 279; Scharf 1980, 111–12). Overall, however, the legislation hurt women workers in a number of ways.

First, 25 percent of the codes remained unaffected by the equal pay provision. Ware notes that only half of the women in the workforce were affected by NRA codes (1982, 38). But even industries covered by the legislation found ways around the equal pay provision. The "July 1929 clause" "stipulated persons paid below minimum NRA levels on that date could continue to be so paid" (Scharf 1980, 112). Other industries exempted "employees engaged in light and repetitive work"—read: female workers—from the minimum wage standards (112). And NRA rules allowed industries to pay 80 percent of the minimum wage to "inexperienced" workers, most of whom were women and black workers (Foner 1980, 280). In short, employers found numerous ways to circumvent NIRA codes, including "speedups," "stretch-outs," tampering with records, and numerous "tricks by which employers manage[d] to cut wages while at the same time attempting to present the appearance of full compliance with code regulations" (qtd. in Foner 1980, 284; see also Hutchins 1934a, Scharf 1980, 110–38).[1]

Married women who worked outside the home—a sizable percentage of the entire female workforce—became scapegoats during a time of job scarcity and found little protection from the law (Ware 1982, 29). Secretary of Labor Frances Perkins decried women who worked for "pin money," a misnomer obscuring the fact that most women worked to put food on the table. Section 213 of the Economy Act of 1932 "allowed the firing of one spouse if both husband and wife worked for the government" (Strom 1983, 361). Almost all of the workers fired under this provision were women. Other places of employment that restricted the work of married women included banks, public utilities, and school districts (Ware 1982, 28).

Some occupations were only partially covered by, or were completely exempted from, NRA codes. These included domestic and agriculture work, jobs that employed 66.5 percent of black workers and 90 percent of all black female workers (Foner 1980, 280; Ware 1982, 30).[2] Racist practices were encoded in the NRA legislation. As Foner points out, "Wage rates with differentials of up to 30 percent were set in the South under NRA codes. Southern employers let it be known at the code hearings that if they were forced to pay higher rates, they would fire black workers and hire whites" (1980, 280). Hence, blacks aptly referred to the New Deal's NRA as the "Negro Removal Act" (281).

One potential bright spot of the act was section 7(a), which stipulated that workers could join unions and "bargain collectively through representatives of their own choosing." Called "the spark that rekindled the spirit of unionism within American labor" (Bernstein 1970, 37), section 7(a) was especially beneficial for women working in garment, textile, and food processing industries, all of which were subject to seasonal layoffs and irregular work (Scharf 1980, 117; Foner 1980, 281–90). After the passage of section 7(a) the United Textile Workers increased membership from 27,000 to 40,000 (Foner 1980, 285) and the International Ladies Garment Workers Union (ILGWU) raised its membership to 200,000, a 500 percent increase over one year (Ware 1982, 42). These and other unions across the country led countless strikes and work stoppages throughout 1933 and 1934, including a general strike of 450,000 textile workers in New England and the South, thousands of whom were women (Foner 1980, 286).[3] Despite the sanction given by the NRA to union organizing, employers found ways to undermine section 7(a) through loopholes and specious interpretations of the code (Bernstein 1970, 38–40). Thus, even this aspect of the NRA had mixed results.

Above all, Roosevelt was politically expedient. He came to the presidency "at a time when it was good politics to improve working conditions, increase income, and promote the organization of workers; but in all these matters he waited until it was politically opportune and possible to do them" (Edelman 1957, 182). New Deal legislation and its often questionable results represent one among many factors, or rhetorical constraints, that shaped the lives of working-class women during the Depression.

The history of working-class women's lives shows that this group was not passive in the face of laws, regulations, and social norms that rendered them second-class citizens. In the three decades leading up to the Depression, working-class women—often with the help of more well-to-do sisters—paraded for suffrage, picketed for fair wages, and led rent and food strikes. These activities provide a historical backdrop for understanding the actions of women during the Depression. Mid-nineteenth-century and Progressive-era activists left behind a rich store of activities from which CP activists and working-class women of the 1930s could draw ideas and inspiration.

## Beginnings on the Picket Line

Just as labor historians have noted that women have always worked,[4] it is equally true that women have always agitated for gender and class equality. Contrary to perceptions that the labor movement was primarily male centered, women and girls played an important part in extra-discursive actions such as walkouts and strikes as early as the 1820s. These actions stand as precursors to what would be a long history of militant actions by women workers. In the early 1800s, in mill towns across New England where females dominated the trades and were exploited as a source of cheap labor, young girls protested wage cuts alongside male comrades and led their own all-women's strikes (Foner 1979, 29–30). In February 1834 an eight-hundred-strong strike in Lowell, Massachusetts, was significant for the tactic protesters took to persuade others to join the struggle. The women walked through town, visited other mills, and gave spirited speeches in an attempt to rally fellow workers to the cause (34). This was one of the first of many "flying squadrons" that would be used in labor struggles into the 1930s. Flying squadrons were "groups of traveling strikers who moved from one mill town to the next, demonstrating at the gates of factories where workers had not yet joined the strike" (Foner 1980, 286).

In addition to participating in some of the first walkouts in the burgeoning industrial northeast, factory women voiced their concerns in letters published in magazines such as *Factory Girl, Factory Girl's Garland,* and *Factory Girls' Album and Operatives' Advocate* (Foner 1979, 61). These documents initiated a long history of letter writing by working girls and women who used this medium to authenticate their experiences and to call attention to their conditions. Working-class women of the 1930s similarly employed letter writing as one among many tools for justifying their positions as workers in the paid labor force. Indeed, parallels can be drawn between letters from the two periods. Like the letters penned by women of the Depression era, those written by 1800s mill workers provided detailed descriptions of life in the factory as a way to authenticate the women's experiences, and they provided calls to action in order to motivate readers who found themselves in similar situations (Foner 1979, 67).

From the early 1800s through the 1930s, worker organizations and unions were most often dominated by men, and many openly denied women access.[5] The Knights of Labor, perhaps the most influential labor organization of the late 1800s (prior to the rise of the American Federation of Labor [AFL]), was unique in allowing women in its ranks and providing a space for the articulation of concerns specific to women. The group, 10 percent of which were women, supported equal pay for equal work and woman's suffrage. As Tax remarks on the legacy the Knights left for future women labor activists (1980, 47), "In such favorable conditions, strong women leaders quickly began to develop and achieve recognition within the Order, and in fact the development of such women was one of the chief contributions of the Knights to later stages of organization." Additionally, the Knights welcomed "domestic workers," including "housewives, servants and housekeepers," and recognized "work within the home as a vital part of the community's total production" (Levine 1983, 328). But in contrast to the housewives of the 1930s who similarly organized around concerns specific to motherhood and domesticity, the Knights upheld a sentimental ideal of the home and woman's "proper" place therein.

When denied access to male-only trade unions, which happened frequently through the 1800s, women formed their own organizations, such as the Factory Girls Association and Female Labor Reform Associations in New England mill towns; the United Tailoresses' Society in New York; the Daughters of St. Crispin, which was the first national trade union for women in U.S. history (Foner 1979); and the Working Women's Union in Chicago (Tax 1980).[6] These organizations represent the first attempts at workplace organization by women and for women.

In the late 1800s and early 1900s, women also organized as mothers and housewives, laying a foundation for the housewives' movement that gained notoriety in the 1930s. Community and familial ties created a web of support through which women developed a political consciousness that tied domestic well-being to the workings of the marketplace. During trips to the market, "women shared experiences and built alliances around common needs, problems, and injustices. As negotiators for scarce resources, women also came into contact with the distributors and dealers of those goods, reinforcing their importance in regulating and adjudicating the community's moral economy" (Cameron 1993, 95).

Women's heightened awareness of economic concerns translated into actions aimed at lowering the cost of living. Between 1902 and 1910, Jewish housewives on New York's Lower East Side organized numerous food and rent strikes and, through their actions, called attention to the ways the broader economy impacted their families and homes (Orleck 1995, 26–31). They put neighborhood networking to use and articulated an argument highlighting the interrelated nature of production and reproduction that would be repeated by their daughters and granddaughters in future labor struggles. Much like Clara Lemlich Shavelson and Rose Nelson, who led housewives in the 1930s, Cecilia Schwartz incited women to protest the rising cost of meat by illustrating the power they held as consumers. In a 1908 speech she pointed out, "'If we don't buy from the butchers, they won't be able to buy from the wholesale dealers. The result will be that the wholesalers will find themselves with a lot of meat on their hands. They will then sell cheap to our butchers and we will get our meat cheap'" (qtd. in Orleck 1995, 27). Housewives demonstrated with equal enthusiasm in rent strikes, such as a 1907 strike in New York described as the "best organized of the early-twentieth-century housewives' actions, and the largest rent strike New York had ever seen" (Orleck 1995, 29). Pauline Newman, a garment worker and soon-to-be-famous labor leader, organized the strike garnering the support of housewives as well as self-supporting women. Orleck notes that the strike "had mixed success" (30). Of the ten thousand families who participated, about two thousand received a reduction in rent. Additionally, the strike initiated community discussion of rent control, which became law in the 1930s.

In some respects, it was the inability or unwillingness of Left organizations of the period—for instance, the Socialist Party of the early 1900s and the Communist Party USA (CPUSA) of the 1930s—to address the concerns of women as housewives that prompted this group to act out on their own behalf. Likewise, the Industrial Workers of the World (IWW), founded in 1905, was not attuned to the unique needs of women either as laborers or as housewives,[7] but the organization can be noted for its efforts to make the home and family "the very center of [its] agitational practice" (Gosse 1987, 12; see also Faue 1991, 10–11). Leaders of the IWW relied on vivid images and emotional language in order to connect "the small, daily blows, the drawn-out immiseration of real people bound up in familial units with the suffering of the whole class to which these same people less visibly belonged" (Gosse 1987, 13). At a material level, IWW leaders successfully garnered the support of housewives—a group oftentimes marginalized from the workplace—in strikes and walkouts. The women proved eager to participate in strikes, in some instances "fighting off scabs with rolling pins, brooms, and pokers" (Tax 1980, 128).

Elizabeth Gurley Flynn (who would later become an active member of the CP) was one of the few in the IWW specifically to address women and their concerns. "She alone acknowledged the inequality and domination built into the division of labor in proletarian families" (Gosse 1987, 7). In her speeches and writings, Flynn discussed loveless marriages that amounted to little more than "sexual enslavement" (1915, 102), critiqued the burden of "household drudgery" (1916, 135) borne by women alone, and lamented the workplace conditions faced by women, which were the "same as man's only worse, infinitely worse in every occupation" (1915, 101). Flynn was also quick to call out the sexism of male comrades who would rather have their wives and daughters remain in the home performing housework than see them participate in a strike (Tax 1980, 128). Flynn's influence notwithstanding, the "IWW strategy for women remained one of workplace organizing alone" (130).

The well-known labor activist Mary Harris "Mother" Jones was present at the IWW's founding convention in 1905. Notorious both in and outside of labor circles, Jones used her persona as "mother" to nurture her constituency and to motivate its members to act militantly (Tonn 1996). She was especially popular among coal miners and worked as an organizer for the United Mine Workers for a number of years. Ella Reeve "Mother" Bloor, the CP activist (explored in later chapters), was Jones's junior by thirty years, yet the two led somewhat parallel lives and may have have crossed paths during their decades-long activist careers.[8] Both were beloved by the men and women they led, both displayed oratory skills capable of arousing the most weary and downtrodden, and both enacted a persona of militant motherhood (see Brown 1999; Tonn 1996) that proved successful in organizing entire families in struggles against corrupt bosses and company-owned towns across the country.

To fill the void in efforts to organize working women, the Women's Trade Union League formed in 1903. Dubbing itself the "women's branch of the labor movement and the industrial branch of the women's movement" (Jacoby 1975, 126), the WTUL sought to unionize women and to lobby on behalf of a group that faced dual axes of discrimination. Despite intragroup conflict between working-class members and middle-class "allies" (Dye 1975a; Orleck 1995; Tax 1980; Triece 2001), the organization made an impact by supporting significant labor uprisings in the first decade of the 1900s, such as the famous Uprising of 30,000 in New York City. The Uprising of 30,000, a strike of shirtwaist workers that began in late 1909, remains one of the most important walkouts in labor history. The action illustrated in dramatic terms the gains to be had in collective actions that had coercive force. Workers, particularly women and girls for whom this was an initiation into the world of public speaking and action, learned the importance of solidarity or "sticking capacity" in struggles against bosses who most often had local governments and militias on their side.[9] Clara Lemlich, who would go on to organize housewives in the 1930s as Clara Lemlich Shavelson, played a central role in educating workers and rallying them to the cause (Orleck 1995, 58–61; Tax 1980, 205–40).

Perhaps most important, the uprising of shirtwaist makers served as an inspiration for tens of thousands of workers throughout the 1910s and quite possibly for activists of the Depression era who, in the early 1900s, gained their first exposure to labor radicalism as youngsters in the factories and mills of the Northeast. With varying degrees of success, workers in the cloak, textile, and garment trades, as well as corset makers and white-goods workers, halted their machines and through collective action won reduced hours, higher wages, and, in some cases, union recognition. With picket support and relief aid provided by the WTUL, in September 1910 forty thousand men's garment workers walked out of shops and paralyzed the industry in Chicago (Foner 1979, 350–54; Weiler 1984, 114–39). The next four years saw similar walkouts numbering in the thousands in garment factories in Cleveland and Milwaukee; in the corset industry in Kalamazoo, Michigan; among silk workers in Paterson, New Jersey, and coal miners in Colorado; and in the well-known "bread and roses" strike of Lawrence, Massachusetts, textile workers (Cameron 1993, 117–69; Foner 1979, 346–73; Long 1985, 52–85; Scharf 1984, 146–66; Weiler 1984, 114–39).

Cameron's (1993) description of the beginnings of the 1912 "bread and roses" strike of Lawrence mill workers underscores significant parallels between early twentieth-century labor activism and the tactics employed by working-class women during the Depression. "Throwing down their aprons and grabbing picker sticks . . . the women shut down their machines, marched out of the mill, and called for others to follow them. The following morning, massive waves of strikers wove their way up and then down Canal Street. Standing on each other's shoulders and shouting orders, men and women made 'stump speeches' sending 'flying squadrons' of operatives through all the other mills to recruit supporters and shut down machines" (124–25). Much like the housewives who agitated during the 1930s, the wives and mothers of Lawrence "played an especially critical role bringing pressure not only on recalcitrant neighbors but on those members of the working-class community dependent on workers' wages. Grocers, shopkeepers, landlords, and others tied to the neighborhood economy were targets of women keenly aware of the connections between cuts in wages and holes in the stomach" (133).

During the 1930s, women similarly relied on neighborhood networking and engaged in creative and confrontational tactics to call attention to the contradictions inherent in a socioeconomic system that singled out sex-typed jobs and scapegoated married women even as they struggled to feed their children and keep a roof over their heads. One could argue that it was community-based activism, initiated primarily by working-class women, that broadened and sustained labor struggles through the 1930s. As the following chapters demonstrate, women's experiences as mothers, homemakers, and workers in the paid labor force enabled them to better understand the links between production and reproduction, the centrality of unpaid domestic labor to the economy, and the importance of a solidarity that encircled union members, housewives, and community leaders.

## Women Writers of the 1930s

Analyses of women's presence in the public realm during the 1930s focus primarily on women's literary contributions. "Rather than continue the trend of decrying women's absence from the public sphere," Rabinowitz argues, "a rich selection of women's voices and visions circulated during the decade" (1991, 3). Her study, along with a number of others, focuses on "revolutionary" women writers of the 1930s with an eye toward developing theoretical frameworks for capturing the complexities of sex and class as these categories shape women's writing (see Coiner 1995, 1996; Hapke 1995; Nekola and Rabinowitz 1987; Staub 1994). In *Labor and Desire,* Rabinowitz studies the theory of "gendered classed subjectivity" developed in women's revolutionary literature of the 1930s, which "narrates class as a fundamentally gendered construct and gender as a fundamentally classed one" (1991, 8). In a similar vein, Coiner looks at the work of Tillie Olsen and Meridel Le Sueur in order to understand how they managed the tensions between feminist and Communist Party ideologies and challenged patriarchal norms and values in mainstream as well as leftist proletarian literature (1995, 6, 7).

Other studies focus on women writers of nonfiction as reporters and journalists in Communist and other Left presses. Staub (1994) examines the work of Tillie Olsen in Communist periodicals such as the *Working Woman* and *Western Worker* for the persuasive strategies she employed in giving voice to or authenticating the lives and experiences of the working poor. According to Staub, Olsen's writings were powerful as a "means for the redress of past grievances, as well as the need not only to criticize corruption and injustice, but also to affirm alternatives" (130). Nekola and Rabinowitz (1987) similarly validate the work of women reporters of the 1930s in *Writing Red,* an anthology of women's fiction, poetry, and reportage of the 1930s. Their collection includes well-known Left writers such as Agnes Smedley, Tillie Olsen, Meridel Le Sueur, Mary Heaton Vorse, and Dorothy Day who appeared in a number of radical journals and covered an array of topics, including women's strike activities, women's dual work burdens, women's status in China and the Soviet Union, and the particular problems of black women workers.

## Women and the Communist Party

Scholars have also examined the roles of various leftist organizations and radical unions in improving workers' lives during a decade that saw 75 percent of the American population living at or below the subsistence level (Foner 1980, 256). A number of these works take a bottom-up view examining rank-and-file participation in specific strikes and relying on records and testimonies from folks considered "average workers."[10] Studies of the CPUSA have examined party leadership, policies, strategies, and shifting ideological emphases, but very few of these have given much more than a passing glance at the contributions of women, who comprised over 30 percent of CP members by the end of the 1930s (Shaffer 1979, 90; see also Draper 1957; Klehr 1978; Ottanelli 1991).

Perhaps women's invisibility in historical accounts of the CPUSA is due in part to the party's own neglect of the needs and concerns of this constituency. Scholars who examine women's roles in the CP vary in their interpretations, but most conclude that the CP's attempts to foster women's rights had "mixed results" (Shaffer 1979, 110). Women's concerns with sex bias in the workplace and oppressive gender norms governing home life were often ignored or overtly dismissed as secondary to class revolution and the concerns of heavy-industry workers, most of whom were male (see Shaffer 1979; Strom 1983). Throughout the 1930s, women were "underrepresented in the CP's leadership and among its candidates for public office even relative to the proportion of women in the party" (Shaffer 1979, 78, 90). Ware (1982) and Baxandall (1993) offer testimonies of women that reveal their frustrations with party leaders, some of whom were their husbands, who excluded them from meeting participation and decision making (Baxandall 1993, 155). Within the party, "women were viewed . . . as mothers of sons and creatures of sentiment, not carriers of reason" (154; see also Gosse 1991).

Despite these noteworthy shortcomings, many have pointed out the importance of the CP in advancing women's rights during the Depression (Baxandall 1993; Brown 1999; Gosse 1991; Shaffer 1979; Ware 1982; Weigand 2001). According to Ware, "[T]he Communist Party was one of the few to encourage public discussion of women's issues during [the 1930s]" (1982, 124). Similarly, Shaffer notes that during the Popular Front (1935–39), the CP "produced some of the most thorough and concrete analyses seen in the United States of the conditions of working-class women" (1979, 110).

A number of women advanced to leadership positions in the party and wielded considerable influence, particularly when it came to concerns facing women. Margaret Cowl, who along with Anna Damon led the Women's Commission during the 1930s, worked on issues pertaining to women's recruitment and women's rights in the workplace (Shaffer 1979, 80; Ware 1982, 120). Elizabeth Gurley Flynn held a position on the Women's Commission as well as the National Committee. She was also a regular contributor to the *Daily Worker.* Other leaders include Ann Burlak, activist among textile workers and head of the Rhode Island CP; Anita Whitney, who ran for a number of political offices on the California CP ticket; Clara Lemlich Shavelson and Rose Nelson, leaders of the housewives' movement; Grace Hutchins, an activist and author of a well-known book on women's work in a capitalist society; and the renowned "Mother" of the CP, Ella Reeve Bloor.

In the early 1930s, the CP gradually widened the lens that had been narrowly focused on shop-floor concerns to include neighborhood and household issues that shaped working-class families' lives. Gosse attributes the change in party emphasis to a strategic opportunity during the summer and fall of 1930 when "many desperate men and women, including local Communists without any direction from their Party," employed "grassroots survival actions" that proved effective in preventing evictions and lowering food and rent costs (1991, 127–30). Men and women went door to door organizing neighborhood Unemployed Councils, as well as special organizations for housewives and mothers. Gosse notes that in early 1931, party leaders "published directives for the Unemployed Councils that at last unambiguously transferred their focus from the wage-earner to the family" (131).

Although it was the early to mid-1930s before party leadership finally recognized the importance of family and neighborhood concerns, the CP activist Ella Reeve Bloor (not to mention a host of other working-class activists) had incorporated such issues into her organizational campaigns throughout the early 1900s.[11] Brown (1996) argues that Bloor's "community-based organizing style" laid the groundwork for the Popular Front of the mid-1930s. As a Socialist and organizer for the Cloth Hat, Cap, and Millinery Workers in the 1910s, Bloor envisioned a future that saw "men and women working together as equals for the common good of working-class communities: shop-floor issues were explicitly linked to community life" (Brown 1996, 215). Bloor's rhetoric echoed that of Leonora O'Reilly (1911b), a Socialist activist of the early 1900s, who described her audience as "aspiring souls, feeling, thinking, acting together to shorten the hours of labor, to establish a living wage, to improve the conditions of life and labor everywhere" (227).

The *Working Woman,* a CP publication, represented an important venue for conveying the perspectives of working-class women such as Bloor and relating the militant actions of neighborhood councils that effectively lowered food and rent costs throughout the Depression. There exist few studies of this magazine, which had a paid circulation of eight thousand by the mid-1930s. Shaffer views the *Working Woman,* along with a daily women's column in the *Daily Worker,* as a structure within the CP that "helped counter sexism in the party" and "gave women support" (1979, 95). Others have taken a more pessimistic view of the magazine. Nekola and Rabinowitz see the *Working Woman* as a "fascinating illustration of the feeble attempts to link class and gender within an official Party publication" (1987, 5). In a similar vein, Baxandall concludes that one "could hardly call [*Working Woman*], in any phase, feminist or for the liberation of women" (1993, 154). At the very least, the efforts of the

*Working Woman* and other CP ventures to reach out to working-class women deserve deeper analysis in order to fully understand the party's relationship to women and women's equality.

The analyses in the following chapters represent one of the few attempts to explore this magazine specifically for the rhetorical strategies employed to negotiate the contradictions working-class women faced as mothers, housewives, and workers in a capitalist society. In contrast to the findings of Baxandall (1993) and Nekola and Rabinowitz (1987), my research reveals that the *Working Woman* articulated a nascent materialist feminist ideology and served as an important outlet for working-class women whose needs and concerns were all but ignored by pervasive New Deal rhetoric and often overlooked by CP hierarchy.

Additionally, in chapters 2–4 I will broaden common understandings of New Deal politics and its impact on women by exploring women's reactions to this political agenda as manifested in their rhetorical strategies and confrontational tactics. More specifically, I will be looking at the ways women challenged the paradoxes that arose when their material circumstances did not concord with dominant ideologies. In carrying out this project, one goal is to restore what Scharf (1980) refers to as the "forgotten woman" of the Depression to her rightful place in labor history. Scouring archives and retrieving artifacts of working-class, immigrant, and African American women remains an important endeavor if communication scholars are to understand fully the roles that rhetoric has played in shaping history and fostering social change. Taking on the call to radically "reread" or "reinvent" the 1930s (Mullen and Linkon 1996; Rabinowitz 1991), I reexamine in the following chapters what happened to efforts for woman's equality during the 1930s. A look at women's activities in the CP suggests that concerns for women's rights did not go away during the decade of the down-and-out man but took multifaceted forms. Women's confrontational tactics in the CP point to the continued need to examine the roles that extra-discursive tactics have played in struggles for social justice. And women's responses to the contradictions arising when material necessity crossed gender norms provide rich sources for analyzing how women negotiated paradox and initiated a materialist feminist worldview while leading lives which were made difficult by the demands of mother, worker, and activist that pulled them in multiple directions. As Shaffer noted, "[C]onsciousness of liberation does not arise fully coherent and in a neat package; but in partial and even contradictory ways" (1979, 110–11). At the same time, there is reason for optimism concerning the potential for humans to articulate and engage collective agency to confront and alter the structures or constraints that shape their lives and delimit their actions.

## Paradox and Emergent Discourses

From the early 1800s to the present, prevailing images in popular, political, and religious discourses have portrayed the family and home life as a sphere of love and tranquility, an escape from the cacophony and sometime cruelty of the workaday world. The popularity of "family values" rhetoric in the 1990s attests to the persistent nature of this familial ideal (see Cloud 1998b). Images of a secure and comfortable home environment are particularly salient during times of unrest or discord in realms outside of the home and emerge as a backlash against challenges to the economic and political status quo (Cloud 1998b, 393; Triece 2001, 137–76). During the Depression of the 1930s, images of the home took on increasing significance as an escape from the unemployment, breadlines, and bank runs occurring beyond the front stoop. This familial ideal represented a paradox for working-class women who witnessed firsthand the ways that workplace hardships extended into the home.

### Perspective by Incongruity

Numerous scholars have explored the historical roots of familial images in an effort to demystify what has become a natural or assumed ideal. We find a distinct relationship between prevailing ideas about the family and gender roles and changes in a society's economic structure (see Abramovitz 1988; Barrett and McIntosh 1991; Coltrane 1996; Coontz 1988; Matthaei 1982; Zaretsky 1976). In preindustrial America, the lines between work and home life were blurred. The family itself was seen as an economic unit, the locus of both production and reproduction. Growing and preparing food to eat and sell at the market, making clothes, and providing for the family's basic necessities were activities central to family life and they governed familial relationships. Fathers played a major role in their children's lives as tutors and moral guardians. Women and children worked alongside men in the fields and performed other important duties to contribute to the family's survival (Coltrane 1996, 29; Matthaei 1982, 102).

The advent and growth of industrial capitalism around the early 1800s, however, fundamentally changed the family unit, most notably in that it widened the separation between work and home and further reified patriarchal gender roles for men and women.[12] Images of the home as a distinct refuge from the work world are part of an ideology of separate spheres, which took root in the early 1800s to support the changing economic system. Increasingly, production took place outside the home, in factories, where men were expected to sell their labor power for wages. Women's work remained tied to the home. Although it was not uncommon for their work to involve income-generating activities (for example, taking in lodgers, doing piecework), the majority of it involved repetitious, arduous, unpaid domestic chores—cooking, cleaning, bearing and raising children, and, not least, purchasing and consuming products now mass produced in factories.

To support the more pronounced separation of production and domesticity, a doctrine or ideology of separate spheres arose, which among other things conveyed the values and behaviors deemed fitting for the family and specified gender norms appropriate for each sex. "Manliness became equated with success in the economic competition" (Matthaei 1982, 105); womanhood was tied to virtuousness and morality, necessary characteristics for managing a stable home and family. In short, through a doctrine of separate spheres, the values and activities that were made to appear naturally fitting for a family were, in fact, central to the perpetuation and growth of capitalism.

Relevant to our discussion here is the way in which the doctrine of separate spheres alleged a separation between public and private realms and idealized home life. Maintaining the myth of a rigid distinction was important for the growth and survival of capitalism on many fronts. For one thing, the distinction justified a privatization of duties that had previously been considered the domain of the community. Whereas in preindustrial America, child rearing was considered a communal affair, the "decline of home production and the coming of the Industrial Revolution reshaped the relationship between family and work, promoting the idea that the family and child rearing were separate from other aspects of life" (Coltrane 1996, 32). The privatization of what were previously considered public issues turned attention away from broad-based social structures and focused it instead on the family as both the source of and solution to a host of social ills. In short, the family—and particularly women in their roles as mothers and wives—became convenient scapegoats for problems deeply rooted in the broader socioeconomic system (Cloud 1998b, 388). Additionally, the apparent separation of public and private reified a gender division of labor and ensured that necessary reproductive duties (cleaning house, doing laundry, feeding and raising children) were performed by women at no expense to the state. And finally, the notion of separate spheres and accompanying gender roles justified wage differentials when women did enter the paid workforce. Women in the workforce were most often viewed as "temporary" workers (since their natural or proper place was considered the home) and as a source of inexpensive labor when male workers were in short supply (as during wartime) or when male workers demanded higher wages.

On one hand, the doctrine of separate spheres afforded a degree of autonomy to working-class and more affluent women in their roles as wives and mothers. Coontz notes that for the working class the family represented a "place where workers could assert their own standards of comportment, escape factory regulation, and resist middle-class interference into their leisure life" (1988, 301). Still, however, the words and images that praised the glories of home life rang hollow for those who could barely afford to put food on the table. The links between home and work appeared particularly stark for African American women who performed domestic and reproductive duties for well-off white families (Abramovitz 1988, 30).

While the doctrine of separate spheres obscured the interrelated nature of public and private, working-class women struggled to make the connections known through a strategy termed "perspective by incongruity," which was played out at the rhetorical and extra-discursive levels. The influential rhetorical scholar Kenneth Burke developed the concept of perspective by incongruity to explain how words can be used to generate new, previously unthought-of interpretations of our surroundings. Perspective by incongruity involves "extending the use of a term by taking it from the context in which it was habitually used and applying it to another" (Burke 1954, 89). By decontextualizing, or extracting a term from its usual context, perspective by incongruity creates new associations and hence new ways of interpreting an event or concept. Perhaps most important, perspective by incongruity is not a neutral process. It is "not simply the pairing of terms from normally dissociated fields of experience or terminologies," but is rather a part of "ideological critique . . . and thus social change" (Blakesley 2002, 171).

Perspective by incongruity provided an effective rhetorical strategy for women who attempted to upend the doctrine of separate spheres. As those held primarily responsible for making a comfortable home on scant wages, working-class and poor women witnessed daily the impact that one's work environment had on home life; the two spheres were not, in fact, separate. To call attention to and deconstruct this paradox, women dissociated the image of the home from its usual connotation of warmth and repose and provided a new association that effectively linked public events with private well-being. Ella Reeve Bloor was one CP activist who was particularly well known for emphasizing the links between factory and community (see Brown 1999).

Additionally, women challenged the paradox arising from the doctrine of separate spheres through extra-discursive actions that publicized and politicized household matters traditionally deemed private. For example, through organizations such as the Mothers' League and the United Council of Working-Class Women, women orchestrated bread and rent strikes and neighborhood boycotts, and they physically blocked evictions of families unable to pay rent. These actions acquired meaning through language—for example, the use of flyers, meetings, and corner speeches—yet their significance went well beyond words. Through use of physical presence or absence, women disrupted commerce, slowing or halting the production and/or distribution of goods, which meant little or no revenue for business owners and landlords. To the extent they had economic or material consequences, such actions—which I explore later as a form of "coercive persuasion" (Simons 1972, 231, 232)—often spoke louder than words.

As noted above, an integral part of the doctrine of separate spheres established specific gender roles that were seen as "naturally fitting" for each sex. The contradictions between gender role ideals and the realities of women's lives represents a second paradox facing women of the Depression.

### Justifying the "Woman Worker"

In her sweeping analysis of religious and popular discourses of the mid-1800s, Barbara Welter (1966) identified a "cult of True Womanhood," which prescribed the attributes of the ideal woman. Above all, the "True Woman" was characterized by piety, purity, submissiveness, and domesticity. As naturally pious, a woman would lend her moral suasion to cleaning up corruption in the workaday world; her purity ensured that she remained virtuous for her future husband. Submissiveness and domesticity were essential attributes for woman, whose "proper sphere" was the home. A wife was expected to remain dependent on her husband and to make the household her primary object of interest and concern. She was deemed naturally suited to homemaking and was glorified as a mother and the moral guardian of the home.

The reality of women's lives stood in stark contrast to this prevailing and persuasive rhetoric. Women have always worked outside the home, giving lie to the dictates of True Womanhood. Therein lay the roots of a paradox that characterized their everyday lives. Though women were supposed to be pious and pure, they were exposed, out of necessity, to the corrupting influences of the paid labor force. And despite notions of women's natural tendency towards submissiveness and domesticity, women operated heavy machinery and labored alongside men in the very public spaces of mills and factories.

In the early 1800s, New England textile mills hired thousands of young women and girls who worked twelve or more hours each day for $1.75 a week (Foner 1979, 20–26; see also Kessler-Harris 1981; Matthaei 1982). By 1890, females—most of them young and unmarried—made up 17.1 percent of the labor force (Matthaei 1982, 141). The "working girl phenomenon," as Matthaei refers to it, was a result of a number of factors, among them, gender role expectations within the family. Young girls were expected to dedicate themselves "to the service of [their] families" (148). Poor families, attempting to adhere to the cult of True Womanhood by keeping wives out of the labor force, instead sent daughters to work in factories to supplement the family income. It was often the case that the income brought in by young girls was used also to pay for their brothers' educations.

The reasons are numerous and complex, yet one thing remains clear: women worked because they *had* to, because their livelihood and the livelihood of their families depended upon their income. As one women said in a letter to the *Daily Worker* in 1930, "If you are a woman, you will understand what it means to work in the factory and keep house. I have been working, even when my husband had a job, in order to make ends meet. Now he is out of work since last October, and don't ask me how we get along on my miserable earnings. But without it we would starve" (qtd. in Foner 1980, 257). Most jobs performed by women were unskilled and low paying. By 1900, the paid labor force counted five million women among its ranks (Foner 1979, 270). Over 50 percent of these women were domestic servants, waitresses, or workers in factories or mills (Kessler-Harris 1981, 80). With continued industrial expansion and the growth of corporate capitalism, women increasingly found jobs in offices and department stores (Scharf 1980, 4, 5). In general, women and girls occupied a variety of positions laboring as laundresses, cloakmakers, cigar rollers, stenographers, waitresses, shirtwaist makers, domestic servants, and mill workers, to name a few. Despite working equally long hours, white women received less pay than their male counterparts, sometimes 75 percent less (Kessler-Harris 1982, 155; see also Foner 1979). Black women endured discrimination due to both race and sex and were relegated to even lower-paying, more arduous positions, primarily domestic and agricultural (Foner 1979, 268).

With the onset of U.S. involvement in World War I, women took on jobs traditionally reserved for men in munitions plants and airplane factories and as streetcar conductors (see Enloe 1983; Foner 1980, 59–98; Greenwald 1980; Honey 1984; Triece 2002). Evidence suggests, however, that this work had little real impact on the gender and race discrimination that affected women's workplace experiences (Foner 1980, 80–98; Greenwald 1980, 13–

32). Most women in the labor force during World War I were not new to this realm, and fewer than 5 percent were first-time workers (Kessler-Harris 1982, 219). White women stepped up from their old, usually unskilled, jobs and into newly opened positions vacated by men now in the military, though they still earned lower wages and faced hostility from male coworkers. Black women moved from agricultural and domestic positions to fill unskilled jobs vacated by white women and were subjected to discrimination based on their race as well as their sex.

Women comprised over 20 percent of the total workforce by 1930 (Ware 1982, 23). Though we most often picture the "down-and-out male" when we hear of the Depression, this economic downturn left over 3 million women unemployed (Foner 1980, 257). Some scholars point out, however, that women were not hit as hard during this decade. The "percentage of women employed actually increased" during the 1930s (Ware 1982, 35). The reason has largely to do with the sex-typed nature of women's employment. Occupations hardest hit by the economy were auto, steel, and manufacturing, jobs dominated by men. In contrast, clerical, trade, and service occupations—deemed "women's work"—were less affected (Milkman 1976, 79). As had always been the case, black women endured much greater hardship than white women. They were more likely to be unemployed, were more often subjected to dangerous working conditions, and faced even lower earnings than white women (Foner 1980, 261, 262).

If women were present in the paid labor force, they were sure to protest the inhumane conditions under which they worked. Their protest actions were another way that women defied the dictates of True Womanhood. Factory walkouts, picketing, leafleting, public speaking, resisting evictions, facing arrests and jail time, and instigating neighborhood-wide store boycotts were anything but traditionally ladylike; yet, women engaged in all of these actions in their attempts to receive fair and just treatment in the workplace. In particular, in order to confront the paradox that arose when gender norms contradicted material need, women relied on a rhetoric of justification, in which they employed two strategies: differentiation and transcendence. Through differentiation, women called up the necessity of their work in the paid labor force, while transcendence emphasized women's right to work outside the home. Additionally, women engaged physically in strikes and walkouts, often alongside male coworkers, in order to call attention to their roles in the paid labor force.

Rigidly defined gender roles circumscribed women in their capacities not only as wives, mothers, and workers, but also as activists. Norms dictating that women remain submissive, dependent, and domestic went against fundamental dictates of effective public speaking. Hence, a third paradox facing working-class activists of the Depression arose when they attempted to persuade their fellow female comrades to transgress gender norms and take the public platform.

## Challenging Contradictions

Historically, public speaking has been defined as "manly," an activity requiring characteristics associated with maleness, that is, rationality, linearity, and assertiveness. The presence of a female speaking publicly, then, was paradoxical. If she was a "true woman" she could not, by definition, be an effective speaker. Were she to convey the attributes of a good speaker, she would strip herself of her womanhood. Though the presence of women speaking and acting publicly gradually became more widespread by the 1930s (for example, a number of women held prominent positions in Roosevelt's administration), it was still not the norm. Working-class women, in particular, faced a number of barriers when attempting to speak out on their own behalf. In addition to gender norms that dictated submissiveness and domesticity, poor and working-class women were often saddled with the double shift of work in the home and factory, so they had little time to gain needed public-speaking experience. And if they were able to overcome normative and time restrictions, they often faced sanctions from close-minded husbands and male comrades within the CP. Female activists of the CP who were able to rise to leadership positions and exercise influence in the labor movement, then, faced a unique obstacle when they addressed their working-class sisters. Much like their predecessors of the early 1900s labor movement (see Triece 2003), they had before them the task of transforming an audience comprised of poor women, oftentimes inexperienced in activism and assuredly encumbered with workplace and/or familial duties, into a group capable of speaking out and altering their living conditions.

Campbell initially explored the obstacle that audience posed for feminists in her 1973 essay, which framed women's liberation rhetoric as an "oxymoron." She noted that if women wanted to achieve their goal of promoting female independence and self-sufficiency, they had to reject "certain traditional concepts of the rhetorical process" since these "features encourage submissiveness and passivity in the audience" (78). Campbell argued that public speakers often adopted an "anti-rhetorical" style in the form of consciousness-raising, which enabled them to deal with the constraints posed by the audience.

A look at the rhetoric of CP women during the 1930s suggests they employed two strategies to transcend the paradox concerning audience. First, activists such as Ella Reeve Bloor relied on appeals to a second persona or implied auditor (Black 1970). That is, rather than shape appeals to the real or actual audience (who may be unable or unwilling to enact the speaker's goals), CP women created what Black (1970) calls a "model of what the rhetor would have [her] real auditor become" (113). The concept of the second persona implies that certain fundamental changes, or a reconstitution, in the audience is desired or required in order for the speaker to accomplish her goals. Reconstitution refers to the ways that messages can "liberat[e] listeners to think and act more creatively, intelligently, and humanely" (Hammerback 1994, 184; see also Charland 1987; Jensen and Hammerback 1998; McGee 1975).

Communist Party activists also overcame the obstacle of audience through enactment, a rhetorical strategy whereby the speaker "incarnates the argument, *is* the proof of the truth of what is said" (Campbell and Jamieson 1978, 9). Ella Reeve Bloor, perhaps the most visible female CP activist, provides a good example of how enactment operates both rhetorically and extra-discursively. For instance, Bloor often took her young children with her on speaking tours, creating an uncommon platform spectacle but reinforcing the potential of mothers as activists and underscoring the argument concerning the link between public and private. Highlighting children in protest efforts dates back at least to the early 1900s when Mother Jones led a group of children textile workers from Philadelphia to New York to publicize their plight. Again in 1912, children took center stage as Lawrence, Massachusetts, textile strikers sent their little ones to sympathetic homes in the New York area for safety during their months-long struggle with Lawrence textile owners and police (Tax 1980, 257–61). No doubt, Bloor was aware of the sympathies that such sights aroused in addition to the resonance that such images held for her specific audience of women. In a tribute to Bloor on her seventy-sixth birthday, a fellow CP activist, Ann Barton, wrote, "The story of Mother Bloor should be a challenge to all women, telling them what one woman did, what women can do. Her life story should be a challenge so that women who read this will answer that they too will fight shoulder to shoulder with Mother Bloor in the cause to which she has already given so many years of a rich life" (1937, 6).

## Women and Paradox in the Twenty-First Century

Numerous communication scholars have examined paradox, both what it is and how it operates.[13] Paradox may be approached more specifically as a hegemonic constraint that seeks to maintain the status quo in gender relations in the home and workplace. It is important to examine not only or primarily how paradox plays out rhetorically, but how those most affected by the paradoxical rhetoric responded to it. The words and actions of female activists of the CPUSA provide a unique means to explore these issues. While the CP was one of the few organizations of the 1930s to address the concerns of working-class women in a systematic way, its response to the "woman question" remained ambivalent as sexist attitudes persisted throughout the predominately male hierarchy. Communist Party women such as Bloor, Flynn, Hutchins, and Shavelson often had to work hard to get their voices heard not only by the general public, but often by those in their own organization.

Women of the Communist Party USA, have remained understudied despite their enormous contributions in shaping the Communist Party's Popular Front and in challenging political policies and cultural codes that continue to discriminate according to race, class, and gender (see Loader 1975). The artifacts these women left behind deserve closer scrutiny in our efforts to understand how women, past and present, respond to and attempt to expose the contradictions that perpetuate sex and class discrimination. As one contemporary scholar attests, "the experiences of the women [in the CPUSA] illuminate problems which are important to any woman today struggling with the relationship of Marxism to feminism, of the personal to the political. They are experiences we must learn from, not relive" (Loader 1975, 10).

The 1930s was not absent a feminist movement. Women of the CPUSA articulated a nascent materialist feminist ideology that was often quite successful in gaining the attention of fellow working-class women, husbands and male comrades in the CP, and mainstream politicians. One strategy employed by these "forgotten women" of the Depression was perspective by incongruity, the subject of the next chapter.

# TWO

# Negotiating the Public/Private Split

The scene of high unemployment, constant layoffs and pay cuts, and hungry families, Johnstown, Pennsylvania, was much like the hundreds of other mining and mill towns across America in the early 1930s. The struggle against such conditions was just as persistent as the hunger they produced. Most militancy came from an unexpected source: housewives. "We must fight—not starve," wrote the wife of one unemployed worker in a letter to the *Working Woman* in 1931 ("Johnstown Working Women"). Her words echoed the oft-repeated CP slogan "Don't Starve! Fight!" which gained credence in 1931 (Gosse 1991, 129).[1] The extreme conditions facing families in Johnstown and similar places no doubt motivated this woman and others like her to speak out. In towns and cities it was not uncommon for children to forage in garbage dumps for food to eat. In hard-hit mining areas, families subsisted on roots and grass; babies and youngsters were given black coffee because there was no milk. The woman who wrote to the *Working Woman* sounded a clarion call to action for the women of Johnstown. "Housewives and working women, organize together, for we are the most oppressed, more so than the men. We are at home seeing our children crying for food. How do we feel when we have not even a piece of crust to give them? . . . [C]omrades and women workers, we are the ones who suffer from unemployment and low wages. Slaving from sun up till sun down in order to give our children what little we can. We must all join in the working-class organizations. Be in the fight for better conditions for our families."

For this woman, home was not a safe haven sheltered from the business of mines and mills. Families were bound as much by the need to survive as by affective ties. The reality facing countless families of the working poor stood in startling contrast to images of the family that evoked privacy, warmth, and repose. As the writer indicated, women, in their roles as caretakers and home-makers, were often likely to recognize the influence of the workplace or public sphere on what was thought to be strictly private, the domestic sphere. To call attention to these connections, working-class women employed a number of rhetorical and extra-discursive strategies. The letter to the editor noted above provides a good example of how women recontextualized images of the family by stripping them of their idealized trappings thus encouraging a different interpretation of this hallowed institution. As explored in this chapter, women employed decontextualization, irony, and metaphor in order to evoke strikingly different conceptions of authority figures and established traditions. Kenneth Burke's notion of perspective by incongruity sheds light on the strategies employed by these women.

## Perspective by Incongruity and Impious Associations

Burke points out that humans go through life with a set of common-sense notions of "how things were, how they are, and how they may be" (1954, 14). "Piety" is the term Burke applies to illustrate how common sense operates in our lives. Piety is a "system-builder, a desire to round things out, to fit experiences together into a unified whole. Piety is *the sense of what properly goes with what*" (74). Perspective by incongruity involves the disruption of the pious, disconnecting "proper" associations, "violating the 'properties' of [a] word in its previous linkages" (90), in order to create new perspectives. Through decontextualization, juxtaposition, irony, and metaphors that create "impious" or unorthodox associations, public speakers create new identities, interpretations, and worldviews.

Perspective by incongruity involves dissociation, the process whereby typical or standard linguistic associations are torn apart. For example, the wife of an unemployed worker referred to a "Hoover prosperity of starvation and unemployment," creating an entirely new context for the word "prosperity" ("Johnstown Working Women" 1931). In contrast to the typical notion of prosperity as fullness and abundance, she encouraged a new interpretation of prosperity that linked it to scarcity and despair, thereby implying an abundance of scarcity. Such new interpretations require "purposeful forgetting," which along with perspective by incongruity is a "necessary component of ideological critique and thus social change" (Blakesley 2002, 171). Thus it is not surprising that working-class women, particularly those close to the Communist Party USA, would rely on this strategy in their struggles for economic parity.

In the writings and speeches of CP women, perspective by incongruity operated through dissociation, irony, and metaphor, all of which effectively aroused in readers or listeners contrary perspectives on various respected institutions, such as the home and motherhood. Similar techniques have been employed by political cartoonists (see Bostdorff 1987) and contemporary activist groups (see DeChaine 2000). For instance, Queer Nation, a group advocating gay rights, distributes flyers and pamphlets depicting jarring juxtapositions of photographs and captions that force a reinterpretation of mainstream values. Straight people who are confronted with these artifacts, DeChaine notes, "may be 'shocked' by the images, but that shock might, it is hoped, carry a double-inflection of meaning: not just an affront to traditional sensibilities, but more importantly, a 'shock of recognition' that brings people to a higher level of critical self-awareness" (2000, 297).

In addition to using words that effectively shocked readers into a new understanding of themselves and their surroundings, CP women employed militant actions that, through their enactment, represented a form of "extra-discursive impiety" that upended traditional notions of womanhood and clearly revealed the spuriousness of home life tranquility. As used throughout this book, the phrase "extra-discursive reality"—to be distinguished from discourse, or human language—refers to actions and events that exist independently of, though are understood through, human language. According to this theoretical perspective, the relationship between discourse and the material or extra-discursive is dialectical, meaning each shapes the other, but their respective influences are not equal. Language has consequences in the material world, but this is not to say that language is material in the same way as factories and homes. Economic forces or those that enable a society to feed and clothe and thus sustain its people are the most influential in the last instance (Engels [1890] 1978, 761). The extra-discursive actions employed by women physically challenged material structures in such a way as to have an impact on the material welfare of suffering families.

These actions were significant for the ways they contained elements of both coercion and persuasion (Simons 1972, 237, 240). Persuasion came in the form of justifying the struggle and convincing others to join the fight. Yet, in a capitalist system where their labor power is ultimately the only power that workers have over owners who control the means of production, coercion was oftentimes indispensable. To the extent that workers engaged or withdrew their labor power, they forced owners concerned about profits to give in to their demands. In addition to standing side by side with husbands and brothers on the front lines of pickets, housewives exercised their collective influence as consumers through boycotts that quickly convinced butchers and bakers to lower their prices. Viewed within the context of the disenfranchisement created by capitalism, these coercive actions can be better understood not as "immoral" or "illegal" but rather as the necessary and sometimes only means by which powerless groups obtained basic rights. These actions may be seen "not merely [as] the extension of domesticity to the political realm" but rather as "forms of protest that pointed to the emergence of class politics in the urban sphere of social reproduction" (Faue 1991, 9).

In sum, CP women relied on dissociation, irony, and metaphor in order to rend recognized institutions and public figures from their established contexts, and they often employed extra-discursive actions such as store boycotts and picketing; flying squadrons; eviction blockades; milk, bread, and rent strikes; grocery stores raids; and welfare office sit-downs. Through perspective by incongruity, activists created new associations and new ways of seeing what may have been considered natural or timeless and thus unchangeable. This rhetorical strategy provided an effective means for calling attention to the paradox women faced as workers, wives, and mothers who struggled against a system that made their home life anything but tranquil and secure.

## Creating New Perspectives through Dissociation and Irony

In discussions of the family and its relation to the broader society, it is important to consider historical context and to distinguish between the ideal and the reality of family life. Despite popular notions that promote the nuclear family as timeless and cross-cultural, the family has changed greatly over the centuries more or less in relation to a society's economic structure. In brief, preindustrial American families represented the locus of both home and work life. Families were more or less economic units, with husbands, wives, and children participating in daily sustenance activities, such as growing and preparing food, making clothing, performing household and farming chores, and preparing goods for sale in the market. This is not to say that there was no sexual division of labor within the family. It is just to say that the chores performed and jobs held by men and women did not always fall neatly along traditional gender lines. Women often engaged in "men's work" as merchants and shopkeepers (Matthaei 1982, 29), and men played a central role in child rearing and instruction (Coltrane 1996, 29). Still, the husband remained the property owner and head of household while the wife retained no economic or political rights upon marriage. Men were associated with activities in the public sphere, while women were defined in terms of their familial relationships with husbands and children. As Matthaei notes, "In general, husbands took up commodity production, while wives centered in self-sufficient production" (1982, 31).

Regardless of the ambiguities surrounding gender and labor in colonial America, it is clear that the rise and spread of industrial production exacerbated the extant sexual division of labor. The increasing separation of commodity production from the home reinforced patriarchal gender relations and gave rise to a new role for the family. With necessary goods mass produced in factories and purchased from stores, the family centered less on economic and more on affective ties, and women's roles as mothers and wives came to be more closely aligned with the emotional work of socializing children and soothing husbands after a hard day's work in the factory, mill, or mine.

Two ideologies popularized in the early to mid-1800s—the doctrine of separate spheres and the cult of True Womanhood—constructed an idealized image of the family and reinforced woman's roles therein. The doctrine of separate spheres communicated the idea that family life and work life were separate realms, complementary and largely untouched by one another. Work life, which was associated with masculinity, was part of the public sphere, worldly, rational, and marked by competitive ties. In contrast, according to this ideal, the family was woman's sphere; it served as a refuge from the clamoring of the public realm. As the feminine domain, the family was structured according to affective relations. Morality and virtue, viewed as natural womanly traits, imbued family life.

Though the traditional nuclear family as established in the doctrine of separate spheres was an ideal rather than a reality within reach for most families, we need not deny the persuasiveness in the doctrine's utopian impulse (Cloud 1998b, 390, 391) nor should we overlook the very real measures that family provides, such as emotional security (Barrett and McIntosh 1991, 21) and, particularly for working-class families, a degree of autonomy not found in the daily grind of the factory (Coontz 1988, 300, 301). Yet, a closer look at the testimonies of poor, immigrant, and African American women from the 1900s forward reveals the interconnected nature of public and private spheres. It was an interrelationship highlighted time and again by those who were held responsible for the quality of a domestic atmosphere that was not left untouched by issues in the workplace. As Cameron explains, "Unending efforts to secure the 'bare necessaries' for their family, necessarily brought women into the public arena of the market, not only as consumers of commodities, but also as negotiators for scar[c]e resources and advocates for familial and community needs. Whether haggling at the market, falsifying papers, or out-maneuvering landlords, women acted in ways that assumed an inherent unity between 'private' and the 'public,' and they perceived of themselves as intimately involved in the comings and going of each" (1993, 112).

From firsthand experience, women realized the spuriousness of separate spheres rhetoric. In 1914, living in circumstances not unlike those her working-class sisters would encounter in 1930s coal towns, Mrs. M. H. Thomas pointed out the extent to which family welfare hinged on the whims of mine owners who also owned families' homes and the stores where they were forced to shop ("An America Pogrom"). Thomas, the wife of a Ludlow, Colorado, miner, noted, "A man dare not report a piece of unsafe roofing here, he would just be fired and blacklisted if he did" (172).[2] Twenty years later, housewives made the same observation, often in public forums such as magazine articles, letters to the editor, and speeches. Specifically, women activists of the Communist Party employed the rhetorical strategies of dissociation, irony, and metaphor, and they engaged extra-discursive tactics in order to startle audiences into assuming a new perspective that undermined separate spheres ideology.

### Creating a New Context for "Home"

"Time has come for the public to know how I have to struggle to raise my children; at times I don't have anything to feed them but bread and coffee, some time not even that," proclaimed Fanny Sepich, the wife of a coal miner in Pittsburgh (1931). Time and again working-class wives and mothers described with no lack of detail the havoc wrought on their home life by unemployment, wage cuts, and even New Deal policies. For these women, public and private realms were decidedly not separate. Their straightforward descriptions, found in letters to the editor, speeches, and pamphlets, are significant for the way they strip the image of the family of its affective trappings, laying bare the side of family life that most clearly reveals its links to the economic world. In Burkean terms, CP women created "impious" associations by violating "common sense assumptions about what properly ought to go with what," thus revealing "hitherto unsuspected linkages and relationships which our customary vocabulary has ignored" (Whedbee 2001, 48). They encouraged a new perspective on the realities of home life by dissociating the image of "home" from its traditional context and placing it in a newly crafted context that more accurately reflected their daily experiences. For audiences who had a similarly raised consciousness concerning class issues, these narratives rang true and perhaps motivated them to organize to fight the conditions that adversely affected their families. For others who were less cognizant of the influence of the economic system on familial sufferings, harsh descriptions of home life shocked the reader/listener into a new recognition of where the root of the problem existed.

To its credit, the Communist Party offered one of the few outlets available to housewives to articulate their own unique experiences in the home during the Depression.[3] Regular columns such as "Woman's Voice" in the *Working Woman* and "The Women's Angle" appearing in the *Daily Worker* provided space for women to voice their concerns and vent anger directed at the ways that capitalism was making their lives miserable. Working-class women of the CP often pointed out that, in their roles as wives and mothers, they—more than their husbands—were hardest hit by the economic situation (Bloomington 1936b; "Effects of Unemployment" 1930; "Johnstown Working Women" 1931; "Miner's Wife Tells" 1931; "Steel Drive Is Spurred" 1936; Van Veen 1931c). Mothers struggled firsthand with tightened budgets, "making do" on black coffee and crusts, and clothing children in rags. "The wife of the unemployed gets the worst of it. She is the one to answer her children's cry for bread. . . . All the misery of the shortage of keeping the family from starvation in time of unemployment falls heaviest on the housewife," asserted a *Working Woman* article in early 1930 ("Effects of Unemployment"). The following year, with no improvement in workers' conditions and winter fast approaching, Sadie Van Veen (1931c) similarly observed that "it is the mothers that must scrimp and make the little pay cover many needs of life. It is the mothers of jobless families that are tortured by the cries of children for food."

These statements indicate the extent to which working-class women identified with the social expectations of wife and mother. Yet, the statements convey an incisive critique of the paradox that working poor women faced on a daily basis. On one hand, poor women were expected to carry out the duties of good wife and nurturing mother just as were their sisters of means. At the same time, however, the capitalist system created a context that made it difficult, if not impossible, for poor women to carry out these very duties. They knew that public and private were not separate spheres.

The significance of these domestic descriptions becomes apparent also when we consider the historical context in which these women spoke out. The economic uncertainty of the early 1930s led to a cultural conservatism concerning sex roles and the family. The weak economy (manifested, for example, in unemployment and job scarcity) threatened the nation's "manhood" as well as the masculinity of individual men. As a result, "Americans were reluctant to examine or tamper with traditional roles within the family at a time when it was viewed as perhaps the only remnant of stability" (Coiner 1995, 39). Thus, the descriptions of home life provided by working-class women represented a particularly profound contrast to prevailing perspectives and had the effect of awakening readers/listeners to a new understanding of "home."

In addition to speaking out as housewives, women also revealed how their experiences as workers outside the home affected their duties as mothers (see "International Women's Day" 1931; "Negro Widow Cheated" 1933; "Organize the Farm Women" 1934; Price 1936; "We Need Women Fighters" 1931). Farm women worked fourteen- to sixteen-hour days providing produce for the nation's children but could not afford fruits or vegetables for their own families, noted one CP activist writing in a 1934 issue of *Party Organizer* ("Organize the Farm Women"). Another woman highlighted the plight of unemployed women, describing it as "more acute than that of unemployed men." In addition to the pressures of being out of work, they—perhaps more than their male counterparts—came face-to-face with the lack of milk for the baby and the shortage of fuel for warmth and cooking ("We Need Women Fighters" 1931). A black domestic servant wrote a letter to the editor of the *Working Woman* that underscored the ways that race discrimination worked in conjunction with class and sex in making black women's experiences an even greater burden. Her story was not unlike that of many women in today's society who experience the repercussions of the 1996 repeal of long-standing welfare legislation. Writing in 1933, E.C. from New York told of how she had to leave her eight-year-old son home alone while she cleaned a well-to-do white woman's home from early morning until eight in the evening for only $1.75. She concluded her letter with a rhetorical question pointing up the dilemma facing women forced to balance the demands of worker and mother: "Now I ask you. My boy is eight years old. How can I live and bring him up under such conditions?" ("Negro Widow Cheated" 1933). In these examples, the issue of women's "double yoke," or double-shift workday, was subtly invoked though, as scholars have pointed out, CP leadership remained reluctant to acknowledge or address this concern with much enthusiasm (Coiner 1995, 45). The next chapter explores in greater detail the ways that working-class women reconciled their dual roles as worker in the home and worker in the paid labor force.

The foregoing examples point to the ways that CP women's rhetoric functioned through perspective by incongruity to create "impious" or atypical linkages between home life and the miseries effected by the economic sys-

THE UPPERS *and* THE DOWNERS

THEY DON'T WORK

THEY HAVE

THEY WANT MORE

BANK

THEY WORK

THEY HAVEN'T

NO RELIEF

① ② ③

tem. Additionally, incongruous or unorthodox perspectives were elicited through juxtaposition and metonymy, which called attention to the ironies inherent in the capitalist system, such as the necessity of extreme poverty to enable extreme wealth.

### Critique through Irony

Burke (1945) notes that irony functions through dialectic. As he observed, "Irony arises when one tries, by the interaction of terms upon one another, to produce a *development* which uses all the terms" (512). Working-class women frequently relied on juxtaposition of seeming opposites. Their rhetoric was filled with images and narratives that placed "poverty" and "wealth" side by side, which resulted in a new understanding of both of these experiences. Rather than allow the commonplace perception of the two phenomena as opposites, separate, or unrelated, the juxtaposition called up their actual interrelationship thus enabling the irony to emerge. Capitalism, a system allegedly built upon "free" enterprise, relied on the "slave labor" of the majority of the nation's citizens. For most, freedom meant the "freedom" to work at slave wages or starve. The use of juxtaposition called attention to these ironies.

A cartoon appearing in the June 1935 issue of the *Working Woman* offers a clear example of juxtaposition that put the relationship between poverty and wealth in sharp relief (figure 1). The strip is divided into five frames with each frame divided in half horizontally. The top half of the frame depicts "the uppers," meant to represent the upper class; the bottom half shows "the downers," representing the working class. Each frame provides an illustration along with a phrase that encapsulates the respective experiences of the rich and poor. For instance, the first frame, in the top half, shows a wealthy, overfed couple being chauffeured in the back seat of a car and states, "They don't

Figure 1. "The Uppers and the Downers." Cartoon appearing in the *Working Woman,* June 1935.

work." The bottom half of this frame shows a line of women bent over sewing machines and states, "They work." Through the juxtaposition a statement is made: the leisure of the elite comes at the expense of the toiling masses. The third and fourth frames continue with the upper half stating, "They want more . . . so they raise prices," and showing the wealthy couple hugging bags of money and grabbing for profits. The bottom half of the fourth frame depicts working women holding open empty purses and says, "They can't pay." In the final frame, the line dividing the top and bottom is literally and figuratively disrupted. In this frame, the line that separates the two halves appears to be bumped out of place by a sign held by a working woman, which reads, "Strike June 8." In a figurative sense, the message is that the working women's strike will disrupt the "uppers'" life of leisure. What is significant about this cartoon is the way that the two halves of each frame work together to create a specific message concerning the interrelated nature of wealth and poverty under capitalism. The "uppers" in this cartoon can benefit only to the extent that the "downers" work and suffer. The irony, of course, is that a nation of such seeming wealth and prosperity can harbor such widespread poverty.

Anna Damon, who along with Margaret Cowl headed the CP Women's Commission in the 1930s, provided a new perspective on war for *Daily Worker* readers in 1932. By contrasting what war meant for the rich with its significance for the poor, Damon (1932a) called attention to the irony in a system that can spend millions on death but is not willing to invest in programs to keep its own citizens alive. The U.S. government, Damon wrote, "is feverishly preparing for a war which will kill millions of workers, refusing at the same time to grant one cent for Unemployment Insurance to the 15,000,000 starving workers and their families. For the working women, war means fresh monstrous sacrifices, poverty, starvation and death. For the rich war means making fresh billions of profits." It is in and through the dialectic—spending versus refusing to grant money; fresh monstrous sacrifice versus fresh billions of profits—that a new perspective is brought forth. Damon's juxtaposition forced a reinterpretation of war that sees it as a wasteful act that destroys rather than protects home life.

Quite often, particularly in the pages of CP periodicals, juxtapositions were gender based, with images of fur-clad, bejeweled wealthy women contrasted with poor women who were malnourished, unemployed, and homeless (see Chasin 1930; "Families in N.Y. City" 1931; "How to Live on 95 Cents" 1931; Van Veen 1934; "Woman Domestic Worker" 1931). These examples rely on the trope of metonymy, the function of which is to "convey some incorporeal or intangible state in terms of the corporeal or tangible" (Burke 1945, 506). In this case, metonymy reduced complex issues surrounding capitalism and attendant unemployment and poverty to the concrete image of the wealthy woman and her expensive accouterments.

Photos of wealthy women and actresses dotted the pages of the *Working Woman* in the early 1930s and stood in stark contrast to the stories and pictures of women who worked in sweatshops, lived under bridges, and who, along with their children, were evicted from their homes. "In metonymy, perspective by incongruity occurs when an orientation is provided by the graphics and an incongruity by the discourse" (Bostdorff 1987, 55). In many examples, pictures of smiling well-to-do women were momentarily inviting until the reader's eye fell to the caption below the photo or to one of many articles on the same page detailing the sufferings of the unemployed and working poor. The juxtapositions of text and image called up the irony in a situation where such disparate experiences can occur within the boundaries of one town, city, or country.

For instance, one page in the March 1931 issue of the *Working Woman* depicted a society woman, Mrs. Henry G. Gray, who is "wearing a fortune in gems, enough to buy food for hundreds of workers' families for a year." An article appearing next to the photo tells of the wives of miners in Pennsylvania who, along with their children, have picketed with their husbands against wage cuts and layoffs that have led some families to a state of near starvation ("International Women's Day Finds Miners" 1931). Similar juxtapositions appeared in the December 1931 and February 1934 issues, in which images of an actress and a "rich dame" were placed next to testimonies from the unemployed in Detroit, Pittsburgh, Cleveland, and other cities around the country ("Women in Michigan Auto Cities" 1931; "Unemployed Women Raise" 1934).

The responses of reformers, social workers, and civil servants to the widespread problems facing poor families often came in the form of suggestions that, from workers' perspectives, were ineffective at best, and at times completely inane. The irony in such "advice" was exposed in CP women's responses, which described the circumstances they faced on a daily basis ("'Buy More Clothes'" 1931; "Don't Starve—Don't Stuff" 1933; "Free Lunches" 1931; "'Go Elegant'" 1933; Hutchins 1935; Small 1934). Grace Hutchins, the CP activist and author of *Women Who Work,* bristled at the advice of dieticians who encouraged families to get at least three to four servings of meat a week and who suggested that a food budget of twenty-three cents a day was sufficient for a family of five. With frustration, Hutchins (1935) compared the rise in meat prices between 1933 and 1935 with the amount given to families receiving relief in order to show the impossibility of meeting the recommended weekly requirement of meat. Hutchins concluded by pointing out that the "meat barons" were the ones who gained in this picture: the profits of the largest meat trusts were between two and ten million dollars.

Other women took aim at advice from fashion and entertainment pundits who entreated women to "Go elegant" ("'Go Elegant'" 1933), to "Wear more elaborate clothes" ("'Buy More Clothes'" 1931), and to "go glamorous" come evening (Small 1934). "How elegant can we look in a dress made over three times?" asked one writer ("'Go Elegant'" 1933). "'Don't see how we're going to get clothes this winter,'" a farmer's wife was quoted in the same article. Sasha Small (1934), a well-known CP activist, responded to advice to "eat on the terrace" found in the *Ladies Home Journal:* "Eating on the terrace! How about the possibilities of losing the whole house that is facing so many families who managed to accumulate enough to buy one, to say nothing about the families who live in fire traps from which they are in daily danger of being evicted" (10). And the advice from a member of the executive board of the National Conference of Catholic Charities to boost the economy by wearing "more elaborate clothes" and demanding "trimmed hats" was shown to be absurd through its juxtaposition with an article detailing the exploitation of women and their young children who do home work or "work given out by the factory owners and produced in the kitchens and bedrooms of the tenements under the sweat shop system" ("Children and Mothers Enslaved" 1931).

In short, CP women employed irony in order to call attention to the interrelationship between wealth and poverty. They accomplished this through dialectic or the juxtaposition of images and narratives that created an incongruity and led to a new perspective on women's position within capitalism. In conjunction with dissociation, irony provided a rhetorical means by which these activists could call attention to the paradox of separate spheres rhetoric, which their experiences proved to be a myth.

Ella Reeve Bloor contributed to discourses that attempted to upend separate-spheres rhetoric. But rather than rely on dissociation and irony, Bloor employed metaphors of the family and motherhood (Brown 1999) in order to humanize class struggle and to call attention to the ways that economic matters invaded family life.

## The Rhetoric of Ella Reeve Bloor

Known as "Mother" to tens of thousands of workers and farmers across the country, Ella Reeve "Mother" Bloor was perhaps the most renowned woman of the Communist Party. In celebration of Bloor's seventy-fifth birthday, Anna Damon said of her, "She has inspired us with her great courage, with her great heart; she has helped us in whatever work we may be doing by example, by advise [sic], by encouragement; she has taught us the meaning of selfless devotion and loyalty to an ideal" (1937, 3). Despite her fifty-plus years of work in Socialist and Communist organizations and her tireless speaking and advocating for the nation's farmers, unemployed, and working poor, little scholarly work has been devoted to Bloor's life.

Bloor was significant within the CP for her community-based organizing and her appeals to motherhood and family, which enabled her to connect with her listeners (see Brown 1996, 1999). Bloor's reliance on the trope of motherhood played into a long tradition of women's public speaking that employed such references as a way to justify women's political activism. Scholars have debated the efficacy of employing maternal appeals in women's arguments for social change.[4] On one hand, arguing from a position as mother and/or relying heavily on metaphors of motherhood may further reify essentialist notions that reduce women to their biology. Further, such arguments may reinforce beliefs that women are inherently self-sacrificing and nurturing, "hence hampering efforts to achieve advances for women as individuals" (Hayden 2003, 197). Additionally, reliance on maternal appeals may obscure the broader political implications of the issues to which one is attempting to call attention.

From a different perspective, maternal appeals may be viewed as an effective way for women to influence public policy and economic reform. Tonn argues that "maternal roles had particular efficacy for women as union agitators" (1996, 2). In her study of Mary Harris "Mother" Jones, Tonn explores how characteristics of mothering—namely, nurturance and militancy—lent themselves to the task of organizing and motivating oppressed miners. Hayden examines the rhetoric of women participating in the Million Mom March held in 2000 and argues that women employed "maternity to challenge the dominant social and political order and to promote an alternative set of values based in their daily interactions with their children" (2003, 196).

The use of maternal appeals in women's rhetoric of the nineteenth and early twentieth centuries is particularly significant given the rhetorical situation women faced as speakers. One hundred years ago, women had fewer rhetorical options for justifying their participation in efforts at social reform. Speaking in their roles as mothers was often seen as the only way for women to gain a hearing since dominant beliefs denied women the attributes deemed necessary for effective public speaking. The very idea of a rhetor negated all qualities traditionally associated with femaleness (see Campbell 1973). During the 1930s when Bloor was speaking out, the economic hardships of the Depression were framed primarily in terms of how they affected the primary breadwinner, who was assumed to be male. Less attention was given to private-sphere issues, such as women's abilities to control the quality of life in their homes and communities. Bloor's use of appeals to motherhood, then, should be seen as a strategic way to build rapport with her listeners and to politicize issues that she knew were often swept under the rug by mainstream politicians and fellow CP comrades alike.

Furthermore, Bloor's familial language and the ways she used her role as "mother" were not maternalist in the usual sense. Brown (1996) distinguishes between traditional notions of maternalism and Bloor's deployment of "motherhood." Brown notes that from a traditional standpoint, maternalism "assumes that women have a special capacity to nurture, and suggests that women and men have naturally separate spheres" (538). In contrast, Bloor's use of motherhood "was not sentimentalist, essentialist, or naturalist, but instead part of her construction of a serious ideology about the need to reproduce life and culture humanely. . . . For her, home and community were primary locations for the creation of class consciousness and class struggle" (539). Put differently, Bloor recontextualized motherhood, family, and protest in order to highlight the connections between public and private spheres.

Years before Popular Front policy became official within the CP, Bloor was working at a grassroots level in industrial and farming towns across the country, listening to the concerns of families and assisting them in their organizing efforts. Bloor's activist work demonstrates her devotion to and belief in the family and in community. Some of the more narrow minded within the male-centered CP hierarchy may have viewed Bloor's activism as innocuous and therefore acceptable, insofar as she remained within the limits of "women's concerns" and to that extent stayed "out of the way" of what was thought to be the more "serious" organizing of men in the workplace. Nothing could have been further from the truth, however. Bloor's concerns for family were never limited to the literal individual family. Bloor's "family" was the family of the working class. Working-class concerns were, thus, concerns that affected the entire family and the community as a whole—not just factory or mill workers. This belief is reflected in her correspondence and speeches as well as in the activities to which she committed herself. During the 1920s, at the height of CP masculinist rhetoric emphasizing the shop-floor issues of working *men* in heavy industries, Bloor was speaking to the needs of the entire community. "For her, working toward unionization and integrating community and shopfloor issues was not part of 'front' or auxiliary work which could be prioritized below 'real' Communist Party work. Unionization, community-based organizing, and integrating men and women into work for community betterment were legitimate CP work" (Brown 1996, 231).

Bloor framed working-class struggles as a family affair, using perspective by incongruity to form a new image of both "family" and "protest." According to Bloor, the purpose of working-class protest was "to create a world 'where such things as starvation of little children and the fear of poverty will not exist,' to bring 'happiness and security for all our children'" (qtd. in Brown 1996).[5] Bloor's rhetoric was not unlike that of Mother Jones who, in the early 1900s, encouraged her audience of miners to "visualize themselves as a 'family,' which increased their sense of belonging and moral duty to others" (Tonn 1996, 13). In a 1932 speech to farmers gathered in Washington, D.C., for the First Farmers National Relief Conference, Bloor defined family in broad terms that included members of all farm organizations in addition to thousands of unemployed workers who gave open support to the farmers. As she recounted her involvement in the strike of the Farmers Holiday Association, Bloor provided her listeners a clear picture of this family of workers: "One of the greatest achievements of that strike struggle came to me fully in that parade. All the way along the line were thousands of workers, unemployed most of them, and these workers would shout to the farmers: 'We're with you boys.' And the farmers in the parade would shout back to them: 'That's right, boys, we're with you. If you have to strike, we'll feed you.'" Additionally in this speech, Bloor conveyed the importance of family loyalty when she described children's' participation in the strike. "So the farmers came from far and wide with their wives and children. At one time there were 200 children picketing and that helped greatly because it is pretty bad when a man is going to break strike to see so many children against him" (1932b).

In addition to appealing to family unity, Bloor highlighted family preservation, another characteristic of mothering (Tonn 1996). Bloor "protected" her worker family by identifying threats to that family and in turn motivating her audience to stand up to and challenge forces that threatened worker solidarity. In a speech to miners sometime around 1933, Bloor (1933c) took the tone of a mother admonishing her children as she urged her audience to relinquish racist attitudes and set aside petty squabbles in order to support struggling workers in other parts of the country. She said, "Comrades, let us have *unity—not on paper—not just cold letters*—but unity of workers and farmers—*unity of our ranks.* Brothers—brother miners, don't be jealous of each other—you are all good workers—some can read, some can write, some can organize—let us push and pull collectively, pull together." Bloor also identified threats outside of worker ranks in her 1932 speech to attendees of the First Farmers National Relief Conference (1932b). She told of how striking farmers stood up to the "misleaders . . . the real estaters and lawyers [who have] come here to misrepresent us. Now we come here to attend to our own business, and we are going through with it."

Similarly, in a speech to milk farmers in Philadelphia the following year, Bloor framed the farmers' strike as a struggle for the entire family. She referred to her own experiences as the wife and mother of "dispossessed farmers" in order to establish credibility and to convey the fact that farm-related issues affected not only farmers but women as wives and mothers (1933b, 1). She continued by stating that the farmers were going to strike "for more than the cost of production. . . . [T]hey are going to strike . . . for their homes, for their wives and children. We believe that the wives and children have the first mortgage on all our farms and we are going to strike for them" (3). And as countless examples demonstrate, farm wives (and the wives of mill and mine workers) joined their husbands in striking for themselves and their families.

Bloor's maternal appeals were often directed specifically toward women, constituents whom she knew to be most often ignored by or isolated from broader worker struggles. Such language was exemplified in a 1933 article appearing in the *Working Woman* in which Bloor emphatically stated that "the working women-through their own suffering, their own struggles have learned to fight, and *together* we shall fight all imperialist wars, all starvation and unemployment, and *together* we shall do our part to build a new society, with happy motherhood, and healthy, happy childhood as the cornerstone" (1933a). Bloor issued a similar call to women in 1937, urging them to show solidarity with the women of Spain who were waging their own battle against oppression. "We pledge ourselves to mobilize our women to organize in unions, in homes, in communities, to unite the women of America against our enemies, poverty, child labor, exploitation of women in all industries, unemployment, outrageously high cost of living, terrible housing conditions in every city in America." Bloor's inclusive language encouraged women to understand their own families' concerns as stemming from a broad-based social system, which affected working-class families collectively and which required collective struggle in order to overcome.

Bloor's own experiences as a wife and a mother as well as her many cross-country campaign tours enabled her to see the interconnected nature of home, community, and workplace and prompted her to address this nexus as it affected women's lives. Yet she always linked issues of home and community to broader political and economic systems and structures. In short, her familial language, employed in the context of working-class struggles, provided a way for Bloor to politicize institutions deemed private and therefore apolitical in dominant discourses. For example, in a radio address broadcast nationally on 30 October 1936, Bloor rallied her listeners to vote for the CP presidential candidate and to support a host of worker-farmer struggles. Bloor spoke specifically to her female listeners. Reminding them of the influence that politics has on home life, Bloor (1936) stated, "Á vote for Landon [the Republican presidential candidate] means less milk for babies, inadequate clothing for children, no jobs for your husbands, a wave of persecution against women in industry." She continued by addressing the specific needs of farm women: "You have watched drought scorch the land. You have watched the speculator and banker rob your husband and your family of what they have earned through the sweat of their brow. . . . The Communist Party stands pledged to fight for the rights of the farming women and their families."

Another notable element of Bloor's familial language was her use of specific instances of women who embodied strength and displayed resistance. These vivid examples served two purposes. First, as will be elaborated in chapter 4, stories of militant young women engaging in workplace and community struggles gave Bloor's listeners an image of what they themselves could become. Second, references to the actions of women activists recontextualized a culturally dominant icon of family and home, "Woman." In her October 1936 radio address, for example, Bloor related her adventures while on a 14,000-mile tour campaigning for workers' rights, making special mention of the women she encountered who were "taking [the CP] campaign so seriously." She also lauded participants of the numerous housewives' strikes, which, she said, "exerted a tremendous political influence."

These examples highlighted the political elements of women's lives, providing another way for her to link the seemingly privatized family with worker struggle. Put differently, Bloor's rhetoric represented an emergent discourse, which emanated from the gap between culturally dominant discourses that mythologized "womanhood" and the realities of working-class families' lives. Brown notes that "in recognizing the personal as political and the community as inseparable from the workplace, [Bloor] foreshadowed the feminist and New Left movements of the 1960s" (1996, 347).

Likewise, Bloor utilized, and indeed embodied, "motherhood" in specifically political ways. Both her rhetoric and her actions created a new context for "motherhood," one that linked this traditional institution to a politicized working-class family. The words used by fellow working-class activists to describe Bloor indicate the way that Bloor used her status as "mother" for nonmaternalist ends. On one hand, Bloor was frequently described in terms connoting traditional motherhood. Comrades mentioned her "warmth," "compassion," and "remarkable ability to merge completely with the masses" (Todes and Small 1937). Her son, Carl Reeve, explained how Bloor played the traditional role of mother in many workers' lives: "many hundreds of people come to her with their personal troubles and problems because she is interested personally in all kinds of people, in their families, and in their development" (1937, 28). Workers referred to themselves as "sons" and "daughters" of Mother Bloor, while "Bloor herself had been referring to her Communist comrades as family since the early 1920s" (Brown 1996, 537).

At the same time, in contrast to these traditional descriptors of motherhood, Bloor was characterized as "energetic," "fiery," "spirited," and "courageous." She voiced workers' "never-realized dreams and [fought] like a lioness to make those dreams come true" (Conroy 1937). Earl Browder (1937), the general secretary of the Communist Party, was among the many who lauded Bloor's tireless agitating on behalf of the nation's poor. He said of Bloor, "She has given her time, her inspiring energy, her great enthusiasm and ability to almost every phase of [the labor] movement. Wherever workers were engaged in struggle for the right to organize, the right to better their lot, the right to live—Ella Reeve Bloor was there with them helping them, teaching them, showing them the way and encouraging them with her own great courage" (17).

Bloor's militant actions on behalf of labor—often engaged with fellow mothers and sometimes her own children and grandchildren by her side—further contributed to a politicization of the institution of motherhood. In her early years of activism, Bloor took her small children with her on speaking and organizational tours (Barton 1937, 12–13). In later years, she was accompanied by her granddaughters. The spectacle of a mother with her small children speaking publicly on behalf of a progressive cause served to undermine traditional ideas of mothers as serene, self-sacrificing, and submissive to the men in their lives. Bloor's very presence—not to mention the topics of her speeches—created an impious association between mothering and public activism.

As "mother" to the workers, Bloor was jailed numerous times for her roles in strikes and uprisings. While jailed for her participation in a strike of female chicken pickers in Loup City, Nebraska, Bloor received letters from supporters across the country, including one from a farmer's wife in Pennsylvania who was inspired by Bloor's courage and stated that she "would gladly take [Bloor's] place behind those gray walls of injustice" (Bloor 1935). Another letter further reinforced Bloor's status as a beloved mother: "How long I have watched your courageous work. Keep up your splendid courage. Many love you that you know not of" (Bloor 1935).

The powerful combination of compassion and bravery exemplified by Mother Bloor was also seen in October 1933 when Bloor spoke at the funeral of an Ambridge, Pennsylvania, steelworker murdered by police. The Ambridge Massacre, as it was known, was yet another tragedy that marked the history of labor struggles in the early 1900s. In this battle, striking steelworkers were terrorized by police who murdered, jailed, and threw workers out of town and "declar[ed] 'open season on the Communists'" (Cush 1937). Bloor made her way to the funeral while most of the town's workers were understandably too afraid to attend. In the presence of police who had attended the funeral, one of whom was poking his gun at Bloor's side, Bloor walked to the edge of the grave and "in a clear, calm, confident, defiant, determined tone, her hand held high, in the last, solemn, salute to the worker . . . said 'I speak in the name of the Communist Party'" (13).

In sum, Bloor successfully avoided reinforcing traditional restrictive notions of motherhood by subverting the concept. Her rhetoric politicized what was deemed a privatized institution and thereby created an impious association between motherhood and public activism. The success with which Bloor created a new perspective of motherhood is revealed in descriptions of Bloor that interweave references to her "warmth" and "compassion" with stories of her bravery and militance. Bloor believed that both elements were necessary for appealing to, and gaining the commitment of, those most exploited by the economic system. When it came specifically to working-class women, Bloor "used a rhetoric and imagery of motherhood to open up class politics and to find a way to broaden class language to appeal to an audience concerned with family, community, and social life" (Brown 1999, 559). For the working class as a whole, Bloor's used her role as mother to create community among workers and to motivate working-class families—two goals necessary for sustaining labor struggles throughout the 1930s.

## Labor's "Joan of Arc"

Perhaps one of the few Left activists whose decades-long dedication to labor struggles rivaled that of Mother Bloor, Elizabeth Gurley Flynn began her activist career at a tender age. She was giving speeches at the age of fifteen on "What Socialism Will Do for Women," and she was arrested for the first time a year later "for blocking traffic and speaking without a permit" (Baxandall 1987, 2). Flynn cultivated her activist and oratory skills as a member of the Industrial Workers of the World (IWW) from 1906 until the early 1920s. It was not until 1937, during the party's Popular Front period, that she joined the Communist Party. The party's shift toward more inclusive, grassroots organizing was attractive to Flynn, who "favored mass-based popular movements rather than sectarian politics" (Baxandall 1987, 38). Yet, Flynn grappled with the CP's organizational approach to labor struggle. She "detested the CP's discipline and constant political intrigue" (Baxandall 1994, 132) and found the party's "monolithic unity" to be stifling (Olmsted 1971, 106–8).

Her ambivalence notwithstanding, Flynn dedicated herself to the party's cause in hundreds of speeches in the late 1930s. Like Mother Bloor, Flynn had a reputation for holding her listeners rapt as she spoke in defense of political prisoners and against the spread of fascism. "The simplicity of her words and the clarity and the vibrant tone of her voice, echoing like the rich peal of a large bell in the higher registers, full and pulsating in the lower registers, compelled the attention of her listeners" (Camp 1995, 140). According to the Socialist Norman Thomas, Flynn "put life into a meeting as practically no other speaker could" (qtd. in Camp 1995, 140). A friend wrote to Flynn when she was hospitalized in June 1940, "The amount of love that you seem to evoke among the people is one of the most astonishing of phenomena—or would be astonishing if we did not understand it so well" ("Letter to Flynn," 1940).[6]

Communist Party leaders, well aware of Flynn's popularity, deployed her as a "medium for the ideological messages from above" (Baxandall 1987, 40; see also Camp 1995, 144). Some party members trivialized Flynn's contributions, describing her as a "'simple unsophisticated' earthy woman with no patience for abstract thought" (Baxandall 1987, 40). Theoretical acumen aside, Flynn was most at home when addressing ordinary working-class folks, particularly on issues relevant to women and their experiences as mothers and workers. Like Bloor and her working-class sisters, Flynn oftentimes called attention to the ways in which matters of production affected the home, and much of her rhetoric was infused with a "militant motherhood" (Tonn 1996) that was particularly appealing to the women in her audience who were charged with feeding and clothing their children on husbands' meager wages.

In a radio address given in late April 1938, Flynn relied on imagery of springtime and rebirth in order to illustrate the ties between work and family life (1938a). In her explanation of the history of May Day, Flynn created an apt metaphor for the labor movement, one that recognized that issues of reproduction (for example, food, shelter, warmth, child rearing) were intimately tied to work outside the home. In the past, Flynn explained (1938a), May Day "welcomed the coming of Spring, of warmth, light, and fertility. The power and heat of the sun awakened Mother Nature. . . . Even in the backyards of blackened steel town or among the coal camps an apple tree in bloom brings signs of spring to gladden the spirit. In the Middle Ages, the people who had ploughed the earth and planted the seed, gathered on the village green to celebrate. . . . *So it was appropriate that this natural people's holiday should be selected in America as a political labor holiday as well. Labor, the productive force, is the true son of Mother Nature, entitled to her fruits*" (emphasis mine). In effect, Flynn pointed out, production and reproduction are part of the same circle; each is necessary to sustain the other.

In subsequent speeches, Flynn made more open appeals to mothers and to motherhood in an attempt to point out the ways that economics affected home life. In these instances, Flynn displayed a "militant motherhood" in which she "challeng[ed] those who threaten[ed] [her] constituency and . . . challeng[ed] [her] audience themselves to resist" (Tonn 1996, 3). Flynn's references to motherhood in the context of militance and confrontation exemplify perspective by incongruity. In essence, Flynn dissociated motherhood from the traditional context of passivity, domesticity, and gentle nurturance. In Flynn's rhetoric, mothering took on a new understanding that included solidarity and anger directed at the economic and political powers-that-be.

Speaking to women in western Pennsylvania sometime in 1939, Flynn made the case that the Communist Party was the most effective means for fighting the "small handful of idle profiteers [who] stand in the way" of "peace, prosperity, and happiness" (1939). Women, especially "the mothers whose hearts are torn today with anxiety over their children and the future," are the ones who will benefit from Socialism. Flynn's rhetoric was characterized by a militant motherhood that cultivated a "sense of collective identity" (Tonn 1996, 5). Flynn concluded her speech with this appeal: "Let us build a fifty-fifty Communist Party in this Western Pennsylvania district of miners' wives, steel workers' wives, and other women who work for wages. We can tap new springs of courage, of militancy, of maternal love, of hope to make this basic area the heart of the Communist Party of America" (1939).

The most eloquent and stirring example of militant motherhood came in Flynn's vociferous condemnation of U.S. imperialist wars, published in the 1940 pamphlet, *I Didn't Raise My Boy to Be a Soldier for Wall Street*. In this diatribe, Flynn (1940a) urged all mothers to protect their sons from the U.S. war machine, which would sacrifice their children's' lives for capitalist profits upon entering the second world war. Flynn called on mothers to march on Washington, if need be, to get their voices heard. "'The female of the species is more deadly than the male,' where offspring are concerned," she proclaimed (5). By associating mothering with death as opposed to life, Flynn startled the reader into a new understanding of the concept. Yet, there is an element of irony in the framing—mothers must resort to death in order to protect their children's lives. Her statement, an example of perspective by incongruity, revealed the confrontational side of motherhood that acts to protect as well as nurture its young. As Tonn points out, "motherhood has always included not just nurturing of children but the pronounced *resistance* against all manner of forces that threaten them" (1996, 5).

Flynn employed forceful language to describe the causes and effects of U.S. involvement in unjust wars. "War is caused primarily by groups of imperialist bankers and industrialists, big monopolies of capitalist interests, seeking to control world markets," she explained (1940a, 7). Those who benefit from war—the "money lords"—seek "to prolong the war . . . and they expect our sons to shed their blood to secure it" (8). But, Flynn notes, it is not just anyone's son who goes to fight overseas. Wealthy mothers supported World War I because "[t]hey knew their sons . . . would not be in the frontline trenches. Their sons were swivel-chair soldiers, 'dollar-a-year' patriots, snoopers, safely situated 3,000 miles away from the bloody battlefields" (3). Flynn stated flatly, "If Wall Street wants this war, let the rich, middle-aged bankers and brokers go to war. Let *their* sons go to war—not ours" (8).

Flynn's antiwar rhetoric was particularly compelling for the description of the ravages of war on the children of mothers on both sides of the line. During wartime, mothers "will see our sons marched towards 'the enemy'—other plain mothers' sons—herded like cattle in parallel slaughter trenches. There they will be bombed from the skies, torn by shrapnel, maimed, wounded, crippled, gassed with deadly fumes, shell-shocked, or killed outright on the battlefields" (1940a, 4). Throughout the pamphlet, Flynn spoke directly to her readers in their roles as mothers. She told them that although they might not be members of the Communist Party, they had more in common with each other as mothers than they did with the "war-makers" (15). Further, Flynn appealed to that side of mothering that acted forcefully in the face of threats to one's young. In a tone marked by urgency, Flynn impelled readers to become active in resisting the war. "Act quickly. . . . *Act now* for peace. . . . Pass resolutions in your organizations. Send them to your Senators and Congressmen. Make them sharp and imperative instructions to them to *keep us out of war this time and no fooling about it either*" (14). She even suggested that women visit their local veteran's hospital in order to "see these poor twisted wrecks of humanity" who were casualties from previous wars. "Mothers of America, you will surely then say clear and firm, 'We Didn't Raise Our Boys to be Soldiers for Wall Street!'" (7).

Flynn's position on women and war changed just one year later when Hitler invaded the Soviet Union. In keeping with the official Communist Party line, which now viewed fascism as a threat to Communist Russia, Flynn and her comrades "quickly became as emotionally pro-war as [they] had only yesterday been anti-war" (Camp 1995, 165). In 1942, Flynn published *Women in the War,* in which she urged women to answer the wartime call by entering factories and *"mak[ing] arms* for our fighting forces and our brave allies" (1942b, 6). "The women of the nation are essential to winning the war. They are the reservoir of labor. In ever-increasing numbers women will be called out of the kitchen on to the assembly line. It is a matter of patriotism. . . . Women are cheerfully answering the call" (6). Denunciation of Wall Street greed and images of battlefield slaughter were replaced by descriptions of women who were ably and dutifully filling factory positions. Still, throughout the pamphlet, Flynn advocated equal pay for equal work, equal treatment for black women, equal participation in unions, and federally funded child care.

Flynn's experiences in the CP and her struggles to balance public activism and family responsibilities exemplify the ways that working-class women were forced to confront and reconcile a number of paradoxes surrounding their roles as women, mothers, workers, and activists. For one thing, Flynn was a woman in a male-dominated organization that gave superficial attention to issues affecting women. Unlike her male comrades, Flynn (and her activist sisters) was often forced to choose between dedication to her sex and allegiance to her class. Put differently, Flynn could play the role of Communist Party activist or women's rights activist, but oftentimes not both at the same time. For Flynn, the issues of the working class came first and foremost throughout her life, even when it caused internal dissonance (see Olmsted

1971). Baxandall notes that publicly, Flynn "follow[ed] the twists and turns of the party line in her speaking and writing, despite the reservations she described in private diaries" (1994, 133). As a result, her position on issues important to women often changed. For instance, though she fought for birth control during World War I, as a CPer she wrote a column opposing abortion, "citing Stalin who outlawed abortion and rewarded women for raising large families" (Baxandall 1994, 133).

Additionally, like many other female activists, then and now, Flynn felt forced to choose between her role as mother and that as activist. It was a dilemma that her male comrades who were also parents (including the father of her child) never had to make. She left her only son, Fred, in the care of other family members while she engaged in labor struggles and also while she went to Oregon for a ten-year hiatus from activism. According to Baxandall, these years of separation were hard on Fred, "who had always resented his mother's lack of attention and finally punished her by cutting off communication altogether" (1987, 33, 34). No doubt, the separation was also a strain for Flynn, who struggled with feelings of guilt even as she was doing important work in working-class communities and advocating on behalf of wrongfully imprisoned labor activists (see Camp 1995, 179, 180).

Still, Flynn's dedication to the Communist Party did not stop her from openly criticizing male comrades for not putting enough emphasis on the organization of women and their advancement to leadership positions (Camp 1995, 172, 173). Frustrations such as those experienced by Flynn are what led many working-class women to form organizations of their own, such as auxiliaries, when they decided to join labor struggles.

## Organizational and Extra-discursive Tactics

Perspective by incongruity is a discursive strategy that, in the example of Communist Party women, functioned through dissociation, irony, and metaphor. Incongruous or atypical associations and images awakened readers/listeners to new interpretations or understandings of their lives as women and as workers and thus succeeded in motivating women to speak out against the conditions that hurt their families. But CP women did not limit their challenges to the realm of discourse. They formed organizations and engaged in extra-discursive actions through which they physically challenged economic and political policies. I would argue that these organizations and actions functioned similarly to perspective by incongruity in their ability to create impious associations and to disrupt the sanctity of home life and motherhood.

## Women's Auxiliaries

The activities of CP-influenced union auxiliaries were the means by which many poor women got their first taste of involvement in the broader struggles of labor. A closer look at auxiliaries points us to a number of significant issues. First, the presence of women's auxiliaries calls up the issues radical women faced when they wanted to step outside their homebound roles and take a more active part in class struggles. It's important to ask, then, what was the role of women's auxiliaries within the labor movement? How did women's auxiliaries stand vis-à-vis the Communist Party and male unionists? Second, the actions of women's auxiliaries were notable for the ways they created a sort of "extra-discursive impiety" or unorthodox linkage between militance and motherhood that forced a reinterpretation of traditional notions of caretaking and homemaking.

"Auxiliary" implies an ancillary or secondary role, like that of a helpmate to the "real" or primary organization. The history of auxiliaries points to the ambivalent stance that male unionists and CP activists held toward women's roles in labor struggles. Baxandall states that during the 1930s and 40s "women were organized into ladies' auxiliaries, which made coffee, organized day care and built morale by staging rallies" (1993, 153). Only "occasionally" did these groups take action and when they did, it "tended to occur when it was too dangerous for men to act on their own behalf" (153). Female CP activists and ordinary working-class women attested to the barriers they faced when they attempted to organize themselves into something more than a tea party. During a coal miners' strike in the early 1930s, in which over eighteen hundred auxiliary women participated, a CP organizer noted that the women "were compelled to organize over the heads of the [United Mine Workers] officials" who had "openly forbid the organization of the women's auxiliary" ("Work among Women in the Mining Fields" 1934).[7] Male union leaders of the Progressive Miners of America (PMA) tried to "change the fighting auxiliaries into harmless sewing clubs" and "gossip circles," noted one *Working Woman* contributor (Kling 1935). A letter writer had expressed similar frustrations in the magazine a few months earlier. "The reactionary officials [of the PMA] have been stamping out every sign of militant activity and tell us to keep our noses out of men's business and not to go picketing, but to stay at home, make bed sheets, cook and hold parties, but our officers seem to forget there is hardly anything to cook and nothing to sew" ("From a Coal Town" 1935). The pressures of their husbands and society at large kept many women locked into traditional gender roles, with many PMA branches "holding dances, parties and affairs." Communist Party activists who attempted to use auxiliaries as a way to involve women in the CP were confounded by findings in 1937 that a good number of auxiliaries were "only tea parties" (see Perry 1937).

Yet, some women leaders viewed such social functions pragmatically, as a way to overcome another barrier: women's reluctance to join an organization that engaged in less-than-feminine actions. Auxiliary leaders and CP activists exercised persuasive ingenuity to convince less enthusiastic women to join auxiliaries (see "A Day Unit" 1937; Stevens 1937). Ethel Stevens recognized the reality of the situation in Gary, Indiana, when she said that "women of this strike region had no previous strike or organizational experiences. For most of them it was even a novelty to come to a mass meeting" (1937, 14). Still another issue was confronting the race prejudice of white women who refused to allow black women into their auxiliaries (see Perry 1937). To overcome these obstacles, leaders emphasized the importance of the personal touch—appealing to women face-to-face, connecting with them as mothers and wives. As one organizer noted, "sometimes it is necessary to spend hours with these women, washing dishes and helping them to cook while clearing up confusing things in their minds" (Perry 1937, 10–11). These persuasive tactics were above all practical. Rather than dismiss auxiliary work as a reinforcement of traditional gender roles, it is important to see it as an opening wedge, a door into women's lives that were to a large extent isolated and confining. The CP leader Margaret Cowl affirmed that auxiliaries "set into motion thousands of wives of workers in basic industries. . . . Auxiliaries help the workers win higher wages and the recognition of their trade union. They help to build the trade unions" (1937b, 552).

The testimonies of auxiliary women indicate that this work expanded their opportunities and enabled them to make more apparent the links between public and private spheres. Lasky's interviews with members of the Ladies' Auxiliary to Local 574 of the Minneapolis Teamsters provide insight on the "ambiguous legacy" of women's auxiliaries, but they also underscore the radical potential these organizations carried. Lasky writes, "While reflecting conventional ideas about women's proper place, auxiliary activities also nurtured the seeds of women's autonomy. Indeed, as the auxiliary's responsibilities expanded, 'unfeminine' behavior emerged, and women's militancy threatened to spill over the boundaries of women's separate sphere" (1985, 187). Women in the Ladies' Auxiliary to Local 574 did everything from raise funds and distribute the strike newspaper to occupy city hall "while their leaders negotiated to meet with the mayor" (Faue 1991, 115).

Likewise, a look at the activities of CP-related women's auxiliaries in the steel and coal industries indicates that these women often did much more than make coffee for their striking husbands. Women eagerly joined auxiliaries because they knew from firsthand experience the connections between the struggles of their sons and husbands and the quality of home life. We might say that, in these situations, class solidarity superseded issues surrounding gender bias. Even in the face of restrictions stemming from the influence of traditional gender ideologies on auxiliary work, women acted with creativity and militancy and created a nexus between auxiliary work and home life.

Auxiliaries did more than simply bolster morale. These groups played pivotal roles in building and strengthening unions and organizing women into picket lines alongside men on strike. The daily contact that wives had with their miner husbands made it that much easier for them to exercise their persuasive skills in convincing the men to remain on strike (see "Work among Women in the Mining Fields" 1934). The experiences of the Communist-led National Miners Union (NMU) in the Ohio-Pennsylvania area, the Progressive Miners of America, and the Amalgamated Association of Iron, Steel and Tin Workers in South Chicago provide three good examples of women's militant and disruptive work that contributed to working-class struggles (see "Work among Women in the Mining Fields" 1934; "Build Women's Auxiliaries" 1931; Kling 1935; M. Smith 1930; "Steel Drive Is Spurred" 1936; "Women Auxiliaries Aid" 1931). Mary Smith, a delegate at the Pittsburgh District Conference of the Women's Auxiliaries of the NMU in July 1931, pointed out the significance of women's participation in mine strikes: "Fifty per cent of the population of a mining town is composed of women, and the strike cannot be won with only 50 per cent of the people sharing in the strike activities. But if we get the whole 100 per cent on the picket line, then we have a chance to win" ("Women Auxiliaries Aid" 1931). In an article appearing in the *Working Woman,* Smith (1930) detailed the significant role played by miners' wives who supported the strike.

> Women took a very active part in these strikes. They were on the picket line fighting coal operators, scabs and coal and iron police. An instance was reported that scabs were coming to work in automobiles. They have formed a strong line on the road, stopped the automobiles, took the lunch from the scabs, threw it in a ditch and ordered them to go back. If they did not turn back, they were told by women, their automobile will be smashed and an exception will not be made as far as scabs' heads are concerned. Because of this militancy on the part of women the scabs were forced, in spite of protection by police, to go home and stay there.

Similarly, five years later, women made up at least half of the picketers during a strike in the mine region spanning Ohio, West Virginia, and Pennsylvania, pointing to the strength of auxiliaries in this area. Women also played pivotal roles in decision making, particularly when creativity was needed to skirt company deputies in order to reach men who had returned to the mines with important strike information (Rand 1931).

The militancy of wives and daughters (both within and outside of formal organizations such as auxiliaries) should not be underestimated. One person observed, "Many a strikebreaker lost his dinner pail to the women" of coal auxiliaries in Pennsylvania and Ohio (Borich 1934). And in Johnston City, Illinois, auxiliary women gave one disloyal coal miner "a parting farewell with bricks that he will never forget" (Kling 1935). Wives and sisters of striking railroad workers in Louisiana were equally militant when their husbands and brothers went on strike in 1936. Women formed flying squadrons that stopped trains and effectively forced the resignation of scab conductors and engineers. In Minden, Louisiana, the wives and sisters of strikers "locked the scab crew in the 'caboose,' while they escorted . . . a scab conductor to the telegraph station where he wired his resignation to the division superintendent" ("Women Halt Train" 1936). In Winnfield, Louisiana, after the women boarded the train and attempted to persuade strikebreakers to join the strike, a scab hit one of the women in the face. "In the resulting fray, the scab fireman had all his clothes torn off and left immediately to hide himself in the forest," pointing up the extent to which women went to support their striking husbands and brothers ("Scab Goes Nudist" 1936).

Perhaps the best-known example of auxiliary militance occurred in Flint, Michigan, during the United Auto Workers' sit-down strike of 1936–37 (figure 2). The CP played a role in this event, contributing to the strike fund and providing coverage in the *Daily Worker*. Of the CP's involvement, one woman who participated in the auxiliary stated, "Although I never belonged to a party, I feel that had it not been for the education and know how that [the Socialist and Communist Parties] gave us, we wouldn't have been able to do it" (*With Babies and Banners*). The women's auxiliary was well organized and provided extensive support in the form of publicity, picketing, and the collection of food and money for strikers (Fine 1969, 200). Women performed these tasks with enthusiasm and often put themselves in harm's way in order to ensure that basic necessities were provided. One auxiliary member, who later joined the Women's Emergency Brigade, explained how police tried to stop her from taking coffee and soup to the strikers. The police said to her and

Figure 2. United Automobile Workers of America, Women's Auxiliary, February 1937. Walter P. Reuther Library, Wayne State University.

the other volunteers, "You don't want to go down there, ladies, there's a lot of tear gas down there." And she replied, "I've smelled that before, that don't bother me" (*With Babies and Banners*). In addition to providing food, money, and publicity, auxiliary wives performed the important task of contacting "sit-down 'widows' who complained about the absence of their husbands to explain the strike and to enlist their support" (Fine 1969, 200).

It was the Women's Emergency Brigade, an offshoot of the auxiliary, that was at the center of confrontational tactics that were central to the strike's success. Genora Johnson, the wife of one of the striking men, organized the brigade in the wake of the "Battle of the Running Bulls," a confrontation between police and strikers that turned violent (T. Lynch 2001, 94–95). Wearing red caps and arm bands that said "EB," women of the brigade were "fearless and seemingly tireless," according to one description (Vorse 1969, 76). Members picketed the plants, some of them even spending the night on the picket line (Vorse 1969, 76). And in what was later seen as the turning point in the six-week-long ordeal, they guarded the gate at Fisher Plant 4 preventing police from entering until thousands of picketers could join them in protecting the workers inside.

In addition to turning the strike in the favor of the workers, such actions had an impact on participants' views of labor activism and its relation to life in the home. "Seeing the relationship between union success and the improvement of the material conditions under which they and their families lived, some of the women concluded that they must henceforth involve themselves actively in union affairs," noted Sidney Fine, who narrated the event in the book *Sit-Down* (1969, 201). A brigade participant stated simply, "We wasn't individuals any longer, we were part of an organization" (*With Babies and Banners*).[8]

In Flint and in auxiliaries across the country, though women may have been speaking primarily in their roles as wives and mothers, they acted a very different part. As a result of their actions, women faced jail terms, and in the tragic case of Emma Cummerlato even death, at the hands of police and coal company thugs (Kling 1935). But they fought hard all the same, extending their efforts well beyond the soup kitchen. The auxiliary provided the auspices to carry out confrontational work and it gave women an outlet to challenge the idea of separate spheres. Women knew that the forces that exploited their husbands in the mines and mills also exploited them in the home. "It is the women who have to make the miserable wage go around, to make the relief do," noted one *Working Woman* contributor who spoke of women's auxiliaries among the coal miners of Illinois (Kling 1935). A similar observation was made regarding wives of coal miners in Kentucky: "The women who in the past have always been made to feel that their place was in the home with the kids, and that it was the job of the man to do the fighting, are organizing into auxiliaries. They do not find any home to stay in, no food in the shacks to cook, children sick and crying for food, no shoes or clothes with which to send their children to school" (Drew 1931). Auxiliary women saw their fight as part and parcel of their husbands' struggles, yet they were careful not to personalize their experiences. They grounded their work in a larger political struggle, as a statement from a women's steel auxiliary in Chicago pointed out. "As women of steel we must bend every effort to further our organization and to enlist the support of all our friends through the realization that the benefits of this drive will be shared by the community as a whole" (H. Jones 1936).

Auxiliaries were not the only organizations available to women for engaging in radical actions. Neighborhood councils, unemployment councils, and housewives' councils, to name a few, represented outlets for women to engage in a host of extra-discursive tactics such as bread, meat, milk, rent, and sit-down strikes, which called attention to the interrelated nature of work and home life. These actions can be best understood within the context of the broader housewives' movement of the 1930s.

### The Housewives' Movement of the 1930s

The confrontational tactics of women in the 1930s housewives' movement were rooted in the actions of women on the Lower East Side of New York who, in the early 1900s, initiated meat boycotts and rent strikes in an effort to lower the cost of living. These actions were significant for the ways they embodied both persuasive and coercive elements. Participants were involved in more than a "controversy" or "difference of opinion"; they were engaged in a "genuine conflict" in which "talk between parties" was not enough (Simons 1972, 231). Conflicts involve "irreconcilable differences that are perceived to be so basic" that coercive tactics are often deemed necessary in order to get one's "voice" heard (231). By their bodily presence (as pickets in front of stores or in a sit-down in a welfare relief office) and by their absence (as consumers who boycotted stores), women forced the hand of authorities in a way that words alone could not. In addition to their material significance, at a discursive level these actions reframed understandings of motherhood. Although women were speaking (and acting) out from their position within the traditional gender framework, their arguments were radical insofar as they de-sentimentalized domesticity thereby politicizing women's experiences and calling attention to the social roots of seeming personal problems. "Anger directed at the greedy landlord, the cheating grocer, or the unjust employer can, in the process of female exchange and mobilization, generate into a coherent attack upon an entire system of exploitation, what one former Lawrence [Massachusetts, textile] striker called 'the powers that prey'" (Cameron 1993, 112). The observation of one CP agitator, Christine Ellis (1981), indicated that it was, indeed, women's domestic experiences that became a wellspring of anger and militance directed at public figures and institutions. She saw that "women were usually the most outspoken because they had the children to feed and they had to provide the food for the family. You found women pounding their fists on the desks as well as the men" (30).

Through successful bread, meat, and milk strikes that were carried out through CP-assisted neighborhood councils and associations, women made clear that issues of reproduction were not unrelated to issues of production. This brand of community-based organizing, which characterized the activism of housewives in the early 1900s, had been the mainstay of two CP activists, Ella Reeve Bloor and Clara Lemlich Shavelson, throughout the 1920s.

It was not until the early 1930s that the party, on a more widespread scale, recognized the significance of, and devoted energy to, neighborhood organizing and political actions (Gosse 1991). At first, actions such as food boycotts and rent strikes represented "unlinked local protests. But through the efforts of a small group of seasoned women organizers, these disparate protests were forged into a national movement" (Orleck 1995, 217). Clara Lemlich Shavelson, housewife, mother of three, and experienced radical activist, stood at the center of this movement. In the summer of 1929, she and a handful of Communist housewives formed the United Council of Working-Class Women (UCWW) to serve as an umbrella organization coordinating the myriad neighborhood councils springing up during these years (Orleck 1995, 225). Although it organized and appealed to women as mothers and housewives, the council was wholly political and continuously made links between women's experiences in the home and broader economic and political structures. The group's founding statement observed that "only through the common struggle of men and women in the shops, factories and at home, can the interests of the working class be protected" (qtd. in Orleck 1995, 226).

Bread strikes were common through the first half of the 1930s and represented a significant way that women in the UCWW and other similar organizations became involved in labor-related struggles. In Chicago, the Mothers' League, in cooperation with the Trade Union Unity League (TUUL), a CP organization, successfully led a bread strike that resulted in lowering prices from ten cents to six cents (Morrison 1931). The women were thorough and persistent in their actions. When bakery owners refused to accept their price demands, they called a strike and immediately organized picket lines, which prevented workers from entering the bakeries. Women went door-to-door explaining the strike and urging housewives not to buy from the bakeries nor to buy bread from groceries that were selling "scab bread." To further cover their ground and ensure support, they distributed leaflets and held meetings. Additionally, children were organized by the CP Young Pioneers to join women on the picket lines, making the event a family affair.[9] While on the picket lines, women were not afraid to get confrontational when the situation necessitated it. Picketers in front of one of the bakeries, Banovitz's, were enraged when they saw a scab walk out of the bakery with a loaf of bread. The strikers wasted no time in tearing the loaf from the woman's arms, throwing it into the street, and trampling on it. Women on the picket lines faced arrests and violence from police and "gangsters" hired by bakery owners to scare away the women. But the women were not deterred. After three weeks of picketing, the owners agreed to lower their prices without lowering wages of the bakery workers.

Figure 3. Women and children participating in the Hamtramck, Michigan, meat strike, August 1935. Walter P. Reuther Library, Wayne State University.

The successes of housewives in Chicago and Detroit in early 1931 moti-vated the United Councils of Working-Class Women and other groups to organize their own strikes in New York City and Philadelphia (see "Bronx Bread Strike" 1931; "Short Bread Strike" 1931; "Working Women Fighting" 1931; "Working Women Wage Winning Fight" 1931; "Fighting the High Price" 1935; Reish 1933; Schwager 1933). Women in New York City picketed meat shops and bakeries with successful results. "Butchers were soon so over-loaded with chops and loins and legs and steaks that they realized that the housewives meant business and that meant no business for them" ("Working Women Wage Winning Fight" 1931). The women's steadfast refusal to pur-chase meat had *material* consequences (that is, "no business") for butchers and thus "spoke" loudly. Bread strikes spread from Los Angeles to New York with such success that it took the mere threat of a strike aimed at the Bak-ers' Association in Philadelphia in 1935 to convince bakery owners to refrain from raising prices ("Fighting the High Price" 1935). And wives did not always act alone. In 1933, New York City women joined forces with their baker hus-

Figure 4. Vilma Kowicke and Mary Chumicke leading women in the Hamtramck meat strike, August 1935. Walter P. Reuther Library, Wayne State University.

bands, who were striking against bakery owners' attempts to reduce wages and increase hours (Schwager 1933).

Meat strikes in the East—sparked by ten thousand Los Angeles housewives in March 1935—were particularly successful in the mid-1930s (R. Nelson 1935a, 1935b; Shavelson 1935; "The Detroit Meat Strike" 1935) (figures 3 and 4). Margaret Cowl noted the somewhat disjointed efforts of the strikers, who "[i]n the beginning . . . threw picket lines around small meat shops" (1974, 42). However, she explained, "[T]hrough the efforts of Communist women who were active in the movement, the boycott campaign was directed against the meat trusts, the monopolies who were really responsible for high meat prices. After that, many small meat shop owners joined the housewives in their protest" (43).

On 22 May 1935, Clara Shavelson along with Rose Nelson, another central CP activist and UCWW leader, organized a meat strike aimed at meat wholesalers who kept meat prices artificially high. The actions of the housewives were well orchestrated. They formed picket lines and blocked access to hundreds of butcher shops throughout New York City and the surrounding communities. They formed flying squadrons of three hundred to a thousand women who went from shop to shop persuading owners to honor the strike. Shavelson and Nelson gave daily speeches, and in July, a delegation of house-wives from New York and Chicago went to Washington, D.C., bringing their arguments face-to-face with Secretary of Agriculture Henry Wallace (Orleck 1995, 235–37). In all, the strike was a success and the price of meat was lowered four to five cents on the pound (Shavelson 1935).

A few months later, Minneapolis housewives, some of them affiliated with the CP, initiated their own meat strike under the auspices of the Women's League against the High Cost of Living (Faue 1991, 114). During a five-day strike, women picketed supermarkets and petitioned the government in order to call attention to the link between workplace issues (for example, unemploy-ment) and the quality of home life. "They say that all these 'isms' are breaking up the home but the only 'ism' I know of that is doing that is 'capitalism,'" asserted Marian Le Sueur, a Women's League activist (qtd. in Faue 1991, 114).

The rising price of milk was another issue that activated housewives with the UCWW to play a central organizational role. The struggle for accessible milk was significant for its symbolic value. Milk was the primary form of nourishment for babies. But many working poor and unemployed mothers were unable to afford this important staple and were often unable to breast-feed due to their own malnourishment. Agnes Mitchell, the wife of a coal miner, wrote to the *Working Woman* in August 1931 explaining the wretched conditions faced by families in her region. "Very few mothers are able to buy milk for their small babies, most of them have to feed their babies black cof-fee" (Mitchell 1931). Thus, the fight for affordable milk—particularly when well publicized—was a struggle infused with emotion and lent itself to a sub-version of prevailing images of family life.

In early 1934, the Women's League of Philadelphia organized women in their city to support milk drivers on strike. Characteristic of actions within the broader housewives' movement, the struggles of the Philadelphia women were well orchestrated and extensive. The Women's League organized women into a network of pickets that "chased away the scabs and the police from the neighborhood." Additionally, "pickets were stationed at the homes of the scabs, in order to prevent them from going out of the house" (Pervin 1934). Women held demonstrations and mass meetings and sent speakers to a host of organizations, "including even orthodox churches and synagogues" (Per-vin 1934). The strike had mixed results. Leaders of the AFL settled with the Labor Board and decided to terminate the strike before winning all demands.

Yet the experience was significant for the housewives, who gained speaking and picketing experience and whose coordinated efforts won recognition for the Women's League.

During the summer of 1934, the campaign for affordable milk was well underway, with Shavelson's UCWW at the center (see "Los Angeles Women's Councils" 1934; Rich 1934). In the New York City area, women circulated thousands of petitions, conducted open-air meetings, and held demonstrations in front of large milk companies, such as Borden and Sheffield (see Rich 1934). Sonya Sanders, a CP activist in Bronx County, noted that the women in her neighborhood carried milk petitions in their purses while they shopped and were always "on the alert for signatures" (Sanders 1938, 39). Mothers in Cleveland, Ohio, took a particularly creative tack in order to get needed milk for their babies. Mrs. E. M. wrote to the *Working Woman* and explained that when aid offices cut off milk supplies to families, the "mothers got together in groups and left the babies in the C.E.R.A. [welfare aid] offices screaming their heads off. They refused to come back after them until milk was given. This caused the C.E.R.A. to call in a squad of visiting nurses and turn the office into nurseries. Before they day was over, every one had milk and have had very little trouble on this point since. Ha! Ha!" ("Milk for Our Babies" 1935).

Such out-of-the-ordinary actions were not uncommon throughout the 1930s as workers and mothers within and outside of the CP grew frustrated at the inability of New Deal legislation to address their needs. Petitioning, letter writing, and debating, engaged on their own, were often not sufficient to bring about change. So, in 1932, when the welfare relief of Toledo, Ohio, workers was cut, the workers along with their wives and children marched into an A&P grocery store and took the food they needed ("Toledo Jobless Seize" 1932). The following year, in New Philadelphia, Ohio, two hundred mothers and wives of unemployed men gathered at city hall to demand an increase in food relief for their children. The women "threatened to call a public school students' strike, unless adequate relief was provided by the city" (Hutchins 1934a, 191). Women in Detroit were similarly fed up with their living conditions and so planned a march to the Davison welfare office. Wearing shoes that were falling apart at the seams, they marched into the office and, when denied new shoes, sat down and refused to leave until given new shoes. One of the participants explained the significance of this action. "By sticking together, by a definite fighting program[,] we forced the Welfare Agency here in Detroit to know that we not only needed the shoes but we meant business in the matter of getting them" ("They Got the Shoes!" 1933). Working-class women of the Depression knew from firsthand experience that saying "We mean business" was, at times, not as persuasive as a physical action such as a sit-down that not only conveyed their resolve but also forced the hand of welfare administrators.

These actions were often engaged with babies in arms, creating a public spectacle that further underscored the interrelated nature of public issues and family concerns. Indeed, the UCWW and CP activists such as Shavelson and Bloor often appealed to women specifically in their roles as mothers and played up their own motherhood in an effort to win broader support for their cause. Orleck notes that "after meeting women organizers [such as Shavelson] in the park with their babies, in food markets, and then at street-corner meetings, formerly timid housewives began to feel more comfortable with the idea of joining a housewives' council to deal with their problems" (1995, 228). As the CP organizer Sophia Ocken put the matter, "Our babies are our entrance cards in the class struggle in the neighborhood" (1937, 35)

To ease the involvement of women who could not ignore their caretaking responsibilities, CP women formed "mother and child units" or "woman's day units," which addressed concerns specific to women as mothers and enabled them to engage in organizational activities with their children by their side (see Ocken 1937; "A Day Unit" 1937; Sanders 1938). In the New York City area, a mother's unit successfully obtained relief for a family who had been evicted and for other families whose relief applications had been delayed. The women staged a colorful sit-down strike in which "baby and mother refused to move until relief was secured. . . . Baby carriages all over the [Home Relief Bureau], and a clothesline strung up in the relief station dramatically brought the situation to the public" (Ocken 1937, 36).

Mothers often had no choice but to include their babies and young children in worker struggles. In the mining regions of Ohio, Pennsylvania, and West Virginia, families faced desperate conditions and no one saw that more clearly than mothers and housewives. During the first few years of the Depression, coal miners' wages and hours were continually cut. Families lived in squalid conditions with no running water, no sewage drainage, and little food to eat. These circumstances brought women to the front lines, with children in tow, to support their husbands on strike (see Cooper 1931; "International Women's Day Finds Miners" 1931; "Ohio Children" 1932; "Women Help Lead Picketing" 1931). Jennie Cooper interviewed Mrs. Stella Bonifini for the *Working Woman* in August 1931 about her involvement in the coal miners' strike in St. Clairsville, Ohio. Bonifini explained her frustration at making ends meet on her husband's meager pay: "You have the rent to pay, grocery and butcher bills, and often times doctor bills, for our babies most always get sick since we can't afford to give them the right kind of food." Arrested for throwing stones at scabs, Bonifini defiantly proclaimed, "You send me to jail, and my babies go with me" (qtd. in Cooper 1931). The sight of women such as Bonifini who were picketing and arrested with children at their sides underscored the extent to which women in their roles as mothers were affected by public sphere decisions. These actions also demystified the sentimentality of motherhood and refocused attention on the political dimensions of this allegedly virtuous institution, which required back-breaking work and brought misery for those who could not afford the basic necessities for their children.

The well-organized and oftentimes militant actions engaged by housewives were significant for a number of reasons. First, these events helped to politicize family struggles. Highly publicized events such as bread, meat, and milk strikes created an unorthodox linkage or "impious association" between domesticity or private sphere phenomena (represented by mothers, housewives, children, bread) and public sphere events and individuals, thus calling attention to the interrelated nature of the two seemingly separate spheres. Family issues—appearing on the surface to be private and unrelated to the workaday world—were made public; the social roots of personal life were exposed through these events. Additionally, women's actions violated common-sense notions of what it meant to be a "housewife" or a "mother." By rending these concepts from their usual contexts—characterized by nurturance, quiet self-sacrifice, and virtue—women were able to create a new context for motherhood that called attention to the links between the work of caring and the work involved in commodity production.

On a broader scale, neighborhood actions had an impact on the labor movement as a whole, redefining the boundaries of working-class struggle, figuring a prominent role for housewives who had previously been isolated from the movement. As Mary Smith, a miner's wife, astutely observed, a strike cannot be won with only half of the town's population participating. Women— whether they be workers, mothers, housewives or all three—were indispensable to every working-class struggle ("Women Auxiliaries Aid" 1931).

Finally, extra-discursive actions such as bread, meat, and milk strikes were significant to the extent they blended coercive and persuasive elements in order to achieve tangible, that is, material, gains such as price decreases and additional aid from relief offices. Petitions, flyers, and speeches enabled women to get the word out to sympathizers and to justify the actions to the broader community. But oftentimes it was the threat of lost sales or production that came through coercive tactics such as boycotts and strikes that proved more "persuasive" than words alone. In fact, I wish to argue that, in some cases, communication by itself is not sufficient in struggles with dominant institutions and structures that control the basic means of survival. In such circumstances, extra-discursive actions are quintessential. Petitioning during a meat strike was certainly an important tool for raising awareness and gaining public support. But it was the actual physical blocking of butcher shops, preventing scabs and potential customers from entering, that struck a chord with meat wholesalers, who found themselves stuck with hundreds of pounds of steak and loin, which meant untold dollars in lost sales. In short, communication played a central role; but it was not just the power of words, such as arguments to owners, leaflets, meetings, that won price decreases. The power of the pocket "spoke" to owners in a way that words alone may not have.

## Conclusion

The popular ideology of separate spheres, which portrayed public and private realms as complementary yet distinct, gave rise to a paradox for poor and unemployed women. The ideology and its accompanying connotations of home life did not concord with the reality faced by these women and their families. For the poor and unemployed during the Depression, domestic life was seldom easy and most often was characterized by a daily struggle to feed and clothe children. Basic items such as bread and milk were hard won for many. These day-to-day experiences, in conjunction with continual layoffs, wage cuts, and cutbacks in relief, led many of the working class to recognize the interconnectedness between public and private realms. The testimonies of working-class women reveal a knowledge that their home life struggles were not isolated nor did they spring from nowhere. Rather, women saw that the circumstances and decisions made in the workplace had a direct impact on the quality of life at home.

Working-class women, particularly those in the Communist Party USA, effectively called attention to the gap between ideology and reality. This gap, referred to earlier as a "semantic paradox," motivated women to speak and act out in unique ways. More specifically, women relied on perspective by incongruity, a persuasive device played out at both discursive and extra-discursive levels. Through perspective by incongruity, activists called attention to the interrelated nature of public and private by removing established images of home and motherhood from their traditional contexts in an effort to force a reinterpretation of these sacred institutions. Through dissociation, irony, and metaphor, they created "impious associations" that pointed to the ways that public sphere issues shaped the private realm. Additionally, strikes, boycotts, and sit-downs represented particularly effective ways for women to expose the paradox of separate spheres. These actions represented a form of "extra-discursive impiety" that visually disrupted traditional notions of motherhood and homemaker and materially affected wages and prices by forcing the hand of food wholesalers and store, factory, mill, and mine owners.

Though much has certainly changed in the lives of the U.S. working class since the 1930s, the experiences and protest tactics of CP women hold relevance for us today, particularly in light of an arguably persistent ideology of separate spheres that continues to sentimentalize motherhood and domesticity and masks the relationship between work and home life. The paradox of the public/private split is equally apparent in a contemporary context in which dominant discourses extolling "compassionate conservatism" and "family values" ring hollow when viewed against a socioeconomic backdrop in which seven million are without jobs (Bureau of Labor Statistics 2006) and 18 percent of the nation's children live in poverty (National Center for Children in Poverty 2006). This gap between ideology and reality underscores the necessity of an effort that exposes discursive and economic contradictions, and it represents an opening through which emergent discourses and practices may surface.

Women's participation in the workplace throughout the 1930s resulted in a violation of the boundaries of True Womanhood, another popular ideology that worked in tandem with the doctrine of separate spheres during this time. A second paradox thus arose when the ideology of True Womanhood collided with the material necessity of working-class families. Black women experienced the repercussions of this paradox with particular poignancy since their race worked in conjunction with their class position to prevent them from living up to the dictates of this ideology. The next chapter discusses how women responded to this paradox.

# THREE

# The Paradox of the Woman Worker

A young dress worker in Youngstown, Ohio, wrote a letter to the *Working Woman* detailing the conditions faced by working-class women in her area. The writer made a plea to her fellow workers: "we will not gain anything by slaving our lives away in the laundries, pants factories and raincoat shops. . . . [T]he only way of getting better conditions in a shop and factory and a right way of living is to organize under the auspices of the Trade Union Unity League[.] [A]nd only this way will we get demands[,] that of right of living as human beings, as workers who are making everything and don't get nothin" (Bonin 1931).

Her letter called attention to the dire circumstances facing working poor and unemployed women in the early 1930s, but it also exemplified the fortitude women demonstrated in challenging such conditions. The widespread image of the down-and-out-man raised awareness of the Depression's impact on men; as noted earlier, fewer people were aware of the oftentimes bleaker situation faced by the nearly eleven million women who also made a living as part of the paid labor force in the early 1930s. Women faced cultural and economic sanctions when they entered the workplace. Popular beliefs that women worked for "pin money" and not out of necessity fueled a backlash against women, who were seen as competing against men for scarce jobs. Married women who held jobs were an even likelier target of criticism since they were also "ignoring" their domestic duties. These beliefs carried assumptions concerning gender and the very nature of work and were codified in

NRA legislation in the form of wage differentials that discriminated according to race and sex (Foner 1980, 280, 281; Ware 1982, 38, 39).

Working women's experiences of discrimination and hostility in the 1930s proved that the belief that "woman's place is in the home" was as entrenched as ever, perhaps more so, since, as Coiner notes, "Americans were reluctant to examine or tamper with traditional roles within the family at a time when it was viewed as perhaps the only remnant of stability" (1995, 39). Women workers, then, occupied a place of paradox since the two terms— "woman" and "worker"—were seemingly contradictory.[1] "Woman" implied domesticity, nurturance, and self-sacrifice, while "worker" connoted publicness, competition, and self-reliance. These deeply embedded cultural understandings resulted in a widespread preoccupation with male unemployment (for example, how it affected the family and the male psyche) while simultaneously rendering the employed female invisible (Faue 1991, 62). Throughout the 1930s, women challenged the seeming incompatibility of "woman" and "worker" through specific rhetorical and extra-discursive strategies, which will be explored in this chapter.

Specifically, working-class women's rhetoric regarding their experiences in the paid labor force can be classified as justificatory rhetoric, a "*posture* of rhetorical self-defense" that "asks not only for understanding but also for approval" (Ware and Linkugel 1973, 274, 283). In letters to the editor, published articles, and speeches, working-class women called attention to both their need and their right to work. They relied on differentiation and transcendence, two strategies commonly found in justificatory rhetoric (see Ware and Linkugel 1973; Wood and Conrad 1983). Viewed within the context of the larger woman's rights movement of the past 150 years, differentiation and transcendence parallel two approaches commonly taken by suffragists of the late 1800s and early 1900s in order to justify women's right to vote: argument from expediency and argument from justice. The following discussion locates Depression era arguments within this history and notes the tensions between arguments based on pragmatics (for example, differentiation and expediency) versus those undergirded by political ideals (for example, transcendence and justice).

## Justifying Their Place in the Paid Labor Force

As I described earlier, women have always worked in the paid labor force— from the mid-nineteenth century in New England mills, through the Progressive Era in factories and department stores, and into the 1920s and 30s in a variety of clerical and service-oriented jobs. Then as now, many working-class families relied on two incomes to make ends meet. This was particularly the case during the Depression when incomes earned by wives were necessary to offset wage cuts and layoffs experienced by husbands. During the 1930s, nearly 25 percent of all women worked in the paid labor force (Ware 1982, 21) and married women comprised nearly 30 percent of these workers (Hutchins 1934a, 40). Black families faced even harsher conditions since institutionalized racism compounded the effects of the economic downturn. Foner notes that the "conditions of blacks actually worsened" under New Deal legislation (1980, 280). Nearly 40 percent of all black women worked during the 1930s, most of them in domestic or agricultural positions, neither of which was protected by NRA legislation (Foner 1980, 280–81; Ware 1982, 30).

Although it is clear that their paid labor was needed for family survival, women continued to face discrimination and abuse in the workplace, problems that were only "exacerbated by the Depression" (Ware 1982, 31; see also Hutchins 1934a). Employers found many ways around established minimum hour laws. Despite NRA codes limiting the work week to forty hours or less in most industries, it was not uncommon for women to work fifty or more hours a week (Ware 1982, 27). Employers often made overtime work compulsory. In other industries, such as canning, a twelve-hour day was allowed by law (Hutchins 1934a, 111). Work hours in industries dominated by women were also subject to irregularities and extreme swings ranging from peak seasons that demanded seventy-hour work weeks to slack times when women were laid off (Hutchins 1934a, 111; Ware 1982, 31–32).

Despite their long hours, many women did not make enough to cover basic living expenses during the Depression. As a dressmaker in Milwaukee put the matter, "If I eat I can't pay my room rent. If I pay my room rent I'll have nothing left to buy food with" (qtd. in Hutchins 1934a, 129). Women's low wages were sanctioned by NRA codes—one-fourth of which established wage differentials between the sexes—in addition to a host of provisions that enabled industries to pay women less than men. The NRA legislation stipulated that "inexperienced" workers could be paid 80 percent of the minimum wage (Foner 1980, 280); workers "engaged in light and repetitive work" were exempt altogether from minimum wage standards (Scharf 1980, 112). These rules had the greatest effect on women and black workers.

Although women worked out of necessity—a need intensified by the Depression—cultural beliefs concerning women's "proper" roles continued to place women squarely in the home. The reasons behind the persistence of dominant gender ideologies are complex and varied. One reason, alluded to above, may be related to a perceived need for cultural stability during a time of economic upheaval. The image of a tranquil home life with a nurturing mother at the center was particularly appealing during a time of layoffs, wage cuts, and overall job uncertainty. Second, the belief that women were suited to domestic work became even more entrenched during a time of job scarcity and growing unemployment since it provided the grounds for scapegoating women who worked in the paid labor force. And finally, as was the case in previous decades, dominant gender ideologies were used to justify sex discrimination in the workplace, which benefited manufacturers and kept male and female workers pitted against each other. In short, oppressive gender norms persisted and were perhaps exaggerated in the 1930s for cultural and economic reasons.

Women's acute need to find work outside the home was incompatible with the cultural climate calling for them to remain in the home. The gap between reality and ideology put women workers in a place of paradox. The association of "woman" with home and "worker" with male made it seemingly impossible to be a woman worker. Yet, working-class women challenged this paradox through a justificatory rhetoric in which they defended their positions as workers. Specifically, their reliance on differentiation and transcendence proved effective for challenging a semantic paradox, or a paradox in which "the value associated with the word used to label an object is contradicted by the physical existence, physical characteristics, and/or physical functions of the object" (Chesebro 1984, 166).

Differentiation involves separating a particular fact or object from the context with which it is normally associated and framing it in terms of a new context (Ware and Linkugel 1973, 278). Differentiation is both divisive and transformative. It first detaches an object (in this case "woman") from its typically associated context (the home) and then encourages the audience to view the object within the framework of a new context (the workforce). Through differentiation, the speaker asks for a "suspension of judgment until [her] actions can be viewed from a different temporal perspective" (Ware and Linkugel 1973, 278). In their own defense, working-class women often described their long history of work in the paid labor force, thus creating a new context for "woman," one that more accurately reflected their real lives. Additionally, women created a new lens through which to view their roles as workers by emphasizing the *necessity* of their work—they were not working for "pin money" but rather they labored to put food in the mouths of their children. When workers employed differentiation, they were highlighting a specific scene (Burke 1945, 7–9)—the workplace—which had a compelling influence over their behaviors.

Secondly, women relied on transcendence, a strategy "which cognitively joins some fact, sentiment, object, or relationship with some larger context within which the audience does not presently view that attribute" (Ware and Linkugel 1973, 280). Transcendence recontextualizes. But in contrast to differentiation, which focuses on the particular issue at hand, transcendence rises above the "conventional interpretations placed upon an act" by "enlarging the scene and establishing a context that legitimizes an act" (Wood and Conrad 1983, 316). Transcendence "move[s] the audience away from the particulars of the charge at hand in a direction toward some more abstract, general view of [her] character" (Ware and Linkugel 1973, 280). Women used transcendence to defend their roles as workers by shifting attention away from specific accusations (for example, "Women who work are taking jobs away from able-bodied men") to the larger issue of "right to work" or, as the dressmaker from Ohio stated in the opening of this chapter, the "right of living as human beings, as workers who are making everything and don't get nothin'" (Bonin 1931). In the terms of Burke's (1945) dramatic elements of the pentad, the strategy of transcendence emphasizes agent, or the person or main character.[2]

Telling their stories, giving voice to their experiences, has been the central task of women's movements for equality throughout history, and it was no different for working-class women during the 1930s. Through narration, women retold history—previously recounted by men—from their points of view, specifically, from the perspectives of women who labored in factories, mills, and department stores, and on farms and in the homes of the wealthy. These stories enlarged "woman's space" and pointed to the fact that, historically, women have been equally present in the workplace as in the home. In short, their narratives recontextualized women's "proper" place and thus prompted a rethinking of the values associated with "woman." Their stories represented no less than a "redefinition of reality" (see Wood and Conrad 1983, 316).

In sum, women's justificatory rhetoric contained two emphases: necessity to work and right to work. By stressing the need to work, women placed themselves within the trajectory of industrial capitalism and underscored the importance of their labor in sustaining their families. They emphasized a pressing scene, which compelled or otherwise shaped their behaviors. Women also referred to their right to work, an emphasis that operated rhetorically to shift attention to broader, more general issues concerning human dignity and equality. Within this emphasis, workers highlighted themselves as agents, capable, conscious, and fully deserving of the rights inherent to all humans. Both of these themes, and indeed the very act of storytelling itself, served to authenticate women's experiences as workers and provided a means by which women could confront their paradoxical position as "women workers."

## Working-Class Women's Justificatory Rhetoric

During a time of job scarcity and growing unemployment, women who violated gender norms by working outside the home became easily identifiable scapegoats for the nation's economic woes. Frances Perkins, the secretary of labor in the Roosevelt administration, decried women who worked for "pin money," the dubious term that implied women's income was spent on nonessentials. She also "called for an increase in the wages of men in order to relieve women who did need jobs of the necessity of working and to enable them to fulfill their roles as wives and mothers" (Foner 1980, 278–79). The sentiment that woman's place is in the home was widespread, as indicated by a 1936 Gallup poll that showed 82 percent of respondents disapproved of a married woman's working outside the home if her husband had a job (Ware 1982, 27). Such hostilities had a distinct impact on women's lives in the form of workplace policies that barred married women or fired them outright. In 1931, New England Telephone and Telegraph, the Northern Pacific Railway, and the Norfolk and Western Railway Company fired all or many of their married women workers. Ware notes that a "1939 survey by the National Industrial Conference Board showed that 84 percent of insurance companies, 65 percent of banks, and 63 percent of public utilities had restrictions on married women working" (1982, 28).

Amidst the din of voices decrying women who worked outside the home because they were seen as stealing jobs from men, working-class women emphasized the extent to which they worked out of necessity. Specifically, they employed differentiation as a way to separate the concept of "woman" from the typical context of domesticity. Differentiation was a strategy that encouraged listeners to view women in the framework of a new context. In order to facilitate this recontextualization, women recast understandings of their roles as workers from "gender transgression" to "economic necessity." They accomplished this through vivid and oftentimes lengthy descriptions of their experiences in the workplace and by emphasizing the dire situations that forced them to work.

### Justification through Differentiation

Argument through differentiation represented a pragmatic approach to the issue of women and work much like that taken by suffragists of the early

1900s who turned to arguments of expediency in order to justify women's right to vote (Kraditor 1965, 54–56). In expediency arguments, women appealed to traditionally ascribed roles and gender norms in order to justify their transgression of such restrictions. For instance, in the early 1900s, suffragists argued that giving women the vote would make them better wives and mothers (Kraditor 1965, 55–56).[3] Leonora O'Reilly pointed out what a "woman's touch" could do for politics: "let woman go to work politically to see what an infusion of human sympathy and mother instinct can do in managing the affairs of the State and nation. We must cleanse the political quagmires in which we have sunk. . . . It is for woman . . . to instill into government some of her innate honesty" (1911a, 7–8).

Thirty years later, working women dipped into the stock of expediency arguments when they pointed out that their income was necessary for them to fulfill their roles as mothers who were responsible for feeding and clothing their children. "My husband is a Ford factory worker, out of work for a long time. If I don't work my family will starve," said one worker of the Guardian Laundry and Quick Service of Detroit. Her situation typified that of her coworkers, most of whom were married and most of whom were the wives of former Ford workers who were out of a job ("Laundry Workers Win" 1933). Little had improved for General Motors workers and their families who found themselves in a similar situation three years later. One woman, who later participated in the great Flint, Michigan, sit-down strike of 1936–37, recalled a conversation she had with her husband, who told her to refuse a job with GM if they offered to put her on a machine. "I didn't answer 'cause I knew I was gonna take anything I could get. Back then he didn't have a job, ya know, either work or starve" (*With Babies and Banners*). One woman referred to herself and others in similar situations as "two-job women." She wryly noted, "We come to wonder how it was that women were ever called the weaker sex" (Hutchins 1934a, 55).

As economic conditions worsened throughout the 1930s, workers organized hearings and hunger marches in order to publicize their dire situations. These public-speaking forums, which took place at local and national levels, were significant in part for the participation of women, black and white, who testified to the inability to obtain relief and described children who were hungry and husbands who deserted them or were jobless (see "Bosses Take Advantage" 1931; "Delegates from the New York Councils" 1931; H. Lynch 1931; Robinson 1931; Van Veen 1931b; "Public Hearings in Detroit" 1931). Their speeches underscored the *necessity* for women to work outside the home.

In February 1931, a delegation of 150 unemployed workers, organized by the Communist-backed Unemployed Councils, marched to Washington, D.C., to present a proposed Workers' Unemployment Insurance Bill. Women delegates spoke before Congress testifying to the need for the bill. One such delegate was Lillian May West, a black worker from Youngstown, Ohio, who testified that "she and her husband had been out of work for eight months, and that they and their children were hungry, and they did not mean to stand by quietly and starve" ("Govt. Sneers" 1931). Other women testified to the exploitative conditions in their workplace and to the discrimination they faced due to their age.

In the early 1930s, organizations such as the Workers' Committee on Unemployment and the Unemployed Councils held a series of local hearings in New York, Detroit, Philadelphia, and other major cities. At these events, women workers frequently took to the platform to describe the conditions they faced. At a hearing before the Workers' Committee on Unemployment in New York City in June 1933, one woman testified to her desperate need for work. Having reached the end of all her resources, the woman explained her unsuccessful attempts to secure relief. A relief worker came to her home, "opened a closet and found two dresses hanging within." Upon this discovery, the relief worker "said that she was going to recommend that I receive no aid, because if I could afford two extra dresses I did not need help" (qtd. in Hutchins 1934a, 185).

At a forum held by the Unemployed Councils in the New York area in the early 1930s, a sixty-two-year-old worker justified her work outside the home (intermittent though it was) by pointing out her options—work or starve. "I have been mostly without work for six months and starving most of the time. I live with my nephew who has also been out of work about six months. I get a job doing laundry for folks some times but not very much. They say I am too old to work. But I got to work. I don't want to starve. I may be too old but I can work and I am willing to; but I can't get anything to do" (Van Veen 1931b). Helen Lynch, an outspoken member of the New York Downtown Unemployed Council, shared her story in the December 1931 issue of the *Working Woman* before going on to testify as a delegate at the National Hunger March on 7 December (see "Delegates from the New York Councils" 1931; H. Lynch 1931). Lynch, who had lost her job as a waitress and had lived for a time at the Municipal Lodging House, described the cross section of women who came there in need of shelter and food. "They are of all categories of working women. Factory girls, office workers, institutional working women. . . . Nurses and bookkeepers are here too" ("Delegates from the New York Councils" 1931).

In similar hearings in Detroit and Philadelphia, woman after woman testified of her need to work outside the home for family survival. At the Detroit hearing in 1931, Mary B. declared, "My husband deserted me some time ago, and I was left with three children, six, seven and two years old. I tried to get some work but could not get anything. My gas and electric light was turned off seven months ago. . . . I get two dollars a week from the Welfare, but they are threatening to cut that off because I have only three children. I used to get some milk for the children, but they have cut that off" ("Public Hearings in Detroit" 1931). In Philadelphia, the Unemployed Councils organized the Philadelphia United Front National Hunger March Conference, held on 22 November 1931, which provided a forum for unemployed women from a number of area organizations (see Robinson 1931). At this event, women delegates, both black and white, were chosen to represent the unemployed at the upcoming National March on Hunger in Washington, D.C. The delegates who would tell their stories to Congress on 7 December were representative of unemployed women across the country. Louise Macon, a twenty-seven-year-old black worker, was laid off from her restaurant job a year earlier and her husband was out of work, too. Another black worker, Martha Jeffries, was a widow and mother of one who had lost her job at a chemical factory. A third delegate, Rose Evans, was a white worker trained as a stenographer but unable to find work for the past two years.

National hunger marches took place in 1931, 1932, and 1934. In these marches, thousands of unemployed and underemployed workers from across the nation—black and white, male and female—converged on the White House to demonstrate and petition for immediate relief. Perhaps most notable about these marches was the solidarity of race and gender displayed by delegates, particularly in the context of widely condoned race and sex discrimination in the workplace, which would become codified in NRA legislation just two years later.

The first of these marches, held on 6–7 December 1931, was a mixed success. Upon their arrival in Washington, D.C., the delegates, more than a thousand strong, held a mass meeting in Washington Auditorium, which was attended by about two thousand people ("Weary 'Marchers'" 1931). The *New York Times* described the enthusiasm with which marchers were received. "[W]ith a charge that President Hoover and his administration were trampling the working classes, Herbert Benjamin of New York, a leader in the march, brought more than 3,000 persons to their feet . . . when he asserted the Communist party was the only group left to organize and run the affairs of the United States" (see "Weary 'Marchers'" 1931). The following day, delegates were turned away by President Hoover and Congress, who refused to see them or hear their demands for unemployment insurance. But Anna Damon, a CP activist, noted the spirit, militance, and race solidarity of the women delegates, who numbered 158 of the 1,670 delegates. "The splendid speeches of the . . . women at the conferences in Washington showed that the women of the country are well aware that the struggle for Unemployment Insurance can only be won through mass action of the entire working class . . . [and] that the fight for immediate winter relief must become a daily job of the women factory workers as well as the women at home, employed and unemployed" (Damon 1932b). Though marchers were blocked from presenting their demands in December, in early 1932 women testified before the House Committee on Labor in a hearing on unemployment relief. In the months following the February 1934 march, dozens of women testified before Congress.

It was during this period of mass speak-outs and marches on Washington that the CP activist Grace Hutchins (1934a) published her book *Women Who Work,* a comprehensive examination of women's work conditions across numerous occupations. As she explained in the first chapter, "This book . . . will tell the story of women workers at home and on the farms, in domestic service, in offices, stores, hospitals and restaurants and in factories; how many there are and what they are doing, how the work affects their health, what they earn; their grievances, their demands, their aspirations for a classless society; the story of their struggles—their defeats and their victories" (21). More than anything, Hutchins's book represents a well-argued justification for women's place in the workforce based primarily on women's need to work outside the home.

Working-class women in a capitalist society do not have the freedoms that middle-class women are afforded, Hutchins explained (1934a). "While still in their teens, [working-class girls] are forced to work long hours in the mills, in domestic service, or in the fields, in order to add a few dollars to the meager family income. . . . Throughout their lives [working-class women] are exploited, haunted by the fear of unemployment, of illness, of old age, of destitution. A girl earning $12 a week or less in a mill or shop has about as much 'freedom' and 'opportunity' as a rose-bush in a desert of sand" (8). Each chapter of Hutchins's book details the conditions under which women labor in a host of occupations. In each case, primary emphasis is placed on necessity, which forces women into the paid labor force.

Hutchins's book is noteworthy for the way it highlighted women's experiences in two specific contexts, both of which had been rendered largely invisible throughout the 1930s by mainstream mediated and political rhetorics. First, like the writers of many of the letters to the editor mentioned below, Hutchins gave voice to the millions of unemployed women whose needs were often obscured by the more prominent image of the down-and-out male breadwinner. Unemployed women were just as desperate for jobs as were their male comrades. "Countless numbers of these jobless women have not only themselves to support but dependents, children, older relatives and others who are now left to the uncertainties of 'relief,'" Hutchins wrote (1934a, 181–82). She roundly criticized the discriminatory firing of married women from their jobs as teachers, telephone operators, and civil service workers, explaining that "married women take jobs outside the home because they have to help support the family" (182).

Hutchins also shined a spotlight on the tens of thousands of women who took in home work in order to supplement the family income. Women who testified at investigative hearings in Pennsylvania pointed out the sweatshop conditions under which they labored when they took in home work. Pay was "so low that the women often work far into the night in the effort to make even a few dollars a week" (Hutchins 1934a, 52). Home work had the dubious advantage of enabling women to work for income while keeping up with the unpaid labor of domestic chores and child rearing. Indeed, it was not uncommon for young children to work alongside mothers stringing tags to garments or assembling artificial flowers. *Women Who Work* put a face to the millions of working-class women who entered the paid labor force and provided a justification for women who were challenging the concept of "worker."

Scharf and Ware point to women's justificatory approach as evidence that feminism was "on the defensive in the 1930s" (Ware 1982, 105). These scholars emphasize the "constricted nature of feminist activity" during that decade (Scharf 1980, 136), noting that the pragmatic approach of justification served to confirm "traditional stereotypes about women's primary roles in the family" (Ware 1982, 105). On the one hand, it is true that pragmatic approaches such as the differentiation strategy employed by working-class women (in the early 1900s suffrage movement and in the 1930s labor struggles) were limited to the extent that women tapped into existing gender norms in order to make their case. Yet, I believe that the rhetorical situation in this case is more complex than one involving a simple or straightforward invocation of gender norms or even workplace necessity. Rather, arguments based on justification deserve close scrutiny and perhaps a deeper consideration of the ways they may have served as a foundation for a broader feminist and class critique, as demonstrated through letters to the editor and coercive protest tactics.

Letters to the editor published in the early and mid-1930s often served as a forum for women who sought to challenge the paradox presented by the idea of a "woman worker." These letters by and large relied on the justifica-tory strategy of differentiation, which extracted the image of "woman" from its traditional domestic underpinnings and located it within a new context, the workplace. In order to facilitate this recontextualization for their listen-ers, women justified the new contextual association by emphasizing the need for their presence in the paid labor force. In other words, they turned to their surroundings—or the scene—as a way to explain their actions. But signifi-cantly, they did not "reduc[e] action to motion" as is often the result in rhet-orics that highlight scene (Burke 1945, 131). Instead, as we shall see below, they balanced scene with agent by emphasizing their abilities to stand up and fight back against the conditions that so profoundly shaped—but did not completely determine—their lives.

The act of writing a letter to a widely distributed publication was sig-nificant for a number of reasons. First, through their letters, working-class women gave voice to their experiences. In a way, printed letters served to au-thenticate women's experiences, particularly in a sociocultural context that placed primary emphasis on the travails of the unemployed or struggling male worker. Through their letters, women crafted a selfhood. By author-ing, they author-ized their experiences. Watson's explication of the role of autobi-ography in the lives of the early 1900s women who wrote them underscores the significance of author-ization. Women such as Elizabeth Cady Stanton and Mary Church Terrell "overcame the reticence often typical of their gen-der to write about their lives; the mere act of their writing distinguishes them from many of their predecessors and contemporaries. Some feminist critics have claimed that women do not so much record their lives as write them-selves into existence" (Watson 1999, 1). Such was the purpose that letter writ-ing served for working-class activists of the 1930s.

Second, letters to the editor played a suasive role not only for the writers, but for readers who could identify with the descriptions of hardship and the feelings of outrage expressed in women's writings. The identities of working women put forth by letter writers served as models for readers to emulate. The issue of "implied auditor"—or the ways these letters suggested a "model of what the rhetor would have [her] real auditor become" (Black 1970, 113)—will be discussed in the next chapter. Third, letters to the editor did not only (or simply) authenticate women's experiences, they provided a public forum where women could justify their roles as women workers. And finally, letter writing was significant for working-class women to the extent that it was an active process requiring the organization and articulation of one's thoughts and putting pen to paper. The arguments and anger expressed in these letters suggest the extent to which analysis of—and, at times agitation for—women's rights continued through the 1930s despite perceptions to the contrary (see Scharf 1980, 136). Letter writing was one among the many persuasive means working-class women employed as they struggled to improve their positions as women. It may be viewed as a first step toward more active involvement in organizations and mass actions that brought working men and women together to challenge discriminatory practices.

Staub notes that "the CP was clearly convinced of the need for individuals to articulate their own perspectives: Speaking out, speaking for oneself—these were crucial aspects of politicization" (1994, 113). Letter writing was one way that women workers could "speak out" and speak for themselves. The *Working Woman* published letters to the editor under a number of headings between 1930 and 1935, including "Shop News from Working Women," "Letters from the Shops," "The Mail Box," "Woman's Voice," "Letters from Readers," "In Factory and Office," and "The Reader Has the Floor." These pages gave women a space to articulate and authenticate their experiences as workers whose labor was necessary for family survival. Letters often had a documentary tone, giving a sense that women were registering their experiences for public record. "I am a young girl working in Department 6317, Building 29–4 and I want to say a few words . . . about conditions in our department. For the past few months the bosses have been laying us off right and left," said a typical letter published in 1930 ("Western Electric Speed-Up" 1930). "Here are some of the conditions of women in the National Electric Co.," began a letter in 1931. It continued, "In my department, Braiders, we work nine and three-quarters hours—getting only twenty-three cents an hour." Another letter similarly began, "I am a cannery worker and I thought I would write and tell you some of the conditions we work under here" ("Northwest Canneries Work Women" 1931).

Letters were often quite pointed in identifying bosses, supervisors, and the wealthy who contributed to women's dire circumstances. A worker in the Manhattan Shirt Company in Paterson, New Jersey, wrote with frustration of the constant wage cuts at her factory and noted that the "forewomen are very mean. One named Agnes looks at every stitch with a magnifying glass. Girls are fired when there is a piece of thread on a shirt" ("Penna. Shirt Girls" 1931). A Detroit, Michigan, worker wrote that "our forelady, Rose Charest, is the worst creature to work under. All day long she is running from one place to the other yelling at us and she is the one who cut our wages last time" ("Hardly a Day without a Wage Cut" 1931). A 1935 letter writer described the racist practices of the "slave-driver" James Corrigan, who managed Department 29C of the General Electric plant in Bridgeport, Connecticut ("General

Electric Sweats" 1935). Letters from domestic servants and waitresses told of long hours, scant pay, and condescending treatment from the rich families they served. One waitress related her story of working at the Women's Athletic Club in Oakland, California—a club "where the cream of society come to have a good time" ("Bourgeois Women's Club" 1931). The work day for waitresses often exceeded ten hours and, though there was often good food left over (chicken, roasts, and cakes), it was thrown away rather than given to the waitresses, who were fed day-old salad.

A few letter writers identified themselves as black women workers and gave voice to the intersections of race, class, and gender oppression. "I have been working in the Washington laundries for several years now. The conditions are very poor here," began the letter of a laundry worker ("Negro Women Tell of Speed-Up" 1930). She continued, "We Negro workers are made to feel as if we're worse than our fellow white workers. Once the A.F. of L. [American Federation of Labor] started to organize our laundry, but they wouldn't let us Negroes in it, and you can understand what a flop that was."[4] Another writer noted that the "white girls on our floor get more money for doing exactly the same work colored girls do. And many colored girls do harder work than the white girls, but they get paid less" ("Negro Workers Doubly Exploited" 1930). The October 1932 issue of the *Working Woman* published two firsthand accounts from black female workers. A writer from Alabama narrated, "I was born in Tallapoosa County and raised here and have never seen the day that the boss would give us poor Negroes anything, as far back as I can remember from a little child up to now. They worked my father and mother like convicts and always at the end of the year they could not get us little ones clothing and just enough food to keep us alive" ("My Life" 1934). The other account was written by a woman from New York City who told of her experiences after losing her job as a domestic servant for a wealthy family who gave her twelve dollars a week. "I had to go up on the corners in the Bronx to look for work. I used to stand around or sit on cracker boxes with the other women waiting for someone to come along and offer me a job. Most of the women up there expected you to work for twenty-five cents anyhow. I was even offered ten cents an hour for general housework! And they worked you just like dogs for that money" ("And Mine" 1934).

In addition to documenting—and in the process authenticating—the experiences of female workers, letters to the editor also provided a place where women could provide justification for their roles as paid laborers, a rhetorical move necessitated by entrenched gender norms that continued to associate women with the domestic realm. Letter writers often explained that unemployed or striking husbands, or husbands who had deserted them or passed away, necessitated their entrance into the paid labor force. A textile worker writing in 1933 was quite frank about the fact that women workers would rather raise a family than work outside the home, but "with their husbands out of work, they are trying to raise a family and support it too, out of their own reduced wages" ("No Jobs—No Relief" 1933). Others painted tragic pictures of their struggles to make ends meet after facing the reality that their incomes were necessary for survival. "After my husband was killed while carrying out a dangerous [though] money saving venture at the order of a stingy capitalist boss, I suddenly awoke to the realization that I must get a job or starve," wrote Agnes Wells in a 1931 issue of *New Masses*. A letter from a domestic worker in Oakland, California, began her story, "Widowed, with a child to support, twice evicted, finally got a job as a domestic servant in one of Oakland's rich households" ("Woman Domestic Worker" 1931).

Sarah Victor, a Detroit, Michigan, auto plant worker, declared, "I have been working even when my husband had a job in order to make ends meet. Now he is out of work since last October, and don't ask how we get along on my miserable earnings" (1930). Victor continued her letter, telling of a factory accident that dramatically underscored the lengths to which women would go in order to earn money for their families. At the plant, a speedup caused an accident in which a woman's "finger tip was split in two[.] [B]ut evidently [the woman] could not afford to go home, for after having it bandaged, she returned to her machine and remained until quitting time."

A number of letters came from unemployed women, which put a face to this group of three million whose needs were often ignored in favor of the growing numbers of men in unemployment lines. "I lost my job a month ago; the money I had saved went, and being alone in the world, had no one to look forward to. I called on the Salvation Army for a little to eat and my room rent," wrote one woman in the June 1931 issue of the *Working Woman* ("Slaved at Paris Garter"). Another writer, who worked temporary jobs as a cotton picker in California, related her experiences hitchhiking and jumping trains, a story that challenged the image of the male hobo so prevalent during the Depression ("Lot of Women Cotton Pickers" 1931). She wrote, "I was not the only woman hiking. There were many more like me. Some have children with them." She continued, "I am back on the breadlines in Oakland after seven weeks in the cotton fields. I left without a cent, starving. I came back the same way—starving."

Some letters broached the issue of prostitution as a way to underscore the necessity for women to earn an income. "Prostitution, the oldest of professions, oldest because it is bred of poverty and ignorance, is the only means for women by which a great number of them can get food and shelter," wrote one candid writer in the January 1934 issue of the *Working Woman* ("Low Wages Throws"). A worker at the Murray Body Company in Detroit wrote to the *Working Woman* about the constant wage cuts faced by the women there ("Hardly a Day without a Wage Cut" 1931). "When we come to work in the morning most of the time we must wait for work an hour or two [with no pay.] Then comes work for a few cents. Can a girl support herself on these few cents a day? No! That's why many girls go on the bad road." A letter printed a couple of months later made a similar point. Written by a woman worker in Seattle who had been arrested for participating in labor demonstration, the letter described the numbers of women in jail for prostitution ("Seattle Jobless Girls" 1931). It pointed out, "The majority of the girls in jail were 'ordinary prostitutes,' girls who were forced on the streets by their inability to make a living."

As the above examples illustrate, women's letters to the editor justified the position of the female worker through moving accounts of the conditions that forced women into the paid labor force. These descriptions relied on differentiation, a justificatory strategy that encouraged readers to understand women's public sphere work within a framework of "necessity" as opposed to "gender norm violation." Reliance on this strategy did not, however, mean that letters writers necessarily capitulated to their circumstances. The fact that they worked out of necessity did not mean they were willing to take whatever crumbs were thrown their way. Women often concluded their letters with a call to action, urging readers to fight back, join one of many CP-led organizations, or organize a strike. The wife of a miner in Maynard, Ohio, explained in her letter how she brought home thirty-five cents in pay to feed her four starving children while her husband was on strike. She closed with the exhortation, "Women you must all fight and strike to win your bread and butter for yourself and children" ("Mother of Four" 1931).

Such calls to action indicated an awareness among working-class women of the injustice of their circumstances and provided an opening through which a broader social critique might be launched regarding gender equity. In short, a study of their rhetoric requires attention to the complexities therein, including the needs and influence of the immediate situation, the rhetorical constraints (for example, hostile audiences and/or restrictive gender norms), and the use of a combination of strategies and/or emphases. In the aggregate, these elements created a compelling testimony. In addition to using differentiation, which underscored that necessity drove these individuals into the workplace, working-class women also employed a strategy of transcendence whereby the debate over women in the workplace was shifted to a higher moral ground resting on the issue of equal rights.

## Justification through Transcendence

The strategy of transcendence has its roots in the arguments of the nineteenth-century woman suffrage movement, which emphasized that, insofar as women were humans, they were deserving of the same basic rights accorded to men. The early suffrage movement leader Elizabeth Cady Stanton's speech "The Solitude of Self" has been called "the epitome of the natural right argument" (Kraditor 1965, 46). In her speech, Stanton emphasized the "individuality of each human soul," arguing that "if we consider [woman] as a citizen . . . she must have the same rights as all other members, according to the fundamental principles of our government" ([1892] 1989, 372). Arguments from "natural rights" or "justice," as they are called, competed with—and at times were employed in tandem with—arguments based on expediency well into the twentieth century (see Cott 1987).

Working-class activists of the 1930s relied less on transcendence than on differentiation for reasons that are numerous and complex. The difference may indicate the extent to which working-class women were themselves influenced by dominant gender ideologies stipulating that their "proper" place was in the home. Differentiation implied that women worked outside the home *only* out of a necessity that, when removed, would prompt women back to the home. On the other hand, heavy reliance on arguments of necessity may point to a rhetorical astuteness on the part of women who recognized that this strategy required of its listeners less cognitive restructuring and may have elicited more sympathy. Still, some letter writers referred to ideals such as equal rights, unity, and worker solidarity in an attempt to shift the argument of women's paid labor to a higher moral ground and to accentuate that women worked not only out of necessity but because it was their inherent right. Discussion of women's rights emphasized women as agents, as moral beings capable of acting on their own behalf. In some senses, this emphasis on agent, as seen through the strategy of transcendence, provided a complement or balance to the earlier described emphasis on scene, as it attributed qualities such as autonomy and self-awareness to the workers.

A writer named Jennie told of the working conditions of women in the food industry ("Food Workers in Chain Stores" 1930). Her statements are not only documentary in tone, as were the letters mentioned above, they also carried a confrontational cast. Food workers "represent one of the most exploited sections of industry. For the same work the women receive less pay just because they are women," she noted. Furthermore, women "very often have to carry the burden of caring for their homes and children after the long hours of slavery in the shops." Jennie's statements manifested a feminist argument that questioned gender discrimination in the workplace and cultural norms that created a double work shift for women. The letter concluded by emphasizing the need to organize women workers. "The demand for equal pay for equal work is of utmost importance to all women workers in the industry."

Similar letters, written with a sense of fighting spirit, emphasized with a profound simplicity the worker's right to equal pay and decent conditions. These letters are notable for the ways the writers emphasized race and gender unification in arguing for equal rights for all workers. In these arguments, the concrete image of "worker" was linked to ideals such as "human dignity" and what one writer referred to as the "right of living as human beings, as workers who are making everything and don't get nothin" (Bonin 1931). In the February 1930 issue of the *Working Woman,* a letter writer related her experiences standing in line at the Briggs auto factory in Detroit hoping to obtain employment ("Women Workers Being Poisoned" 1930). While in line, the writer had had conversations with fellow unemployed women who told of their desperation to find work and of the poor conditions they faced once they secured jobs. Demonstrating an awareness not typical of her comrades in the Briggs line, the writer concluded, "My answer to you, women of Detroit, is: 'Let us organize in the Auto Workers Union, side by side with the men workers and help make conditions fit to work, for all workers, regardless of sex, color or race.'" With similar emphases, other letter writers related struggles "for the workers' rights" among male and female shoe workers ("Shoe Workers Strike" 1930) and beet workers in Denver ("Work Side by Side with Men" 1931). Of the beet workers, the writer noted, "The fine militant spirit of these Spanish workers should be an inspiration to the American workers. The Spanish women seem as ready to take part in the struggles as the men. Their slogan seems to be 'We work side by side with our men, and we will fight side by side with them.'"

More often than letter writers, CP leaders and seasoned activists relied on arguments of transcendence in order to challenge the paradox of the woman worker. One such leader was Margaret Cowl, editor of the *Working Woman* and member of the CP's Women's Commission and Central Committee (Shaffer 1979, 90). Cowl made frequent speaking tours and her writings appeared in a variety of CP periodicals and in widely distributed pamphlets published by the Worker's Library Publishers. In one such pamphlet, *Women and Equality,* Cowl (1935) made the case for women's right to equality in the workplace by first debunking prevailing notions of women's innate inferiority. "We have often been led to believe that this unequal position of women has always existed and therefore is a natural one," began Cowl. To debunk this belief, Cowl linked women's position of inequality to capitalism and demonstrated that this economic system relied on various "false ideas" in order to sustain itself. "The present inequality of women as compared to men, the unequal position of the Negro toiling population in the USA as compared to that of the white workers, the unequal position of the laboring masses as a whole as compared to that of those who do not work but who own the wealth . . . have a common basic reason, namely: The existence of the exploitation of one human being by another under the system of the private ownership of the things most essential to produce the necessities of life (5).

She continued, "This weaker economic position of women is used to deprive them of equal rights and often to humiliate them" (Cowl 1935, 10). Cowl asserted that in order "to win *complete* equality with men . . . women must become *active* together with the entire working class in the struggle to change the present social system" (11). Cowl did not ignore that many women enter the paid labor force out of necessity. But the thrust of her argument appealed to the ideal of equality—for both men and women workers. In Cowl's argument, the emphasis was not on women who were workers, but on workers who—regardless of sex or race—deserved just treatment in the workplace. She wrote, "The demand of equal pay for equal work for women as part of workers' demands in their strike struggles is necessary, not only to improve the conditions of women workers, but to ward off attacks upon the wages of all workers" (14).

Cowl made similar arguments in "We Must Win the Women," published in *The Communist* in 1937 (1937b). But in this writing, Cowl placed greater emphasis on issues unique to women workers, such as lack of maternity insurance, responsibility for domestic duties, and the high cost of living. Cowl stayed focused on the "struggle for equal rights for women" (548) but explained that specially tailored courses of action were needed in order to achieve equality for working-class women. For instance, since most women worked in unskilled trades, there was a need for "technical training schools for women" (548). Additionally, Cowl argued in favor of the Women's Charter movement, a struggle for women's rights that rivaled the fight for the Equal Rights Amendment, which Cowl and many other working-class activists viewed as bourgeois.

The Woman's Charter movement represents an interesting rhetorical moment for CP women, in which arguments for equality—which emphasized worker rights—intersected arguments that highlighted women's needs.

The movement, initiated in 1936 by Mary Van Kleeck, a middle-class reformer, was supported by a variety of middle- and working-class women's organizations including the Women's Trade Union League, the National League
of Women Voters, the National Consumers' League, the Young Women's
Christian Association, and the CP (Cowl 1974, 41; Ware 1982, 106). Elizabeth
Gurley Flynn (1937a) dubbed the Charter the "women's Bill of Rights," a document that "affirms [women's] established rights and calls upon women . . .
to rally for those not yet obtained." The charter's appeal for Flynn and other
supporters lay in its ability to address the needs of a group whose disenfranchisement stemmed from discrimination on the basis of both sex and class. As
Flynn (1937a) stated, "The Women's Charter will give confidence to women,
increase loyalty to their sex and their class and stir their minds on to the great
struggle for emancipation, of which their activity is an important part."

The Women's Charter document advocated women's equality while also
holding to the need for special protective legislation for female workers. In
Burkean terms mentioned earlier, the charter vacillated between an emphasis
on agent and a stress on scene, between ideals and material circumstances.
The document represented no less than "a battle over the meaning of equality for women" (Ware 1982, 107). For working-class women especially, the
charter attempted to articulate the terms and negotiate the tensions surrounding gender, class, and race.

The document read, in part, "Women shall have full political and civil
rights; full opportunity for education; full opportunity for work according
to their individual abilities. . . . [T]hey shall receive compensation, without
discrimination because of sex" (qtd. in Ware 1982, 106). Additionally, the
charter stated, "Where special exploitation of women workers exists, such as
low wages which provide less than the living standards attainable, unhealth-
ful working conditions, or long hours of work . . . such conditions shall be
corrected through social and labor legislation, which the world's experience
shows to be necessary" (qtd. in Ware 1982, 106–7). These two provisions in
the Women's Charter point to the rhetorical balancing act that CP (and other
female) activists negotiated in arguing for women's rights in the workplace.
The first statement, which emphasized *women as workers,* justified women's
roles in the workplace by relying on transcendence—referencing ideals such
as "civil rights" and "full opportunity." The second statement, and the one
sparking the most controversy, emphasized *workers as women,* in an attempt
to recognize the unique situation or scene at hand ("where special exploitation of women workers exists . . .").

The Women's Charter—as well as countless debates surrounding definitions of, and approaches to women's equality—was attempting to balance not only differing emphases but, more important, differing philosophical worldviews. Transcendence, which is an agent-centered strategy, is undergirded by idealism, a philosophy that stresses consciousness, will, the self, or spirit as the starting point of history (Burke 1945, 128, 171). In contrast, the scene-oriented approach of differentiation is tied to materialism, which highlights material conditions as an all-encompassing force that determines or compels behaviors (128, 131). The charter's supporters refused to ignore the profound impact that workplace conditions (scenic elements) had on working-class women's lives. Yet, they did not fall prey to a fatalist position whereby the scene completely overpowered the agents/women. Rather, they called attention to women's "rights," "dignity," and "spirit" in an attempt to convey that women workers were not only determined *by* (scene) but determined *to* (act on their own behalves). Unfortunately, this attempt to balance philosophical viewpoints was not without contradictions (see Tonn 1995). Ultimately, for numerous reasons, the movement failed, disintegrating a few years after its initial launch.

The argumentative pull between needs and rights rhetoric within the CP reflected debates occurring within the broader women's rights movement, which centered on the issue of protective legislation for women in the workplace. Working-class women and their advocates, such as the Women's Trade Union League, argued vehemently in favor of special legislation that would protect women in the workplace by restricting their hours and occupations. Deplorable workplace circumstances created an urgency prompting activists to highlight the unique needs and conditions of women that necessitated immediate relief. The 1908 Supreme Court case *Muller v. Oregon* was decided in favor of protective legislation; justices were convinced by arguments that "women are fundamentally weaker than men" and that "women's physical stature and the performance of maternal functions place her at a disadvantage" (qtd. in Kessler-Harris 1982, 187).

Yet, "the organizational energy and skill required to pass protective legislation conflicted with the continuing struggle toward women's equality" (Kessler-Harris 1982, 206). Alice Paul and the National Woman's Party (NWP)—an organization composed predominantly of middle-class and professional working women—advocated passage of the Equal Rights Amendment, which would do away with any legislation that made special provisions on the basis of sex. In their opinion, protective legislation institutionalized sex segregation in the workplace. "If . . . a law is passed applying to women and not applying to men, it will discriminate against women and handicap them in competing with men in earning their livelihood," noted one NWP member, Jane Norman Smith (qtd. in Kessler-Harris 1982, 206).

Communist Party activists such as Elizabeth Gurley Flynn—whose views were undoubtedly shaped by her experiences of childhood poverty—viewed the ERA through a quite different lens. "[A]long comes a group of smug prosperous ladies who never worked for a day's wage at long hours on tired feet in store or factory to propose an 'Equal Rights' Amendment," bemoaned Flynn as she ran for Congress in 1940 on the CP ticket (n.d.).[5] Indicating the extent to which class inflected the ERA debate, she continued, "It [the amendment] sounds plausible until you hear that the duPonts endorse it, and the Manufacturers' Association say it's a grand idea! If you're a wise working women you think 'Something phony here!' You bet there is!" (n.d.). Like other CP activists and working-class women, Flynn opposed the ERA on the grounds that minimum wage and maximum hour laws that had been won through bitter struggle "would be thrown out under [the] proposed amendment" (n.d.).

The CP's Women's Charter was clearly influenced by both sides of the protective legislation debate, a debate that for the most part did not see resolution and, according to one labor historian, "split[] the feminist ranks" (Kessler-Harris 1982, 206). Still, Cott maintains, the "woman movement as a whole maintained a functional ambiguity" whereby the competing perspectives were often blended in a rhetorical move that recognized the uniqueness of womanhood and the universality of personhood (1987, 20).

The presence of various tensions in the rhetoric of CP and other working-class activists reminds us that this organization and its members operated within and were influenced by the larger culture of the period. So while the CP's female members invested a good deal of energy in arguments that justified women's roles as workers, there were moments of rhetorical ambivalence, specifically, points in CP rhetoric at which the idea of "woman" remained in contradistinction to the idea of "worker."

## The CP's Ambivalence toward the Woman Worker

As noted earlier, some scholars have argued that the CP's support and encouragement of women's auxiliaries was proof that the CP was not devoted to full integration of women into the worker's movement. From this perspective, auxiliaries may be seen as helpmate or second-rate organizations in which women were relegated to traditional domestic duties (for example, serving coffee or making food for men on strike) while the "real" work of labor struggle was left to the men. Women's auxiliaries warrant a more complex analysis; as organizations, they both contributed to and challenged traditional ideas concerning women as wives, mothers, workers, and activists. On one hand, the CP's male leaders were known to encourage women's ghettoization in auxiliaries in order to keep them out of the rough-and-tumble of labor confrontations or even to undermine the work of auxiliaries altogether. In contrast, the CP's women leaders went to great pains to make auxiliaries more than "tea parties"—to transform them into organizations instrumental to the cause of all workers, regardless of gender or race (Cowl 1937a, 26).

Despite women's proven militancy and leadership abilities within the party, many of them faced hostility or "benign neglect" (Baxandall 1993, 144) from male comrades who would not or could not see beyond traditional sexist beliefs and practices. Cowl (1974) pointed to "male supremacy" as one reason behind the lack of sustained involvement of working-class women in the party. She asserted, "There was an indifference to the mass women's movements and they were not really accepted as part of the working-class movement of the United States" (44). Baxandall takes a somewhat harsher view of women's experiences, noting that "women were viewed in the party as mothers of sons and creatures of sentiment, not carriers of reason. . . . There were contradictions, as women were expected to be ordinary hausfraus and weak, and yet wonder women—but not capable of leadership" (1993, 154). Marie Harrison Pierce, a CP activist from Waco, Texas, put the matter this way when writing in the *Party Organizer:* "We must realize that even though women in America are not forced to wear the veil, that even though they have the right to vote, there are still many hangovers of women's inferiority, and that workers do not shed this as a coat when they join the Party" (1936, 17).

Although a number of women reached prominent positions within the party (see Brown 1996, 1999; Ware 1982; Weigand 2001), "other women met increased sexism further down the ranks" (Ware 1982, 122). Oftentimes the hostility came from husbands who were threatened by their wives' newfound sense of independence and assertiveness upon involvement in labor struggles. "The men deliberately kept [their wives] from advancing," noted one CP activist (qtd. in Baxandall 1993, 150). Women aired their frustrations with husbands in letters to the *Working Woman* and the *Daily Worker* (Ware 1982, 122). "My place organized into an Industrial Union and now I am a union girl," wrote an Italian worker in the June 1933 issue of the *Working Woman* ("How Can I Make My Husband Understand?" 1933). "I was elected as a delegate to conferences and every word became attached to my mind and entire being. . . . But my husband is not in favor of all these new ideas and we have fights, he thinks that I do something wrong in back of him." The *Working*

*Woman* editor responded to this woman's quest for advice by pointing out that "many husbands . . . still cling to the old ideas that the woman's place is at home. They try to discourage the women from taking part in the fight to improve the conditions of her family." The editor then encouraged readers to write in and share their own experiences dealing with husbands who were resistant to their union involvement.

The issue of male chauvinism was addressed throughout the 1930s in the *Party Organizer,* particularly with regard to how it affected the recruitment of women into the party. Lip service is not enough, explained one contributor in the September–October 1931 issue ("Work among Women" 1931), who wrote, "It is about time the entire Party, men and women, got a new slant on how to draw the women workers into our campaigns and struggles. We should stop stating policy and then adding 'and the women, Negro, and youth.'" The writer stressed the need for "special methods of work" in order to bring women into the unions and to "build women's auxiliaries into a permanent functioning part of the union." Ann Burlak (1934), the CP leader known for her commitment to organizing women in the textile trades, expressed similar sentiments three years later. "I feel that many of our Party functionaries in the field still take the fact that it is necessary to develop women leaders, with a grain of salt" (54). Her plan for overcoming male apathy was simple: "for every male worker we take into the Party, let us take in a woman worker, and develop the best among them into leading positions in the Communist Party."

The CP's inability to see beyond traditional gender norms also surfaced, oftentimes subtly in the pages of the *Daily Worker* and even the *Working Woman* in the form of articles and regular columns that addressed women in their roles as mothers, homemakers, and on occasion, beauty objects. Though not officially titled as such, a "woman's page," which appeared regularly in the *Daily Worker* beginning in the mid-1930s, captured the ambivalent position of the CP toward women activists. The page carried "The Women's Angle," a column that detailed women's strike and union activities, which provided legitimacy to women's roles as activists. The page also carried "Watch Your Manners," a column offering advice from "Polly Propper," which spoofed its counterpart in popular magazines and newspapers.[6] The answers guided female readers into roles that challenged traditional gender norms. In reply to a young woman who wrote asking if she should marry a poor gentleman with whom she is love or wait, Propper states, "Marry him and both of you join in a demonstration for unemployment insurance. It will be proper to march linked arm in arm and singing" ("Watch Your Manners" 1936). The "Women's Angle" and "Watch Your Manners" notwithstanding, the remainder of the "woman's page" was devoted to soft issues traditionally associated with women. Along with stories of women on the strike line there appeared book and movie reviews and a column on health issues. This page was significant not only for its content (which was decidedly ambivalent when it came to constructing "proper" roles for women), but for its very presence as a place that stood apart from the rest of the paper where, a reader may conclude, the "real" issues of organization, strategy, and conflict were discussed. To a degree, then, the presence of this page reflected the CP's stance toward women in the party. Like the "woman's page" in the *Daily Worker,* real women activists and their concerns never became a fully integrated part of the party's affairs, but more often stood on the sidelines, a footnote unto themselves.

The *Working Woman* was much more open in its support for women in nontraditional gender roles. But it too sometimes appealed to women in their roles as mothers and homemakers. "Household," a column appearing in 1933, provided advice on housecleaning and on cooking nutritious yet inexpensive meals. Women were encouraged to "write in suggestions on how to lighten housework" and to "send in simple recipes." The column, which was retitled the "Household Corner" around 1934, ran a contest for the best dinner menu. The woman whose menu was judged the most "appetizing, nourishing, and cheap" would win a six-month subscription to the *Working Woman.* "Fashion Letter" was another column, appearing around 1935, which appealed to women in their domestic roles. Like the "Household" column, "Fashion Letter" was pragmatic and tailored to the reality of working-class women's lives. The April 1935 page began, "If you have more time than money, here is a simple tunic to make, which, when worn over an old dress . . . will fool nobody" (Barde 1935a). September's version was more ambivalent when it came to conveying counterhegemonic gender ideology. It began with a critique of the king and queen of England, who ran their homes on a $500,000 budget while millions suffered impoverished conditions in India. The column then turned to the necessity of good appearance even during hard times. "Life is awfully serious for most of us now, but don't let us be above that careful grooming which is more important than ever," wrote Gwen Barde, the columnist (1935b). The remainder of the page was devoted to informing readers how to sew the currently fashionable garments.

The presence of household and fashion columns in the *Working Woman* points to the complexities and challenges inherent in women's struggles to challenge through rhetoric traditional gender roles and to justify their participation in what has been deemed "men's work." These pages indicate *Working Woman*'s recognition of the need to appeal to the reality of readers' lives.

Even when women entered the paid labor force and/or became involved as activists, they were still responsible for domestic duties and child care. The issue of audience identification is more fully explored in the next chapter. Here I simply wish to call attention to the ambivalence revealed in CP women's rhetoric as they attempted to challenge the paradox of the "woman worker." Although working-class women went to great lengths to justify their place in factories and mills, as the above analysis shows, many continued to identify with traditional roles of mother and homemaker.

As was the case when they challenged the paradox of separate-spheres rhetoric, working-class women and CP activists did not rely solely on discourse when they challenged the cult of True Womanhood. They mobilized themselves through extra-discursive actions that further highlighted their roles as workers and provided a visible and oftentimes vigorous challenge to ideologies that perpetuated a mythical contradiction between the concepts "woman" and "worker."

## Organizing and Mobilizing the Woman Worker

"During the last two years [women] have proven definitely, in action, that woman's place is on the picket line, fighting side by side with the man for decent wages, decent working conditions and the right to organize into trade unions," wrote one CP activist, Sasha Small, in the *Working Woman* (1935). Small was calling attention to the confrontational actions that women engaged in specifically in their roles as workers in the paid labor force.

Particularly between 1931 and 1937, women workers as diverse as cotton pickers, movie extras, hotel maids, and hairdressers went on strike to demand justice in the workplace. Their fighting spirit ran deep as they drew inspiration from the actions of their working-class sisters decades earlier when confronting institutionalized discrimination.[7] As noted earlier, women's participation in walkouts and strikes began in the mid-1800s with the Lowell textile workers and was commonplace through the early 1900s, peaking with the "great strikes" of 1909–13. In the winter of 1909, thirty thousand shirtwaist makers in New York halted the industry for three months and gave many young women and girls their first taste of the power of collective action. This and other walkouts rallied workers by the tens of thousands and resulted in overtime pay, reduced work hours, and the elimination of arbitrary fees slapped on workers (Foner 1979, 324–73). Perhaps most important, women learned of their strength in numbers, a lesson that would be carried down to those enduring the Depression's hardships.

Figure 5. Waitresses participating in a sit-down strike at a Woolworth store in Detroit, 1937. Walter P. Reuther Library, Wayne State University.

Women's actions during the 1930s stand as evidence that feminist agitation was, to an extent, sustained during this decade (see Scharf 1980; Ware 1982). Women did not necessarily identify themselves as "feminists" nor were their arguments always an explicit challenge to patriarchy and the sexual division of labor. Still, women upended traditional notions of womanhood and domesticity. They participated by the thousands in militant and sometimes deadly strikes; they were arrested, beaten, and jailed; they led men *and* women on the strike lines; and they participated in auxiliaries and in food strikes, which oftentimes facilitated a deeper understanding of the inequalities exclusive to their sex. These examples point out the existence of a militant awareness at times imbued with feminist ideals, which was sustained by thousands of women during the 1930s.

Similar to the housewives' movement detailed earlier, the actions of strikers in the 1930s were noteworthy for their coercive and persuasive elements. First, extra-discursive actions such as strikes, walkouts, and sit-downs were effective insofar as they had material consequences for bosses and owners

Figure 6. "Cigar girls" parade in front of different cigar manufacturers, Detroit, 1937. Walter P. Reuther Library, Wayne State University.

who controlled the conditions under which women worked. Through bodily absence (as in walkouts) or presence (as in sit-downs or strikes that blocked factory entrances), women halted production, a move that almost immediately affected the bottom line (figure 5). Additionally, the sight of women on the picket line challenged popular notions of women as submissive and domestic. Standing on the picket line with signs reading "To Hell with Charity. We Want Unemployment Insurance," "We Demand Jobs," and "Strike on Sweatshops," women called attention to their need and right to work, and they demonstrated a willingness to defy gender norms and place themselves in confrontational situations in order to win fair wages (figure 6).

In a period of institutionalized racial segregation and scapegoating, it is significant that a number of the strikes were characterized by racial solidarity between black and white workers—oftentimes with black workers taking the lead (Foner 1980, 275; see also Larks 1934; Lewis 1933; Sallee 1933; Small 1935; C. Smith 1933) (figure 7). In the early 1930s, black and white women went on strike at the Funstan Nut Company in St. Louis where they eked out a living on

Figure 7. Laundry workers picketing in the 1930s. National Union of Hospital and Health Care Employees Local 1199 Archives, Kheel Center, Cornell University.

three dollars a week in wages (see Lewis 1933; C. Smith 1933). With assistance from the local CP, Carrie Smith organized her fellow black workers on a walk-out on a Monday morning. Smith explained how the white workers joined the strike. "The white girls stayed inside [the factory]. The floorlady told them that all the colored girls were going on a picnic. [O]ne white girl looked out, and she knew what kind of a picnic it was. . . . She saw enough to know that we were not on a picnic. Tuesday morning all the white girls went on the picket line, joined hands with the colored girls and went side by side" (1933, 8).

Cora Lewis, who worked with Smith and local CP activists on the strike, told of the involvement of entire families in the action. According to Lewis (1933), "[O]ne man said . . . that his wife was earning the living and that she went on strike in order to get higher wages, and that if anyone lays a hand on her, they would never live to see the day thru." The strike was a success and workers won all of their demands, including higher wages, "equal pay for Negro workers for equal work," and "recognition of shop committees of union" (Lewis 1933). Foner notes the significance of the strike: "In an era when wage differentials were an accepted way of life, the Funst[a]n nutpickers demanded and won equal pay for equal work for black and white workers alike.

Although white women were active in the struggle, it was the pivotal role of the black women that was responsible for the final victory" (1980, 274).

Like their sisters at the Funstan Nut Company, black workers at the Sopkins Apron Factory in Chicago did not wait for corporate-sympathizing legislators to assist them in achieving fair wages; they organized and went on strike (see Larks 1934; Sallee 1933). Sopkins shops, of which there were at least five in Chicago, hired black women to work in sweatshop conditions, which included wages of three to four dollars a week, no restroom, filthy work areas with no ventilation, and speedups (Larks 1934; Sallee 1933). In June 1933, fifteen hundred Sopkins workers walked out of the factory and remained on strike for two weeks despite arrests and daily beatings from police (Sallee 1933). With the support of the CP-backed Needle Trades Workers Industrial Union, workers won "25 cents an hour for a forty-four-hour week, equal pay for equal work, and no discrimination between white and colored workers" (Foner 1980, 275).

Another area of successful organizing among women came, perhaps surprisingly, in the auto industry. Often assumed to be dominated by male workers, auto plants offered women seven to eight dollars a week for sixty or more hours (Foner 1980, 270). Women auto workers were just as eager as their male coworkers to fight for fair wages and decent hours. In March 1932, workers at the Ford Motor plant in Dearborn, Michigan, organized a hunger march from Detroit to their plant. The group included approximately four thousand men and women, black and white, who set out to present a list of demands to Henry Ford (Sugar 1980, 32–33). Blocked by police cars just a few blocks into the march, "workers fought back and defended their banners. Especially the women led the line to smash through the police" (Barker 1932, 6). Though the marchers remained orderly, police responded with tear gas, fire hoses, and bullets, killing four marchers and wounding many others (see Sugar 1980). The hunger march was not a total loss, however. The Communist-backed Auto Workers Union increased its profile and membership, and another hunger march was quickly planned for the Ford River Rouge plant (Barker 1932, 7).

Just nine months after the hunger march, the Auto Workers Union led a strike of six thousand workers—two thousand of whom were women—at the Briggs auto plant in Detroit ("Driving to Victory" 1933; Foner 1980, 270) (figure 8). "You should have seen the women on the picket line," proclaimed one female striker. "They sang and cheered and pepped everybody up. The men all say the women were amongst the most militant and enthusiastic strikers" ("Driving to Victory" 1933). The women's dedication paid off as they won

Figure 8. Women picketers of Briggs Manufacturing Company, Detroit, 1933. Walter P. Reuther Library, Wayne State University.

"a minimum wage of 30 cents an hour, pay for waiting time . . . and a forty-eight-hour week" (Foner 1980, 270).

The mere threat of a strike from another group of women workers was enough to ward off job losses on a movie set in California (Bloomington 1936a).[8] Frank Tuttle, a Hollywood director, planned to replace the women who worked for a living as movie extras with young "society" women who said they would donate their wages to charity. When the movie extras learned of this plan, they, along with the stars of the cast, threatened to walk out, which proved enough for Tuttle to change his mind about hiring wealthy young women. One worker justified the threatened walkout saying, "Why should rich girls who don't need the money take the bread out of the mouths of extras. . . . They get a thrill. Somebody else misses a meal" (5).

Hairdressers, office employees, stockyard workers, and hotel laundry workers also counted among the tens of thousands of women workers who picketed for workplace justice during the Depression. In 1936, hairdressers in New York City formed their own union and called a general strike to demand a forty-eight-hour week, wage increases, and one week's paid vacation (Bloomington 1936c). The women formed "shock troops" or flying squadrons comprised of hundreds of women who went throughout the city to inform fellow workers of the strike. The strike gained the support of more than a thousand hairdressers in addition to the Progressive Women's Council, the Women's Union Label League, and the Committee for the Support of Locked Out Workers.

The bravery of union women and the effectiveness of their tactics during these years were epitomized in the action of six members of the Office Workers Union in Cleveland, Ohio. In 1936, this handful of women went on strike for the "reinstatement of five of their members" ("6 Girl Pickets" 1936). Their picket line was successful at getting the other workers—mostly machinists who were members of the International Machinists Association—to join the protest. Explaining their reason for joining the women and refusing to work, the machinists noted that "their contract called for safe working conditions and they did not feel it 'safe' to march through the picket line" of women ("6 Girl Pickets" 1936). The action led to the shutdown of the entire plant, which employed over three hundred workers.

Women laboring in what remains one of the most dangerous workplaces—the stockyards—were spurred to action by the CP activist Stella Nowicki after an accident in which a woman's fingers were chopped off by a meat grinder that had no safety guards. Nowicki (1981) and other CP "colonizers" called on the women to sit down on the job.[9] "We just stopped working right inside the building, protesting the speed and the unsafe conditions. We thought that people's fingers shouldn't go into the machine, that it was an outrage" (72). The action resulted in increased union membership and the installation of safety guards on the machinery.

New York City was also the location of a strike of laundry workers in late 1936. To call attention to the workers who picketed Hotel Taft, Jessie Taft (no relation to the hotel owners), the secretary of the Laundry Workers' Union, chained herself to a "pillar of the mezzanine of the hotel" and gave an impassioned speech to the well-dressed crowd below (Schneider 1936). The hotel manager attempted to silence Taft and the young woman was escorted from the hotel, but not before laundry workers picketing outside the hotel had been joined by sympathetic passersby and by black workers from another laundry who joined the Hotel Taft strikers in solidarity.

Throughout the 1930s, women were on the front lines of strikes in a host of occupations. Perhaps more than any other workplace, textile mills were filled with women workers and were hotbeds of strike activity during this decade, culminating in the great textile strike of 1934. Women's experiences in

the textile industry have a rich history marked by significant strikes in Lawrence, Massachusetts, in 1882 and 1912. Community and kin played important roles in these actions and they would continue to shape labor struggles
through the 1930s (see Cameron 1993). Building a foundation of radicalism
for striking textile women and girls in 1934, Lawrence women—both workers and homemakers—halted production, paraded, leafleted, picketed, established soup kitchens and nurseries, and in some cases "united to brandish red
pepper, rocks, clubs and other means at their disposal to maximize worker
unity and promote the common goal" (Cameron 1993, 138).

In the four years leading up to the great 1934 strike, workers by the thousands shut down mills on numerous occasions in order to prevent wage cuts
and speedups. Echoing the spirit of Lawrence, Massachusetts, workers who
shut down the entire mill town in 1912, the textile workers of Lawrence—ten
thousand strong—once again demonstrated solidarity in a strike in February
1931. The CP-backed National Textile Workers (NTW) led the strikers, who
were protesting against speedups and for union recognition (Burlak 1933b;
"Nat. Textile Union" 1931). Notably, the strike was initiated by women workers, who, throughout the ten-day action, were "the most active workers on
the picket line" (Berkman 1931). Women comprised significant numbers on
strike committees, attended strike meetings, and joined the National Textile
Workers (Berkman 1931; "Nat. Textile Union" 1931).

Women's leadership and participation in this uprising were significant
given the context in which they walked out of the mills and into the streets.
As I have described in this chapter, women had to justify their positions in the
paid labor force, even when those positions provided them meager wages and
arduous hours at a time of widespread unemployment (Burlak 1931; "Mills
Shut Down!" 1933).[10] During the Lawrence strike in particular, women were
received less than enthusiastically by some union members and they faced
opposition from priests and police. Time and again, female CP activists noted
the organization's failure to "bring the women closer and to assign important
tasks to them" ("The Lawrence Strike" 1931). Local priests who sided with mill
owners appealed to traditional gender norms as a way to urge women back
into their kitchens (Berkman 1931; "The Lawrence Strike" 1931). The police
indiscriminately used tear gas and nightsticks against strikers, raided workers' homes, and fined and arrested women strikers.

The ten thousand Lawrence strikers won most of their demands, including abolition of the "stretch-out." But just a few months later, in September and November 1931, tens of thousands of workers in northeastern mills
walked out again to fight wage cuts and other injustices (see Berkman 1933;

Burlak 1931, 1933a; "Mills Shut Down!" 1933). Once again, women workers were "in the forefront of the struggle" (Burlak 1931). The longtime CP textile organizer Ann Burlak (1931) noted that in the Rhode Island strikes of November 1931, "the women's and girls' militancy was in many cases better than that of the men." The enthusiasm of female textile workers continued throughout 1933, as thousands struck mills in Rhode Island and Massachusetts and paved the way for the great textile uprising of 1934 (Burlak 1933b).

Fed up with continued wage cuts and speedups, nearly a half million textile workers from Alabama to Connecticut went out on strike in early September 1934. As in previous walkouts, women comprised nearly half of all strikers and were, according to many accounts, the most militant and persistent on the strike line (Colby 1934; Foner 1980, 286–90; Hutchins 1934b). "The women are supporting the major burden of the textile strike," noted a male contributor to the *Working Woman* (Colby 1934). A fellow male textile striker asserted, "We've got women in this town with more guts than the men. . . . You ought to see them grabbin' those bombs and throwin' them back" (qtd. in Hutchins 1934b). Women played an active role in all aspects of the strike, from organizing relief efforts to participating in more confrontational actions, such as flying squadrons and blockades. Militia attacked women in the squadrons with clubs and tear gas. But the women were not deterred as they tossed rocks back at the soldiers. The squadrons were important for the material effect they had on the strike, namely, closing mills and encouraging other women workers to join the walkout (Foner 1980, 286–87). Leafleting alone may not have had the same impact as the physical presence of a thousand picketers outside of a mill holding banners and shouting at workers inside to come out and join the fight.

Women also participated in train blockades that caught the attention of the national media (Foner 1980, 287; Hutchins 1934b). In Macon, Georgia, and Spindale, North Carolina, women and men sat on railroad tracks and prevented trains from delivering textile goods. Of the action in Spindale, the *New York Times* wrote, "Hissing and howling, hurling imprecations at the scabs and demanding that the mills cease operation on pain of being wrecked, the strikers won their point" (qtd. in Hutchins 1934b). In other words, confrontational tactics such as these effectively grabbed the attention of mill owners and had a role in keeping mills and garment factories closed down, since the delivery of necessary goods for continued production was delayed.

Despite the dedication and fortitude demonstrated by hundreds of thousands of textile workers, the sellout of the United Textile Workers (UTW) leadership resulted in a disappointing end to this uprising. The UTW vice-president, Francis Gorman, agreed to the findings of a Roosevelt-appointed investigatory board, which concluded only that "a study be undertaken of wages, workloads, and the 'stretch-out'" in the textile industry (Foner 1980, 289). The board's report did not address the strikers' demands for higher wages, shorter hours, or union recognition. Perhaps the strike may have been more successful had the CP-backed NTW played a central role. The NTW was more radical than the UTW, whose leaders were often easily appeased by Roosevelt and the promises of NRA legislation. Additionally, the NTW fought for civil rights and integrated black textile workers into its union. In contrast, the UTW failed to recognize the interrelated nature of race and gender inequality. Indeed, Janiewski concludes that black women gained very little from the strikes in Durham, North Carolina. She writes, "Led almost exclusively by white men who monopolized the public, decision-making arena by virtue of their sex and race, the unions did not alter the structures of domination which placed black women at the bottom of the social hierarchy" (1983, 102).

Still, the 1931–34 mill strikes held significance for the material gains the women won and for the ways these actions challenged the paradox of the "woman worker." Burlak's account of the Rhode Island strikes pointed to the suasive effect of coercive actions such as walkouts. She pointed out, "The bosses fearing a long militant strike, probably spreading to their other mills, settled with the strikers by giving in to their demands" (1931). From the perspective of mill owners, strikes were effective attention-grabbing tactics, since they spelled one thing: revenue loss. From the workers' standpoint, extra-discursive actions such as walkouts were often the most effective and sometimes the only way for them to "argue" for fair wages and work conditions. In mill towns, owners controlled nearly all aspects of mill workers' lives; for example, bosses owned workers' homes and the stores where workers were forced to shop for food. In this situation, workers' labor power was the most important (if not only) resource workers could employ to win their demands.

The textile strikes of the early 1930s were also significant for the ways they called up the hypocrisy of True Womanhood. In many respects, walkouts and strikes had the same effect as the justificatory discourse examined earlier, in which women justified their place in the paid labor force based on necessity and right. In walkouts and strikes, women were seen fighting alongside male comrades. Oftentimes, these actions resulted in public spectacles where women were treated no differently than men. Women were gassed, clubbed, fired upon, and arrested. In Atlanta during the 1934 textile strike, "mothers of young children" were among those housed at an internment camp set up for arrested picketers (Foner 1980, 287). In short, the idea implied by the cult of True Womanhood—that women were somehow different from men in ways that made them unfit for work in the paid labor force—was called into question. Extra-discursive actions challenged the paradox of the woman worker by demonstrating through physical actions that woman's place was indeed on the picket line.

## Conclusion

Women have always worked outside the home. Since the rise of industrial capitalism, women and girls have stood side by side with men on production lines. They have operated heavy machinery, toiled in fields, labored long hours in department stores, and worked endless hours in the homes of the wealthy. Despite this reality, an ideology of True Womanhood, depicting women as domestic and submissive, remained more or less entrenched, particularly throughout the early 1900s. The gap between popular ideology and working-class women's realities gave rise to a paradox when women became workers in the paid labor force, since "workers" were assumed to be male and "women" were assumed to be domestic. In order to reconcile this paradox, women workers employed a justificatory rhetoric to defend their place in the paid workforce.

Women justified their roles as workers through differentiation, a strategy that called up women's need to work outside the home; and through transcendence, a strategy that emphasized women's right to work alongside men in factories, mills, and on farms. Additionally, like the housewives and mothers described earlier, women workers engaged in extra-discursive tactics such as walkouts and strikes in order to "argue" forcefully for economic justice. Extra-discursive tactics did not take the place of discursive forms of protest, such as letter writing or testifying in public forums. But, when engaged in conjunction with discourse-centered tactics, strikes and walkouts proved not only successful but indispensable in winning fair wages and decent hours in the workplace, since these actions held material consequences for bosses and owners in a way that leafleting or other similar tactics did not always have.

The workplace of the early twenty-first century represents a context for women workers that is quite different from that of the women whose lives were explored in this chapter. Despite notable changes in workplace environment and conditions, however, the reasons women work remain much the same. Women today work out of necessity more than ever and they still face the task of arguing for equal rights in the workplace. Today's working-class families know from firsthand experience that two incomes are, in most cases, necessary for survival. For anyone who remains skeptical of this fact, Warren and Tyagi (2003) advance a compelling argument that undermines the "over-consumption" myth and instead points to a host of economic factors—rising costs of housing, college tuition, and health insurance and a deregulated lending industry—that contribute to financial crises in working-class families.[11] Although women face fewer barriers to advancement and can be found in positions of relative power, they are far outnumbered by their male counterparts, particularly when race is factored in. Additionally, equal pay for equal work is stipulated by law, though this is not reflected in reality. White women earn about eighty cents to the dollar a man earns. For black women that number is sixty-three cents; for Hispanic women, even less: fifty-six cents.

These obstacles to economic equality for women point to the persistence of a gender ideology—however subtle it may be—that links women to domesticity and men to the workplace. Such assumptions are inherent in political rhetorics that blame mothers who work outside the home for a host of social ills, including juvenile delinquency and the decline of family values. Women (especially those with small children) who work outside the home encounter continued scapegoating, despite their demonstrated need and right to earn an income for their labor. This underscores the importance of continued public speaking, debate, and protest around this issue. Indeed, one of the questions facing CP activists of the 1930s was how to appeal to working-class women in order to motivate them to speak and act on their own behalf, particularly in light of this group's historical marginalization from public forums. Rhetorical efforts to create identification with working-class women and to reconstitute this audience into agents of social change are the subject of the next chapter.

# FOUR

# The Paradox of the Woman Orator

"Comrades! We must join together with the other workers. Let us show the capitalists that we are not any more 'know nothings' for we are beginning to learn a whole lot. We will use our knowledge in our own interest. . . . Let us build a union of domestic workers to defend our interests" ("Domestic Workers Too Must Organize" 1931). A domestic worker and correspondent for the *Working Woman* stirred her readers with these words in the March 1931 issue of the magazine. Her rhetoric is noteworthy for the way that it crafts for the listener/reader an agent who is ready and willing to act. The women who read this article may or may not have been experienced in union building or speaking and acting on their own behalf. Yet, the writer addresses her readers not as they actually are, but as she hopes they will become—determined and intelligent workers who are fed up with their circumstances and are ready to initiate change.

Communist Party leaders and activists had to overcome a unique obstacle as they attempted to persuade other working-class women to join the struggle for fair treatment of labor. Historically, the very definition of woman precluded public-sphere participation for this group. Women were considered to be naturally suited to home and child-rearing duties. Likewise, public speaking was deemed a male enterprise requiring virility, rationality, and linear thinking. A paradox arose, then, when a woman became an orator, since womanhood was associated with domesticity and public speaking with manliness.

Yet, history has demonstrated that, despite injunctions against it, women have persistently spoken in public on behalf of issues ranging from abolition, suffrage, and labor reform. As we have seen, women participated in the influential Communist Party USA during the 1930s, and in various labor movement struggles. Women such as Ella Reeve Bloor, Elizabeth Gurley Flynn, Margaret Cowl, Clara Lemlich Shavelson, Anna Damon, Ann Burlak, and others rose to leadership positions within the CP, though not without confronting varying degrees of hostility or ambivalence from male comrades and husbands alike. The following pages examine the rhetorical strategies these activists employed in order to persuade fellow working-class women to transgress hegemonic gender prescriptions by speaking up for women's rights in public settings.

In order to appeal to their female audience members—many of whom were inexperienced in public speaking and/or adhered to dominant norms dictating domesticity—CP activists relied on reconstitution, a process whereby messages can "liberat[e] listeners to think and act more creatively, intelligently, and humanely" (Hammerback 1994, 184). Reconstitution relies centrally on the creation of identification, which, in the example of CP leaders, was garnered through emphasis on three areas: the use of personal contact, the employment of revealing accounts, and the suasive effect of enactment.

## Creating Identification in the Context of Paradox

Kenneth Burke (1950) asserted that the chief aim of rhetoric was identification. Identification occurs when interests between two or more individuals are joined or are perceived to be joined (20). Closely related to identification is the concept of consubstantiality, or the "shared substance" between two persons. Consubstantiality implies what Burke calls an "acting-together; and in acting together, men have common sensations, concepts, images, ideas, attitudes" (21).

### Identification and Reconstitution

The need for rhetoric—and hence identification—arises in situations of uncertainty or ambiguity "when an issue or an idea's merit can be seen from two or more perspectives, each of which may be reasonable" (Blakesley 2002, 22). The paradox of the woman orator was one such ambiguity that required CP activists to take special steps to create identification with their working-class female audience. On one hand, working-class women were influenced by prevailing norms and values that defined them primarily in terms of their home and child-rearing roles. Such norms were persistent and widespread, particularly during an economic downturn in which women who worked were seen as "stealing" jobs from men. On the other hand, working-class women's day-to-day experiences as workers or as wives of under- or unemployed men often provided an impetus to speak in public forums for political and economic reform.

The paradox of the woman orator has presented female speakers with a unique challenge when it came to creating identification, a challenge that was met with ingenuity in the autobiographies of nineteenth- and early twentieth-century activists (Watson 1999, 11–12) and in the rhetoric of working-class women into the 1930s. Since appealing to audience members' currently held values and perspectives may have reinforced dominant gender norms that ran counter to the speakers' goals of motivating women to initiate social change, Bloor, Cowl and other leaders appealed to a second persona, or "implied auditor," which provided a "model of what the rhetor would have his real auditor become" (Black 1970, 113). The concept of the second persona is particularly relevant in this study of rhetoric and social change given the nature of the specific audience. Leaders of the CP were attempting to change not only the domestic and workplace conditions of women but also the perspectives and behaviors of this group. In order to do so, they often had to appeal to an ideal rather than real audience.

Burke identified a link between identification and transformation when he said that "transformation involves the ideas and imagery of identification. That is: the *killing* of something is the *changing* of it, and the statement of the thing's nature before and after the change is an *identifying* of it" (1950, 20). In their attempts to change or transform their listeners, activists like Bloor had to "kill" the misperceptions and hegemonic prescriptions adhered to by many of their listeners. Through their rhetoric, they had to identify a "new" working-class audience member, one who was willing and able to speak and act on her own behalf and in solidarity with others like herself.

Put differently, CP leaders had to reconstitute their listeners. Jensen and Hammerback define reconstitution as the "process by which audiences redefine themselves" (1998, 128; see also Charland 1987; McGee 1975). The concept refers to the ways that messages can encourage listeners to think and act in new, more progressive ways that challenge the status quo (Hammerback 1994, 184). Reconstitution takes place when speakers successfully blend message and persona in such a manner as to encourage identification with listeners who then discover "latent qualities in themselves" (Jensen and Hammerback 1998, 128). Reconstitution is necessary for transformation, and identification sits at the heart of both of these processes.

By establishing identification with an ideal or transformed audience, CP leaders implicitly suggested for their listeners what could be. Theirs was a "rhetoric of possibility," what Poulakos describes as a message that speaks to individuals "in terms of their capacity to become what they are not, and brings to their attention things they do not already feel, know, or understand. Further, it invites them to abandon their familiar modes of thought by challenging their current values and beliefs" (1984, 223–24). For instance, the domestic worker whose words opened this chapter addressed her readers as though they were already "in the know." Whether or not these readers saw themselves as part of a larger "working class," the writer created solidarity through the use of "we" rhetoric. Her message challenged the currently held beliefs of those domestic workers who remained skeptical of unionizing and exercising their rights as workers.

The "obstacle" of audience has been a central problem in the efforts of women activists from the earliest days of women's public speaking and writing. In the early 1900s, the Socialist activist Leonora O'Reilly (who protested alongside the soon-to-be CPer Clara Lemlich [Shavelson]) demonstrated rhetorical ingenuity in transforming her audience into a group of women willing to take control of their workplace circumstances. O'Reilly developed a persona of the "intelligent worker," which effectively balanced an idealized vision of what her audience might become with appeals to the concrete circumstances in which they found themselves (see Triece 2003). For example, in a 1904 speech to shirtwaist makers, O'Reilly repeated the phrases "we know" and "you know," which enabled her to come across as a peer with her listeners, many of whom had little or no union experience. "We all know to day the day of individual effort is passed. . . . You have joined hands in the shop, you know as one link in the chain of industry you count for very little, you know you need the friendship or fellowship of the girl next [to] you" (O'Reilly 1904, 3). Thirty years later, Mother Bloor similarly appealed to a knowing audience when she wrote that "working women, through their own suffering . . . have learned to fight" (1933a). O'Reilly, Bloor, and other labor leaders often spoke to their listeners in a manner that assumed their courage, strength, and willingness to act. Such an approach, it was hoped, would prompt listeners to live up to the image of themselves so eloquently envisioned.

The ways in which CP leaders reconstituted their listeners encourages us to view reconstitution as a process, which oftentimes involves a number of different strategies to ensure successful connection with, and transformation of, one's audience. The following analysis further reveals the extent to which a "feminine style" of speaking is well suited to the goal of reconstitution.

### Reconstitution as a Process

The CP leaders were all too familiar with the challenges of reaching out to fellow working-class women and persuading them to join the cause for labor. The resistance they often faced from the women themselves was compounded by hostility and/or indifference from husbands and male members of the CP hierarchy. This was especially true in the early 1930s before the party officially adopted its Popular Front strategy, which broadened the group's approaches and appeals. Writers in the CP periodical the *Party Organizer* frequently addressed the need for a "special approach" to garner women's support. "What must be recognized . . . is that general agitational and organizational methods are not sufficient to attract women members," wrote a *Party Organizer* contributor in February 1930 ("Women's Work in the Shops" 1930). The correspondent warned that CP organizers "should realize that, due to certain historical, economic and psychological factors . . . the same appeal that might mobilize men into the Communist Party may leave the women workers still indifferent or prejudiced." The writer also called attention to the need for "personal and social contacts" to recruit women. The emphasis on personal contact and testimony, which is characteristic of a "feminine style" of speaking (see Campbell 1989a), can be viewed as an important element in reconstituting an audience of inexperienced and/or reticent working-class women. Before transformation could take place, working-class women had to be met on their own ground.

Establishing a common ground with working-class women opened the way for CP leaders and sympathizers to present a vision of change to their listeners. Through "revealing accounts" (Kirkwood 1992) that detailed past labor successes and homed in on brave women as models, CP leaders painted a picture of the possible, of what could be. Appeals to a second persona further reinforced these visions of the future. Ella Reeve Bloor and Elizabeth Gurley Flynn were particularly adept at speaking to their listeners in terms of what they may become—strong-willed, motivated activists. The previous chapter explored the role such narratives played for their writers. In the following pages, we will examine how these narratives appealed to a second persona and shaped a rhetoric of possibility to inspire listeners.

Enactment, a rhetorical strategy whereby the speaker "incarnates the argument, *is* the proof of the truth of what is said" (Campbell and Jamieson 1978, 9), also played a role in reconstitution. Jensen and Hammerback's (1998) study of the role of the first persona in reconstitution points to the importance of enactment to this process. In order to be convincing, the speaker must "project" or "fulfill" the expectations she sets out for her audience (128). The very presence of Bloor, Flynn, Shavelson, and other CP leaders in meetings, strikes, and door-to-door canvassing spoke volumes when it came to persuading working-class women of their own abilities to become agents of change.

The remainder of the chapter examines more closely these three strategies—personal contact, revealing accounts, enactment—and the roles they played in motivating women to act on their own behalf.

## The Problems of Women Workers

As noted in previous pages, the CPUSA maintained a dubious stance toward issues relating to women's rights. Ella Reeve Bloor's grassroots organizing throughout the 1920s notwithstanding, party attention to the needs of women was all but nonexistent. The onset of the Depression led to a shift within the party toward neighborhood organizing and activism, but these activities were initiated by the rank and file, not the party elite (Baxandall 1993, 148). Gosse explores how the "CPUSA's new awareness of home, family, and neighborhood as political spaces" in late 1930 laid the groundwork for the organization's Popular Front strategy of 1935–39 (1991, 110). The gendered nature of home and family provided an opening through which women could assert more authority within the party; yet, this potential for women's involvement was often left untapped due to the party's ignorance of, or ambivalence toward, the obstacles that needed to be overcome in order to appeal to this marginalized group. "I feel that many of our Party functionaries in the field still take the fact that it is necessary to develop women leaders, with a grain of salt," lamented Ann Burlak (1934, 54). Echoing her frustration, another CP activist asserted that "it is about time the entire Party, men and women, got a new slant on how to draw the women workers into our campaigns and struggles. We should stop stating policy and then adding 'and the women, Negro, and youth'" ("Work among Women" 1931).

The "new slant" was taken primarily by women leaders of the CP who learned the importance of personal contact in order to make their message appealing to their audience. Communist Party activists frequently noted the importance of meeting working-class women on their own ground as the first step toward establishing identification and garnering strike support. One must "win the confidence" of the women before moving on to more controversial labor-related issues, noted one activist. "Avoid starting your conversations with such questions as: religion, marriage, etc., that will shock and antagonize undeveloped women workers" ("Women's Work in the Shops" 1930). Instead, CP organizers met women workers at the factory gates and in their homes and listened to them discuss their concerns surrounding work and family (see Sanders 1938; Stevens 1937; "Women's Work in the Shops" 1930). Sonya Sanders (1938), an organizer in Bronx County, learned firsthand how effective a personal approach could be in transforming women workers. She recalled,

> In the early days of my canvassing, when I rang bells and occasionally heard babies cry, instead of asking the man or wom[a]n who came to the door "why the baby is crying" or "can I be of help"—I would try to politicalize them and give them a sales talk on the [*Daily Worker*]. For my efforts I would get the door slammed in my face. I realized that I would have to start using my head. Now when I knock at a door and sense there is trouble in the home, I ask whether there is anything that I can do. This approach has won many friends and readers. (40)

Seven years later, Margaret Cowl (1937a) was taking this tried-and-true approach with women active in the automobile strikes. Aware that "women sit-down strikers have many more family problems than men workers," Cowl noted that "it was the women comrades who helped these strikers with the so-called simple everyday problems and they won the confidence of these women" (23, 24). Ethel Stevens (1937), a CP organizer, took the same tack when she organized steelworkers' wives in Gary, Indiana. She noted, "We made personal friends with [the wives], went to their homes, talked not only about the strike but also about their own personal affairs."

The organizer and firebrand agitator Elizabeth Gurley Flynn (1938b) displayed a similar awareness of the importance of reaching out to women. Quoting Lenin, Flynn asserted, "'We must get the women with us or they will be against us.'" She continued, "Women in America are so important a political element that the speed with which we move towards Socialism depends upon how rapidly they are included in unions, auxiliaries, campaigns, and in the Communist Party." Women's primary concerns, Flynn well knew, centered around the home and family. "The high cost of food is [women's] daily concern. Anxiety lines their faces right now, with mill and mine shut down." The Communist Party held the answer, according to Flynn, since it "raises immediate issues that reach the hearts and minds of women, better health, homes, and schools" (1938b).

Yet, recruiting women to the party was not easy work. Stevens and other organizers often noted the "patience and then more patience" ("A Unit of Steel Women" 1937) required in order to establish common ground with other working-class women. Describing her experience organizing women in a steel mill, a contributor to the July 1937 *Party Organizer* noted that women who are new to activism often have difficulty staying on the subject of labor during long organizational meetings. The writer explained the approach she took when new members showed more interest in exchanging recipes and sharing household hints. "We never mechanically push anything along. Rather we wait until the next day, then next week. On several points we had to wait until the next month while we helped solve more immediate personal problems for our members" ("A Unit of Steel Women" 1937). Likewise, an organizer in the needle trades asserted that "you can't push anyone into leadership, you have got to guide and develop them into leadership" ("Lessons from Needle Trades" 1934). Yet another activist observed that "the contacts made [at factories] will only be of value if they are systematically followed up through personal approach and in a quiet manner" ("Work among Women" 1931).[1] Stevens (1937) took a deliberate approach to leading the wives of steel-workers into leadership positions. She and her fellow CP organizers "made up a list of about 10 [wives] to whom we paid special attention" and gradually extended their influence until the "list was increased to about twenty."

Organizers in textile and meat-packing trades also explained how their personal approach paid off. "Personal talks" with women workers during a Lawrence, Massachusetts, textile strike revealed the extent to which these women were held back by "priests who preach them to stay home and take care of the house work and their large families after working hours" (Berkman 1931). And in a Chicago packing house, an organizer utilized her "personal friendship with one of the girls" in order to meet women in other departments ("Concentration in the Chicago Stockyards" 1934). Her contacts eventually led to a successful "fight for a half hour rest period."

Perhaps the most effective method for establishing common ground came from Sophia Ocken (1937) and her fellow New York–area organizers, who used motherhood and its attendant issues as a way into the lives of other working-class women. These activists found their own babies to be their "'entrance cards in the class struggle in the neighborhood.'" Ocken realized that though some women may be hesitant to join a strike or industry-related struggle, they were more than ready to stand up for their children on issues pertaining to family relief and neighborhood parks. In this way, they exemplified the "militant motherhood" I elaborated in chapter 2 (see also Tonn 1996). Such willingness is not surprising since activism around child-related issues fit within the bounds of what was deemed "woman's sphere." Tapping their roles as mothers may have had limits since it reinforced (at least to an extent) traditional roles for women.

Yet, it is important to consider the radical potential that such activism held. The women of the New York Mother Child Unit gained experience gathering signatures, speaking to council members, and holding mass meetings. Notably, this unit staged a sit-down in a local relief office to call attention to the need for more relief. The action involved both mothers and babies. "Baby carriages all over the place, and a clothesline strung up in the relief station dramatically brought the situation to the public" (Ocken 1937, 36). Though they were acting in their roles as mothers, these women were gaining public speaking and activism experience. Participation in such activities shaped self-concepts as women gained confidence and were able to see themselves as agents of change who were capable of shaping the lives of their families.

Young girls became a recruiting target for Bloor, who spoke to this group "intimately [and] in [their] own language" in order to make them feel that they were "an integral part" of the labor struggle (Burlak 1937). Ann Burlak, who went on to become a central organizer for textile workers, recalled how Bloor looked her in the eye during one of Bloor's speeches and then pulled Burlak aside after the talk. Speaking one-on-one, Bloor implored Burlak to become involved. Burlak, who was fourteen at the time, noted that Bloor "didn't treat me as a kid. She discussed very seriously with me how I and the other youngsters in that town could help our parents in the class struggle. She asked me to promise her personally that I would organize those youngsters. . . . Within a few months we did have a very good youth club of some 24 kids" (20).

Burlak's recollections point up the success with which Bloor could create a nurturing environment in which to speak frankly to young women who may have been intimidated by the idea of participating in labor struggles. The nurturing practices employed by Bloor and other female CP leaders are characteristic of the "feminine" style of speaking mentioned earlier, which was best suited to the process of reconstitution. Additionally, nurturance played a key role in their overall efforts at agitation. Tonn's (1996) observations regarding the kinship between mothering and agitation are relevant here. That is, successful social movements rely on confrontation but also benefit from a number of behaviors that can be associated with mothering, including "physical preservation, fostering of emotional and intellectual growth, and development of group identity and social responsibility" (2). The attempts of CP leaders to establish common ground with working-class women through personal contact and various social and domestic-related activities promoted the nurturing element so important to efforts at social change.

In the late 1930s, CP organizers became more aware of the need for special efforts to recruit black women to the party. Throughout the 1930s, the CPUSA was one of the few labor organizations actively to recruit black workers and to struggle for civil rights. However, this attention was primarily directed toward male workers. Black women were frequently left out of organizational efforts and often faced outright hostility from white male and female workers. A conference held in June 1937 in New York specifically tackled the issue of black women and union organizing (see L. Thompson 1937). Black and white delegates agreed that "special attention be given to Negro women on the basis of their special problems" (25–26). Louise Thompson, one of the delegates, stopped short of identifying racism as the reason for the lack of black women in the party, but rather noted that many black women "do not feel that they fit in" at party meetings. To counter this, Thompson suggested approaching the women "in a sort of personal way," such as inviting them to social events and "bringing them into our personal circles" (26, 27). In Los Angeles, a black organizer identified as "Adele," noted how she "recruited seventeen Negroes, ten men and seven women," by making visits to their homes and talking with them face to face ("I Visited Their Homes" 1938).

Communist Party activists also organized a host of activities that further enabled them to connect with working women in a personal way. Shop-floor and educational meetings brought both groups together and provided yet more opportunities for sharing perspectives. "Special women's meetings in the shops" gave workers a chance to air their grievances and had the effect of "rally[ing] the women workers together for organized struggles" ("Women's Work in the Shops" 1930). Ethel Stevens and fellow comrades organizing women steelworkers used meetings as a way to listen to workers' concerns, while at the same time giving women much-needed speaking experience. Each meeting centered around a question of concern to the workers. The women were encouraged to ask questions and provide their own perspectives. Stevens noted that "this method is especially important for us because it gives the women a chance to learn how to speak, and it stimulates them to read more of our literature," which prepared them for future meetings (1937, 16). To Stevens's observations one might add that these speaking opportunities bolstered women's confidence and provided a safe environment for women to "try out" the role of orator. Another organizer of steelworkers, "E.J.," reported that her group gave workers concrete tasks to perform, which linked the discussed ideas to their own daily lives ("A Unit of Steel Women" 1937). Organizers within the CP were wise to delegate speaking and organizational tasks. The actual experience of speaking or doing held potential suasive effects as these activities enabled women to see the impact they could have on their surroundings.

Although not CP-affiliated, other prominent unions, such as the International Ladies Garment Workers Union (ILGWU), similarly recognized the need to nurture the speaking abilities of young women (Faue 1991, 110). In the mid- to late 1930s, the ILGWU targeted women with an educational program that taught "skills in public speaking, parliamentary procedure, and organizing" and "it laid the basis for a broader distribution of leadership and activism among the rank and file" (110).

In addition to work-related meetings, CP leaders relied on social events to attract and foster new relationships with women workers. Gradually, these activists became aware of the role that social events might play in their quest to transform the self-concepts and perspectives of women workers, many of whom had little experience with public speaking and activism. As Louise Thompson (1937) remarked, "[I]t is true that political life and personal life tie up together." "S.L.," an organizer of Latin American women, wrote they were "planning more and more social activity, to interchange with the educational activity" ("A Day Unit" 1937, 19). "We are trying to enliven our meetings more and more. We try to combine this with the educational work and with the discussions" (19). The steel organizer Ethel Stevens (1937) similarly mentioned her own efforts to "arrange . . . more social activities" for the workers. Louise Thompson (1937) viewed dances as one way to attract black workers. Her words reveal the importance many CP leaders placed on social activities. "When we have affairs, dances, etc., if we went around we would find young Negro girls who would be glad to attend. If they got there and found they were given consideration, danced with . . . we would find that these are the things that count. . . . They are not so political, but they do mean a great deal" (27).

Establishing common ground between speaker and listener is particularly important in these instances since reconstitution entails a degree of risk taking on the part of the audience. Social events signaled more than a means for introducing fun into the Communist Party; they provided a relaxed environment where CP members and women workers could exchange stories of everyday life as women, wives, mothers, and workers. If these two groups did not at that moment share political outlooks, they held in common their roles as women in a male-dominated society. Dances and cultural outings offered an opportunity to establish what Burke referred to as consubstantiality and in the process to create a foundation upon which to build a deeper and more politically inflected relationship.

Paying attention to the home-related as well as workplace needs of working-class women prompted CP leaders to address child care issues, which often arose when trying to attract new members to the labor movement.

At a CP conference held in New York in late December 1932, one delegate from Lawrence, Massachusetts, spoke of the difficulties of trying to organize women who worked during the day but who were expected to tend to domestic duties at night. With frustration, the delegate explained how women who had attended a meeting had to leave before the meeting was over in order to put their children to bed. "We must work out ways and means for them to come to meetings where they can learn how to organize," she concluded ("Special Attention to Problems" 1933). Other organizers attested to this challenge and further noted the barrier represented by husbands who "still think that their wives will neglect their home and children if they go to meetings" ("A Day Unit" 1937, 17). One answer to this dilemma was to form "mother and child units," which met during the day so that women could bring their children with them ("A Day Unit" 1937; Ocken 1937). Day units proved quite successful though, as organizers noted, children still required attention from mothers during meetings. One unit in New York held its meetings in Central Park with mothers taking turns attending to the children "while the other mothers [held] discussion groups" (Ocken 1937).

The efforts to appeal to a wide variety of women workers through work-related, social, and domestic-centered activities fit hand in glove with the party's Popular Front strategy of the mid- to late 1930s. The Popular Front represented the party's attempt to forge alliances with a variety of progressive groups and to broaden its organizational efforts to include more grassroots and neighborhood issues. During this period, the party "strove to present itself as an American party firmly within American political and cultural traditions" (Shaffer 1979, 76). Shaffer believes that the Popular Front "had important consequences for [the party's] work among women" (76). Although Ella Reeve Bloor had been engaging in the sort of grassroots organizing characteristic of the Popular Front since the mid-1920s, the writings of leaders such as Margaret Cowl indicate the extent to which the Popular Front continued to influence women's organizational strategies throughout the 1930s. For instance, Cowl advocated attracting women to labor organizing through the use of groups such as mothers' clubs, readers' clubs, or social clubs that "would serve as the progressive center in the neighborhood" (1936, 29). Likewise, Jenny Trast, another organizer, suggested "associat[ing] as friends and comrades with women outside of our organization, thus creating interest and sympathy toward our organization" (1937, 22). Cowl's and Trast's observations point to their awareness that such cross-group alliances could serve rhetorical as well as organizational ends.

The creation of identification with women workers was an important strategy in the process of reconstitution. In order to encourage women to change their perspectives of themselves and their surroundings, CP leaders had to establish common ground from which to launch ideas that were new and potentially threatening to their listeners. Having reaffirmed their listeners' presently held values and perspectives, CP organizers relied on a rhetoric of possibility whereby they crafted a vision of their listeners as agents of change capable of addressing their concerns.

## Creating a Rhetoric of Possibility

As noted in chapter 3, letters to the editor written by working-class women served to authenticate and justify writers' experiences as women in the paid labor force. Insofar as these stories represented a rhetoric of possibility, they also held significance for those who read them. Kirkwood (1992) zeros in on the importance of narratives to the "rhetorical enterprise." "Narrative is perhaps the foremost means by which [possibilities of the human condition] are disclosed. Through storytelling, rhetors can confront the states of awareness and intellectual beliefs of audiences; through it they can show them previously unsuspected ways of being and acting in the world" (32).

In short, narratives are an indispensable tool for a rhetoric of possibility. Poulakos describes a rhetoric of possibility as a visionary rhetoric that pertains to "that part of the world that is not. . . . [It] labors to make its listeners envision an absent reality that can be verified only . . . after it has been made actual" (1984, 223). Furthermore, this discourse "asks people to break from the past and the present and to assume the responsibility necessary to create their future" (224). Rhetorics of possibility are conveyed through "revealing accounts" (Kirkwood 1992, 35–37), stories that describe an actor's state of mind that enabled a desirable action on the part of the actor. Revealing accounts obtain their persuasive appeal in one of two ways: through the narrator's commentary, which tells listeners how to interpret the actions; or through sufficiently detailed accounts that enable the facts to speak for themselves (40–44). Relevant to this study is the way that revealing accounts appealed to a second persona. By describing possible actions and states of mind, writers appealed to audiences as they hoped they could become, rather than as they actually were.

The rhetorical act of documenting one's experiences through narrative—particularly through revealing accounts—holds a central place in the history of women's rhetoric. Jamieson explains that since they were "[d]enied access to the public sphere, women developed facility in such private forms of communication as conversation and storytelling" (1988, 82). Storytelling—at times derogatorily referred to as "gossip"—was the primary means through which women passed on lessons to young children and "transmit[ted] the goings-on of the community" (84). Never was this more apparent than in the lives of working-class women throughout the early 1900s who relied heavily on neighborhood "gossip" in order to exchange important information regarding food prices, strike and scab activity, and boycotts (see Cameron 1993).

Stories were also conveyed through autobiographies written by women activists of the early 1900s. These books held significance for the ways they exemplified a rhetoric of possibility that "articulated a model of selfhood for others to emulate" (Watson 1999, 2). Furthermore, "In writing their life stories, these women were expressing the possibility of a new kind of womanhood for others; in recording their life stories, these women were redefining womanhood and personhood for their contemporaries" (2).

Much like early twentieth-century autobiographies, the rhetoric of working-class women appearing in CP publications provides a window through which to examine revealing accounts as Kirkwood has described them. As a mode of communication characteristic of a "feminine style" of speaking (see Campbell 1973; Jamieson 1988), narratives provided the means through which average working-class women could relate a host of workplace actions along with commentary that may lead readers to specific interpretations. Women who recounted stories of their struggles in factories and mills most often mentioned the strength and know-how demonstrated by themselves and their comrades in such struggles. As Kirkwood explains, "[S]ometimes the immanent facts and internal consistency of a story do not allow people to determine *which* possibilities of thought or action it expresses" (1992, 41). In these cases, the storyteller "must 'tell' [readers] what [the action] means." "Militance," "spirit," "bravery," and "solidarity" were the words frequently employed when conveying to readers the mind-set of actors in the narratives.

A letter from a shoe worker in the January 1930 issue of the *Working Woman* provides a good example of one such revealing account. The writer, "M.G.," began by describing how shoe workers fought back after bosses in the shoe factories laid off union members during the slack season. She explicitly mentioned the workers' acumen in the struggle. "Our workers' solidarity, our organizational strength, our strike determination, our class consciousness—these are the weapons that the shoe workers fight the lock-out bosses with!" ("Shoe Workers Strike" 1930).

A similar storyline appeared throughout the *Working Woman,* which told readers of daring workers who fought back against ruthless employers. An article on the dressmakers' strike of February 1931 ("Dress Strike Aims" 1931) related the workers' "splendid spirit of solidarity" despite bosses' attempts to provoke racism. The article further noted the bravery of workers, whose "spirit" was not "dampened" by the actions of brutal police. Articles detailing strikes of mill and auto workers provided similar commentary. Edith Berkman (1933), an organizer of the CP-backed National Textile Workers Union, described Lawrence, Massachusetts, mill strikers as the "bravest fighters against starvation." Ann Burlak (1933a) likewise noted that the "picket lines were the most militant seen." A letter writer describing the solidarity of Detroit auto workers asserted the "women were amongst the most militant and enthusiastic strikers" ("Driving to Victory" 1933).

In each of these narratives, the writer detailed the events surrounding the particular labor struggle and described the part women played in winning the battle. The significance of these stories as rhetorics of possibility comes from the narrators' comments, which conveyed the states of mind of the women involved. Both details and commentary are essential in order for the stories to be persuasive. The theme of spirited workers winning out over unscrupulous bosses can be applied to just about any workers' situation, regardless of whether or not the specific details match. As Kirkwood explains, the details are necessary for conveying the possibility, but "once disclosed the possibility is no longer limited to the performance used to display it. . . . [The] possibilities exceed the contexts in which they first arise" (1992, 37). The commentary is essential for pointing out to readers the states of mind that led to the desirable actions. "When people perceive the states of mind that enable heroic acts, they learn they can do more than admire their heroes' success, and they must decide whether to exercise the means of this success in their own lives" (38).

Other narratives related the transformation of women workers as they learned how to stand up for themselves. These stories convey the thought processes of women who were "waking up" or "beginning to see" the injustice of their situations and their own capability to alter their circumstances. A laundry worker writing to the *Working Woman* in June 1930 declared that her coworkers "who have been asleep for a long time are waking up" to the need to organize into unions and fight for the eight-hour day ("Laundry Worker Tells" 1930). In quite the same manner, Henrietta Bonin (1930), a worker in a pants factory, explained that she and her comrades are "beginning to understand that the reason why the boss can take such advantage of us is because we are unorganized." Ann Burlak (1931), the CP organizer of textile workers, explicitly identified the change in mind-set of mill workers in the Northeast as an awakening to "class consciousness."

Barbara Rand's (1931) account of the wives of striking coal miners, which appeared in the *Working Woman* in 1931, was particularly compelling for its detail of the conversion these women went through as they witnessed the treatment of striking husbands. Rand explained that the wives who formed a women's auxiliary are "no longer shy, backward. The task at hand is a terribly important one. . . . All together, with intense earnestness, everybody makes suggestions." The women were said to handle all sorts of problems including "braving the deputies and state troopers on the picket lines . . . [and] explaining to starved children why there is no bread."

Revealing accounts also came in the form of narratives that highlighted the accomplishments of a specific activist. The story of Mother Bloor's decades-long career of activism was often retold in CP publications and pamphlets (see Barton 1935, 1937; Flynn 1942a; Women's Commission, Central Committee 1937; Todes and Small 1937). Often the narratives of Bloor are sufficiently detailed to make unnecessary any commentary on her state of mind. In contrast to the above mentioned narratives, the Bloor story may have gained its persuasive nature by "showing" a state of mind rather than "telling," as through commentary (Kirkwood 1992).

Characteristic of these accounts is one appearing in the *Working Woman* in July 1931 on the occasion of Bloor's sixty-ninth birthday (Todes 1931). As was the case with other Mother Bloor narratives, this story offered a thumbnail sketch of Bloor's activist duties leading up to her alliance with the CP and included details of Bloor's tireless efforts on behalf of farmers and industrial workers. It supplied sufficient details that would plausibly lead readers to specific interpretations regarding Bloor's mind-set. Still, the author mentioned Bloor's "dauntless courage" and "fighting spirit," in an effort to highlight Bloor as an example for working-class women of all stripes to follow.

In her own speeches and writings Bloor repeated a moving story of Annie Clemence, a union activist known for her work in the Women's Auxiliary of the Western Federation of Miners in Calumet, Michigan, in the 1910s. Bloor's lecture notes—on which she wrote a reminder to use "vivid words"—reveal the importance she placed on this and other compelling narratives (Bloor 1913–14). The Clemence story in particular is so powerful it is no wonder Bloor employed it time and again in order to stir her listeners.[2] In a July 1931 *Working Woman* article Bloor (1931) related how Clemence stood up to soldiers who were intimidating miners during the copper strike of 1913. Bloor's direct quoting of Clemence provided the detail necessary to bring the story to life and to underscore, without explicitly verbalizing it, Clemence's almost shocking bravery. The story goes that Clemence became enraged when she witnessed a soldier tearing a miner's U.S. flag to pieces. According to Bloor, "Annie said: 'When I saw that man's flag cut to pieces, it made me mad, so . . .

I held my flag out in front of me and told them to go ahead and shoot me through the flag. Then the workers all over the US would know what they did to their women and children in the copper country, and what they did to their flag. . . . But . . . they did not have the nerve.'" The admiration Bloor expressed for Clemence throughout the article reinforced Clemence's militancy as a positive action for workers to emulate.

Elizabeth Gurley Flynn offered a similarly inspiring story of her own exploits as a young speaker in the early 1900s. In an article appearing in *Woman Today* (formerly the *Working Woman*) in April 1937, Flynn related her experiences speaking at Industrial Workers of the World (IWW) meetings and free speech protests. According to Flynn, her appearance as a speaker at IWW street meetings was a "novelty," suggesting the challenges women faced when they took the platform in male-dominated contexts and her own bravery in doing so (1937b, 26). Flynn goes on to describe the events of the first free speech fight in Missoula, Montana, in 1910, where she was a central protagonist. She and other IWW members took turns speaking publicly on street-corner soapboxes. Flynn described the workers' courage: "Suddenly the police ordered us to stop. We defied them! We defended our constitutional rights!" (26). She also related their success in outwitting the powers that be. Once arrested, hundreds of workers refused to leave jail thus placing the burden on jailors who had to feed the throng. As Flynn explained, the "taxpayers resented the growing burden of expense. They admired the tenacity of the IWW in those early days. Finally the arrests ceased, all were released and our meetings resumed" (26). In this struggle, Flynn, who was pregnant at the time, was arrested twice.

The *Daily Worker* also carried stories of daring young women, such as the one mentioned earlier that chronicled the actions of Jessie Taft, a laundry worker who chained herself to a pillar in an upscale hotel to call attention to her coworkers who were on strike (Schneider 1936). Like the foregoing narratives, this story is significant for the details, which envisioned for readers the events surrounding the labor struggle, and for the commentary, which tells readers how to interpret the worker's actions. The writer explained how Taft made a rousing speech in support of the strikers as she was chained to the pillar on the mezzanine level. Guests gathered around and "after a few minutes were applauding and encouraging her in her dramatic demonstration." The story unfolded in a sensational fashion as the writer explained how the hotel manager covered Taft's mouth in an effort to silence her after unsuccessfully attempting to unchain her. Meanwhile the crowd grew and continued to applaud her speech. The narrative came to a climax as the writer explained that Taft's chains were hacksawed and the young worker was led out of the hotel.

Significantly, the narrator depicted Taft's behavior as a "courageous action" and noted that Taft "coolly" chained herself to the pillar. Further, Taft was described as a "symbol of the young determined spirit behind the smashing drive in New York to organize" the laundry workers. The narrator's descriptions of Taft and her actions were inspirational for young women who may or may not have had the wherewithal to confront their own exploitative situations in so daring a manner. The stories of Taft, Bloor, Clemence, Flynn, and other brave working women that appeared in the *Working Woman* and the *Daily Worker* represented for readers a possibility of how to be.

In addition to revealing accounts that detailed the actions of a specific activist, Mother Bloor, in particular, facilitated the process of transforming listeners' identities and enhancing their sense of self-efficacy by addressing her listeners as if they were already "in the know" (figure 9). From pre-suffrage speeches of the 1910s to campaign addresses of the mid-1930s, Bloor spoke to women as if they were already motivated and militant workers capable of social change (see Bloor 1917, 1933a, 1933b, 1936). The "working women, through their own suffering, their own struggles have learned to fight, and *together* we shall fight all imperialist wars, all starvation and unemployment, and *together* we shall do our part to build a new society," wrote Bloor in a 1933 *Working Woman* article (1933a). Bloor grounded her rhetoric in reality, mentioning her listeners' "suffering" and "struggles," but she set forth a vision of the future by repeating "together" and "we shall." Bloor also made it a point to appeal to housewives, as in her 1936 campaign address broadcast over the radio (1936). Housewives are smart, Bloor noted, and can see through Republican rhetoric that says relief efforts are the reason for the high cost of living. She said that the "housewife, who does the nation's shopping, knows that the meat trust, the food trust, are waxing rich, as higher prices cut down the amount of milk and bread which a poor family can buy."

Appealing to a second persona and creating revealing accounts represent important strategies that enable reconstitution, a process that takes place over time and, as noted earlier, often begins with establishing common ground through personal contact. Enactment worked in conjunction with these two strategies in order to drive home the possibilities for women.

## Enactment

The concept of enactment—the embodiment of possibilities—points up the way in which a woman's very appearance on a public platform, regardless of her verbal message, made an argument for women's rights to speak. Aboli-

Figure 9. Ella Reeve "Mother" Bloor speaking at a picnic, Akron, Ohio, 23 August 1942. Sophia Smith Collection, Smith College, Northampton, Massachusetts.

tionist, suffrage, and working-class activists of the mid-1800 to early 1900s at times risked their lives by stepping onto the public stage. Once in front of their audiences, their very presence made a case for the idea that women were reasoning humans deserving of the same rights afforded their husbands and brothers. Leonora O'Reilly, the activist who protested alongside Clara Lemlich (Shavelson) in the 1909 Uprising of 30,000, provides a good example of the suasive effect of enactment (see Mattina 1994; Triece 2003). As a lifelong factory worker, labor and suffrage activist, and strike leader, O'Reilly embodied the intelligent and militant worker that she encouraged her listeners to become. Similarly, throughout the 1930s, the physical presence of Ella Reeve Bloor and Elizabeth Gurley Flynn as speakers challenged the paradox of the woman orator by reinforcing the argument that women are capable of speaking in public and have the right to do so.

That Ella Reeve "Mother" Bloor was a steadfast, captivating, and widely popular public speaker throughout the first three decades of the twentieth century is confirmed through the many published comments of friends and comrades who paid tribute to her over the years (see Flynn 1942a; Women's Commission, Central Committee 1937; Todes and Small 1937). Archived handbills and flyers announcing her many speaking engagements further highlight the extent of Bloor's public presence and influence on leftist struggles. In 1918, Bloor ran for lieutenant governor of New York, and the Socialist Party, in which Bloor was involved at that time, circulated a letter to various state locals encouraging them to invite Bloor to speak. The letter's content speaks to the sway Bloor held in that organization, an influence that was noteworthy given women's political status at that time. The letter began, "We have very few women speakers in the party measuring up to Mrs. Bloor's standing. She is widely known all over the State having spoken for most of the locals, and is familiar with the peculiar local conditions in almost every section of the State. As a woman speaker and as a candidate of the Party she will command better attention and receive a respectful hearing, where men speakers may meet with difficulties" (New York State Committee). Despite the wholehearted endorsement of Bloor, the letter writer grappled with the paradox of Bloor, a woman orator, as revealed in the first line of the letter, where Bloor was compared to other *women* speakers in the party. Interestingly, Bloor's sex was seen to be to her advantage since it was believed that as a woman she secured more respect than a man. Her sex notwithstanding, Bloor was admired for her well-noted ability to create identification with her listeners and to sustain their spirits even during the toughest of struggles. Bloor's popularity among women was reaffirmed in a 1918 handbill that stated, "Women Especially (and Men Also)

Are Invited to Hear Ella Reeve Bloor of New York . . . Lecture on Woman and Socialism" ("Women Especially" 1918).

Bloor maintained a steady speaking schedule throughout the 1920s and 30s, often giving more than one speech a day. An undated flyer listed her speaking engagements in New York City, where she addressed the question, "Have you coal, meat, wheat, light, good car service, clothing? Have you a vote, men and women?" ("Nine Mass Meetings"). Bloor spoke to this issue in nine speeches over seven days. The flyer addressed women with the question, "Women, what are you going to do with your vote?" The sheer frequency of Bloor's public appearances underscored her popularity and ability as a speaker as well as her stamina and dedication to the cause of labor.

Throughout the 1930s, Bloor firmly rooted herself in the struggles of farmers and spoke regularly to various farmers' groups in the Northwest, addressing them in a variety of capacities. In 1931 she spoke to farmers of Mountrail County as the state organizer of the United Farmers League; in 1933 she addressed the "Farmers Holiday Meeting" where she shared her experience as a delegate to the Farmers' Emergency Relief Conference, which was held in December 1932 in Washington, D.C.; and an undated flyer announced Bloor's presence as the Communist candidate for Congress from North Dakota.[3]

Bloor's popularity among farmers was remarkable given the challenge she faced. She had to overcome potential opposition not only to her argument but to her very presence on the platform. Campbell's observations regarding feminist rhetoric also apply to Bloor's farmers' rights talk, namely, that regardless of how traditional her argument, Bloor's rhetoric "attacks the . . . most fundamental values of the cultural context in which it occurs" since the assumptions underlying public speaking are "a violation of the female role" (1973, 75). If anything, Bloor was adept at tailoring her message to her audience in order to create identification and thus allay the unease at seeing and hearing a woman speak publicly. Brown notes that "rather than using a revolutionary rhetoric that American farmers would dismiss out of hand, Bloor spent a considerable amount of time formulating a rhetoric of fairness, equality, and family which would appeal to Midwestern and Northwestern farmers" (1996, 311).

At these speaking engagements Bloor stood as an example to farmers' wives, women who were isolated geographically and culturally from labor struggles. In her autobiography *We Are Many,* Bloor noted that the farm women of Nebraska were "the greatest sufferers," having to make a home and raise children in impoverished surroundings and in the midst of drought and dust storms (1940, 242). For these women, Bloor's presence held particular significance as an example of what they could become if they joined Bloor in struggling for farmers' rights.

Bloor's public appearances were eye-catching not only due to her sex, but also because she often had her children or grandchildren by her side. She had two of her children with her—one an infant—when she spoke to striking weavers in Slatersville, New Hampshire, in the 1910s (Barton 1937, 12–13), and two granddaughters accompanied her on a tour of the United States when she spoke in support of CP candidates in the 1936 campaign (Bloor 1940, 286). In at least one case, Bloor was arrested and sent to jail along with her children, who were present with her on the strike line (see Bloor 1932a, 1940). These instances were significant to the extent they upended traditional notions of womanhood as well as motherhood. Bloor was an example of "militant motherhood" (see Tonn 1996), rhetorically, as previous chapters have described, and physically, as the examples of enactment demonstrate. Tonn defined militant motherhood as a feminine rhetorical style that emphasizes "personal experience and personal provocation, narrative and inductive structures, intimate and familial terms of address and *ad hominem* attacks, empathy and shaming, and opportunities for audience imitation, including enactment and dialogic dialectics" (1996, 3).

During more than four decades of consistent appearances on the public platform, Bloor chipped away at notions that women were unfit to speak publicly. A flyer announcing a speech Bloor gave in September 1936 on democracy versus fascism described Bloor as "An *Authority* on Farmer's [sic] Problems and Their Solution" ("For a Free Happy Prosperous America" 1936, emphasis mine). Even at eighty years of age, Bloor was touring the country giving speeches in support of civil rights and condemning Hitler's rise to power. By the time of her cross-country tour in the early 1940s, Bloor's popularity had peaked as she had come to stand as a symbol of the Americanization of Communism. A speech given in July 1942 described Bloor (along with the California CP activist Anita Whitney) as "splendid and dynamic. . . . [Bloor and Whitney] are true leaders of the people—an inspiration to all women" ("Rally to Win the War").

Fellow CP and labor activists bestowed similar accolades on Bloor throughout the 1930s, particularly on the occasion of her seventy-fifth birthday in 1937 (see Barton 1937; Todes and Small 1937). These speakers consistently remarked upon Bloor's public presence as an example for women to follow. Ann Barton noted that "it is to women that Mother Bloor's life has deep and personal meaning. . . . Mother Bloor should be a challenge to all women, telling them what one woman did, what women can do" (1937, 6). Anna Damon, who headed the committee organizing a celebration for her seventy-fifth birthday, asserted that Bloor "has meant so much to each one of us. . . . [S]he has inspired us with her great courage, with her great heart; she has helped us in whatever work we may be doing by example, by advi[c]e, by encouragement; she has taught us the meaning of selfless devotion and loyalty to an ideal; she has shown us how a life full of purpose and meaning and value can be lived" (1937, 3). The comments of Jack Stachel, another CP activist, put the case for enactment into sharp relief. He declared, "Mother Bloor in her life and work represents the most shattering argument against all forms of discrimination still being practiced against women, and the most powerful argument for genuine equality" (1937, 18).

In public-speaking notoriety Mother Bloor was matched perhaps only by her comrade Elizabeth Gurley Flynn, who was referred to as the "Joan of Arc of the labor movement" ("Lodge 500 Welcomes" 1938).[4] On the podium, Flynn exemplified the successful female orator. From her early years as a soap-box agitator, Flynn displayed oratory skill, eloquence, and a deep and abiding dedication to labor's cause. Like Bloor, Flynn maintained a daunting speaking schedule, even speaking ten times in one day during the famous 1926 textile strike in Passaic, New Jersey (Baxandall 1987, 2). In the late 1930s and early 40s, Flynn went on numerous speaking tours, often giving more than one speech in a day.[5] One historian has noted, "In February 1938 alone she attended eighteen meetings, ranging from CP mass meetings, workers' school classes, and YCL [Young Communist League] clubs, to non-communist functions such as a forum on labor history held under the auspices of the Ethical Culture Society, and spoke at least ten times" (Camp 1995, 145). Flynn traveled around the Ohio–West Virginia–Pennsylvania region giving speeches nearly every day during early April and May 1938 (see Women's Commission, Communist Party 1938; "Lower Ohio Valley Section" 1938).

Flynn's bravery as a speaker during these years was significant given that red-baiting was widespread and that she was a woman speaking out in contexts still dominated by men. Her reputation as the "rebel girl" often preceded her, leading on occasion to attempted bans and disruptions of her speeches. When the Plymouth, Pennsylvania, Workers Alliance invited Flynn to speak in October 1939, the organization was prevented from holding the meeting ("Plymouth Is Still America" 1939). Only after protesting the ban and garnering assistance from lawyers and the American Civil Liberties Union was the group allowed to hold Flynn's talk, entitled "Unemployment and Elections."

The handbill advertised Flynn as the "veteran labor leader who has spent practically all her life as an active champion of the men and women of our country who work for a living" ("Plymouth Is Still America" 1939).

Although her fiery speaking style easily earned her the nickname "rebel girl," Flynn demonstrated an ability to remain calm in the face of unnerving speaking situations in the late 1930s, when anti-Communist sentiments reached a high pitch and CP meetings were unlawfully disrupted. On at least three occasions, Flynn's speeches were violently disrupted, although neither Flynn nor her audience were ever harmed. Flynn always maintained composure during these incidents—despite hecklers, tear gas, and police who stood idly and just watched ("Communist Rally" 1939; "Crowd Routs a Communist" 1939; "Legion Leaders Approve Action" 1939; American Civil Liberties Union 1938a, 1938b; "Men Say They Are Legionnaires" 1939). In September 1939, members of the American Legion shouted down Flynn at a CP meeting in Des Moines, Iowa. Responding to one of the hecklers who called her a "'——— liar,'" Flynn retorted, "'You must be a tough customer for your wife to talk to. . . . Why don't you calm down and let's put it to a vote as to whether I continue in this meeting or not?'" ("Crowd Routs a Communist" 1939). The local news account of the event explained that "after an hour of bedlam in which photographic flash bulbs were burst, ice water from the speaker's table overturned and the room generally disarranged, sponsors of the meeting decided to abandon their attempt to continue" ("Crowd Routs a Communist" 1939). During another speech the same year, Flynn defended free speech over the shouts of veterans who responded, "'Free speech, but not for Russia.'" Flynn displayed a bit of humor when, upon concluding her speech, "she said the meeting was an excellent one and that she appreciated the services of the police force, although she did not hope to make Communists of them" ("Communist Rally" 1939).

Flynn was no doubt wildly popular among her comrades. But she spoke before a wide variety of audiences, including high school students, members of the Young Communist League, women's clubs, Irish community groups, mass meetings, and intimate teas (Flynn 1940b, 1943). Archived flyers indicate she was a popular speaker at May Day celebrations. She also taught a series of courses on labor history (see *Pittsburgh Workers School* 1938; "Special Course" 1937; "Story of the Militant Labor Movement" 1938). Her involvement in these events further strengthened her reputation as a central figure in the labor movement.

Yet, it was in her speeches and talks to women and girls that she most readily represented what her audience could become. In the late 1930s, Flynn was a guest speaker at a number of International Women's Day celebrations. She also addressed the specific concerns of women in speeches such as "Woman's Place in a Changing World," "Women's Place in American Democracy," "Women and Democracy," "Women in Industry," "Women Face the Future," and "Women's Future." In 1937, the Young People's Forum (1937) hosted Flynn to address the question, "Which way out for the American girl—jobs, marriage, or . . . ?" The flyer garnered the attention of young women with the questions, "How many of the 14,000,000 unemployed are girls? What is the future for many of them? Can our society adequately provide for them?" The following year, Flynn toured Pennsylvania and addressed "hundreds of women—the wives, sisters and daughters of miners, with women working in industry, and with the women in the trade-union auxiliaries" in an attempt to recruit them to the Communist Party (see Women's Commission, Communist Party 1938). And again, in 1939, when fascism was an ever-growing threat, Flynn gave a speech, "In Defense of Democracy," in Poughkeepsie, New York. The handbill advertising the speech begins with an attention-getter designed to establish common ground with the average citizen. It read, "All Americans value their democracy and the liberties that it gives them. These liberties are being threatened by a small group of 'economic royalists' who are paving the way for fascism in this country" ("In Defense" 1939). Listeners heard Flynn "speak on an American woman[']s creed for defending democracy." Other questions to be addressed were, "Is Woman[']s place in the home? Is Unity between the CIO and AF of L possible? Are communists defenders or enemies of Democracy?" ("In Defense"). In all of these examples, listeners heard a riveting speech given by Flynn, who motivated listeners to confront the system that marginalized them as workers and scapegoated them when they sought work outside the home.

Like Mother Bloor, Flynn led a life of tireless agitation, from her younger days as a Socialist and a Wobbly to her eventual joining of the CP. On handbills, Flynn was described as "America's most famous woman labor leader," a "prominent Irish-American labor leader," a "friend and aid to all youth and workers," and a "famous journalist, lecturer and fighter for women[']s rights." One such document, issued by Friends of the Workers Alliance (1937), proclaimed, "Flynn is back into activity to resume a career that is perhaps the most eventful in all history. Her life is the story of the struggle for freedom in America. From picket line to jail, back to the picket line, on the speakers platform, at strike meetings, back to jail . . . [h]er name re-echoes . . . all that is noble and progressive in America."

In the midst of this popular reception, Flynn expressed her awareness of the ways that gender shaped her experiences as a public speaker. According to Camp (1995), Flynn once told a friend "that what a female labor leader needed was a wife to pack and unpack her bags" (145). In "Brain of a Woman" (n.d.), one of Flynn's many unpublished poems,[6] she conveyed her feelings on being a prominent public speaker:

> One thinks about my schedule, my letters, my articles, my speech
>     tonite[.]
> The subject[,] the place, the people, the results.
> It is calm[,] methodical, it directs my work, my conversations,
> It asks questions, sorts answers, absorbs information, seeks to know more,
>     learn more, be useful,
> Soaks up what I must know to give guidance, and clear answers
> to patient eager workers who listen to me.
> This is the brain that likes to work, to write, to speak, to act,
> This is the brain of the cool[,] collected me,
> The core of me, the unshakeable, unchangeable, dependably,
> reliable me,
> that directs my speech, detects the moment of detachment
> from the audience,
> the lessening and loosening of the electric current between
> speaker and listener.
> Here there is no sex no double standard
> No difference.

The poem was a reminder that a female activist was constrained by norms that her male comrade was not, even if her sex was not an issue when she was on stage. Indeed, one wonders to what extent the last line of the poem actually held true for Flynn and other women. Throughout the 1940s, Flynn continued to work on sex equality in the Communist Party and in labor struggles more broadly despite a lack of enthusiasm from male party leaders (Camp 1995, 172). Frustrations aside, Flynn transgressed the sexual double standard that made "woman orator" a paradox, and she stood as an example of what her listeners could become.

## Conclusion

Historically, public speaking has been described as a distinctly male pursuit requiring "manly" qualities such as "self-reliance, self-confidence, and independence"—all characteristics at odds with what has been defined as "womanly" (Campbell 1973, 75). Thus, the idea of a "woman orator" presents a paradox since womanhood connotes domesticity and public speaking is viewed as a role to be filled only by a man. Communist Party leaders faced an audience-related obstacle to the extent that working-class women of the 1930s bought into traditional notions of womanliness and public oratory appearances, which in turn limited their public-speaking experience. Specifically, activists had to devise methods for transforming their audience into a group willing and able to transgress prevailing gender norms. They accomplished this by establishing personal contact, creating revealing accounts, and appearing themselves in public as examples for women to follow. All of these strategies worked to reconstitute listeners, or to encourage them to think and act in ways that were liberating for themselves and their families.

Previous studies of reconstitution and concepts pertaining to rhetorics of possibility have contributed much to narrative theory specifically, and more broadly to studies of rhetoric and its role in social change. Uncovering the rhetoric and tactics of CP female activists during the 1930s advances studies of reconstitution in two ways. First, the rhetoric of Bloor and other CP leaders points to the way in which the success of audience transformation depends on a variety of strategies that work in conjunction with one another. Second, studying CP activists' efforts to recruit working-class women has shown that a feminine style of speaking goes hand in hand with the process of reconstitution.

It is true that most women in contemporary Western societies do not face the same sanctions for speaking in public that women of the early twentieth century endured. Yet, questions remain concerning women and public speech, particularly given that we still live in a male-dominated society where women must struggle to reach positions of power and to get their voices heard. For instance, what is the relevance of a feminine style of speech in contemporary public-speaking realms? What rhetorical situations call for this style of speech? Dow and Tonn's (1993) study of the rhetoric of Ann Richards, the former Texas governor, indicates the usefulness of this style in mainstream political discourse. Perhaps more provocative is their assertion that the characteristics of a feminine style of speaking contribute to the formation of a feminist public sphere where counterhegemonic ideologies challenge the status quo of women's oppression (287). The scholarly task remains to explore such arenas of resistance and to continue to reveal the paradoxes or reality gaps out of which such resistance may spring.

# Lessons Learned from the 1930s

"The study of women's rhetoric is a study in paradox, pain, and punishment," Carol Jablonski has observed (1988, 164). The experiences of working-class women of the Depression—as homemakers, workers, and activists—certainly attest to this fact. But a closer look at the lives of women such as Ella Reeve Bloor, Clara Lemlich Shavelson, and Mary Smith also points up the complexity inherent in paradox. Paradox can be at once hegemonic and liberatory—delimiting options and at the same time creating an opening for social critique. During the 1930s, ideologies associating woman with domesticity and espousing the home as safe haven represented obstacles for women seeking equality in the workplace and well-being for their families. Yet, these ideologies brought to light a reality gap, which often prompted women to challenge a rhetoric that did not reflect their lives and a system that did not meet their needs. In this concluding portion of the book, I will locate the discussions of previous chapters in a contemporary context in order to explore and better understand how key terms (for example, "family" or "motherhood") have been employed over time in both hegemonic and counterhegemonic ways. The rhetoric of the agitators I explored earlier highlights the importance of connecting seemingly personal issues to the public sphere, thereby encouraging an examination and critique of social institutions and systems that influence our daily lives. Women's protest rhetoric underscores the extent to which meaningful social change should extend well beyond the confines of one's own home and familial relations; and the actions of these women point up the continued importance of a class-based solidarity that has material consequences.

## Familial Discourses and the Paradox of the Public/Private Split

Chapter 1 detailed the doctrine of separate spheres, a popular ideology that took root in the mid-1800s but still held sway in the 1930s. That doctrine maintained that the public world of work and the private world of home were distinct yet complementary realms. Adherents believed that production had little bearing on reproduction—home was a "haven in a heartless world." Yet, the notion that home was a safe haven or respite from the work world rarely accorded with the lives of those in the coal towns of western Pennsylvania or the textile towns of New England and North Carolina. Specifically, in their roles as money managers and mothers of small children, women felt the pain of layoffs and reduced hours in the mines and mills as keenly as did their husbands. Some would argue that the women felt it more acutely since it was the wife who confronted the landlord and the butcher when bills came due and she who soothed her children when they had not enough to eat. As one *Working Woman* writer put it, "All the misery of the shortage of keeping the family from starvation in time of unemployment falls heaviest on the housewife" ("Effects of Unemployment" 1930).

Chapter 2 explored rhetorics that highlighted the extent to which economic factors and decision making in the public realm influenced the so-called private sphere of home and family life. Working-class women of the 1930s used the rhetorical strategy of perspective by incongruity in order to recontextualize popular understandings of the family. Perspective by incongruity involves disconnecting common understandings of "what properly goes with what" (Burke 1954, 74) in order to create new perspectives on various issues. In their own references to home life, working-class women gave lie to traditional idealized images of family that privatized this institution. Through recontextualization, they created a new view of family that effectively linked this so-called "private" entity to the workings and decision making of public institutions. This rhetorical move encouraged a critical examination of social structures and systems (for example, factory-owned towns, speedups, stretch-outs, wage disparities based on gender and race) that made family life difficult if not at times miserable. Ella Reeve Bloor, in particular, was known for her emphasis on the working-class "family." Bloor made organizing a family affair and believed in the integration of "community and shop floor issues" (Brown 1996, 231). In short, CP rhetoric created images of, and made references to, "family" for very specific political ends. According to that rhetoric, families were not isolated nor were they unaffected by activities beyond the front stoop. Seen in this way, the so-called public/private split, which perpetuated the idealization of the family, did not exist.

In contrast to working-class women's broadened understandings of the family, various "familialist" rhetorics continued to privatize issues that were social in origin. These rhetorics represent hegemonic uses of the term "family" and can be traced to nineteenth-century "values of domesticity," which worked to "undercut the opposition to exploitative pecuniary standards in the work world by upholding a 'separate sphere' of comfort and compensation at home" (Cott 1977, 69). Dominant familialist rhetorics frame both hardship and consolation in personal terms. According to these discourses, problems such as poverty, juvenile delinquency, and crime are alleged to stem from families or individuals who lack positive values, initiative, or a sense of personal responsibility, rather than from economic policy surrounding employment, access to quality education, or affordable housing. Scholars have examined the ways in which familialist rhetorics reemerge and regain persuasive appeal during times of substantial economic upheaval or unrest as a reaction to widespread dissent (see Cloud 1998b; Coontz 1988, Triece 2001). In the early 1900s (see Triece 2001) and again in the early 1990s (see Cloud 1998b), familialist rhetorics encouraged individuals to turn inward to home and self-improvement as the solution to problems that in actuality required broad-based collective confrontation. Additionally and not least important, the image of tranquility—or at least the possibility of attaining such—in familialist rhetorics offers the prospect of comfort and a degree of control in a context of economic uncertainty that otherwise may provoke a widespread response to oppression in the form of social movements or labor struggles (see Abramovitz 1988; Coontz 1988; Cott 1977). Social control, then, is the motive underlying familialist rhetorics.

It remains of special importance to examine how familialist rhetorics act as a means of ideological social control in a contemporary context where a "war on terrorism" is waged to battle manufactured threats abroad with the effect of diverting attention from the day-to-day terrors resulting from economic uncertainty that affects our quality of life in the home and the workplace. Contemporary familialist rhetorics are manifested in family values rhetoric and, more recently, in marriage initiatives that seek to codify the traditional heterosexual marriage and the attendant division of labor. Cloud (1998b) examined the ways Republicans and Democrats made heavy use of the ideograph <family values> in order to privatize social problems such as racism and poverty in the context of the 1992 Los Angeles rebellion (393).[1] By centering on the family as both the source of and solution to social ills, <family values> rhetoric encouraged individuals to blame themselves for problems that were systemic in nature and that required a broad collective effort to overcome.

Many of the assumptions underlying family values discourse continue to influence the popular political agenda, now through a rhetoric extolling heterosexual marriage. Marriage promotion discourse—which gained momentum in the mid-1990s and reached an apex in the 2004 presidential election rhetoric—is simply one manifestation in a long history of familialist discourses that espouses values of domesticity (see Cott 1977) in an attempt to assuage public anxiety and unrest in an unstable economic context.[2] In 1995 the Council on Families in America released a report entitled *Marriage in America: A Report to the Nation,* which pointed to the "divorce revolution" as the cause of "poverty within families." The council was nearly unequivocal in claiming that "the weakening of marriage as an institution" was the cause of juvenile delinquency and crime, drug and alcohol abuse among teens, and child poverty. The "steady break-up of the married, mother-father child-rearing unit is the principle cause of declining child well-being in our society," the council asserted.[3]

In early 2004, public discussions surrounding marriage and family were sparked by a move in some states to legalize same-sex marriage. In response, conservative groups such as the Traditional Values Coalition and Focus on the Family, as well as the George W. Bush administration, pushed for a constitutional amendment that restricts "marriage" to the legal union between one man and one woman (despite the fact that former president Bill Clinton had already signed into federal law the Defense of Marriage Act, which defines marriage as a legal union between a man and a woman). Additionally, in early 2004 President Bush proposed a "marriage initiative" to the tune of $1.5 billion dollars to be spent on "training to help [specifically low-income] couples develop interpersonal skills that sustain 'healthy marriages'" (Pear and Kirkpatrick 2004, 1).

More than a semantic quibble and beyond the billion-dollar expenditure, the debate over the definition of marriage represents the latest exercise in government control whereby social problems requiring structurally oriented solutions, that is, solutions that address a socioeconomic system that affects families in their homes, become personalized. Marriage promotion discourse encourages individuals to turn inward to the family or their inner selves in order to ameliorate the pains, frustrations, or challenges stemming from the workplace.[4] As was the case with nineteenth-century values of domesticity and 1990s family values rhetorics, in marriage rhetoric the alleged (and oftentimes very real) comforts provided by the home and family are intended to compensate for the "economic and psychic costs of capitalism" (Coontz 1988, 210; see also Cott 1977).

Put differently, dominant familialist discourses contain a utopian element. This is what makes the rhetoric understandably attractive, but it is also what gives the discourse its hegemonic force. Jameson describes the utopian potential in mass culture as a "fantasy bribe" and notes that "even if their function lies in the legitimation of the existing order . . . [the works of mass culture] cannot do their job without deflecting in the latter's service the deepest and most fundamental hopes and fantasies of the collectivity, to which they can therefore, no matter in how distorted a fashion, be found to have given voice" (1979/80, 144). Utopian rhetorics lend themselves to the process of personalization since they "often elide material constraints and determination in positing a set of ideal solutions to structural problems" (Cloud 1998b, 391; see also Gray 1989). In short, the vision of a happy and stable nuclear family reinforces the capitalist patriarchal status quo by obscuring the need for collective action to disrupt broad-based discriminatory institutions and practices.[5]

The words and actions of working-class women during the Depression provide a useful lesson in countering rhetorics that personalize what are really public issues. Contemporary struggles on the Left may very well benefit from the type of grassroots community organizing that existed in the 1930s, an approach that recognized the ties between home and work and encouraged family and community involvement in activism ranging from standard workplace walkouts that call attention to wage and benefits-related issues, to more creative actions such as caretaker and baby sit-ins staged at welfare offices, which may effectively call attention to childcare issues.

## Rhetorics of Motherhood and the Paradox of the Woman Worker

The doctrine of separate spheres, which legitimated the public/private split, also implied a sexual division of labor in which the public world of work was presumed to be fitting only for men, while women were seen as naturally suited to domestic concerns, especially those pertaining to child rearing. Thus, a second reality gap arose when women entered the paid labor force and violated widespread understandings of what it meant to be a woman (motherhood and domesticity) and what was required to be a worker (manliness).

Working-class women of the 1930s responded to hegemonic attempts at domestication in a number of ways. Ella Reeve Bloor and Elizabeth Gurley Flynn relied on a rhetoric of militant motherhood in order to address concerns of family and mothering in a way that rooted these realms in the public sphere. Additionally, working-class women turned to justificatory rhetorics, as discussed in chapter 3, in order to respond to the paradox that arose when women transgressed their traditional roles as mothers and homemakers when they entered the workforce. Specifically, women relied on two strategies—differentiation and transcendence.

Of particular interest is the way that differentiation was used in order to subvert traditional hegemonic references to motherhood. Rather than evoking popular images that glorified and romanticized motherhood, working-class women often called attention to the hardship and misery associated with mothering in the context of economic deprivation. That is, in much the same way that workers used familial rhetorics in order to recontextualize and politicize, women constructed a new context for motherhood that linked this experience to toil and material want in an effort to counter the image of the happy mother with healthy babe in arms. Specifically, through differentiation women detached the image of "woman" from its typical associated context (the home) and encouraged the audience to view "woman" within a new context, the workforce. Women then explained or justified their roles as workers by emphasizing that their work was necessary in order for them to fulfill their duties as mothers. In other words, they labored in order to put food in the mouths of their children. Although this justificatory move may have reinforced the association between "woman" and "mother," it represented a radical recontextualization, one that called attention to the extent to which motherhood was neither a private affair nor a sacred realm untouched by the workaday world.

Yet, much like rhetorics of familialism, a rhetoric of motherhood can be deployed toward differing political ends, that is, hegemonic or counterhegemonic. The mid-1800s image of True Womanhood, which circulated widely in political and religious discourses, certainly drew on an understanding of the "ideal mother." A true woman was domestic, submissive, pious, and pure—all of the qualities characteristic of the self-sacrificing mother whose entire being hinges on the well-being of her children. The influence of True Womanhood rhetoric is clearly seen through the early 1900s in popular magazines, where romanticized images of motherhood abounded (see Triece 2001).

Also in the early 1900s, hegemonic understandings of motherhood were exploited in order to transform a once politically inflected holiday, Mothers' Day for Peace, into the commercialized Mother's Day that we are familiar with today. As conceived by Julia Ward Howe in 1870, the holiday was meant to be a conjoining of motherhood and activism, a time for mothers around the world to stand up and protest the inhumanities of war. In 1913, Congress made Mother's Day an official holiday and soon thereafter commercial America transformed the day into an individualized celebration of a mother's love and devotion, which, conveniently for business, should be honored with flowers, cards, and gifts. This reconfiguration of Mother's Day no doubt had a particular persuasive effect during the Depression, when images of domestic bliss were used to counteract the uncertainties of economic upheaval. Sadly, Howe's emphasis on mothers, plural and, as Howe noted, "without limit of nationality," was lost to the honoring of mother, singular. Quickly forgotten was Howe's (1870) call for mothers to come together "to promote the alliance of the different nationalities" and the "amicable settlement of international questions." Rather than understand the experiences of motherhood as shaped by the economics of national and international war machines (Elizabeth Gurley Flynn described it as raising boys to become "soldiers for Wall Street"), families were—and still are—encouraged to celebrate motherhood as a private affair that did not extend beyond the walls of the cozy home that mother has made.

Several studies have examined the changing images of motherhood in cultural and political discourses (see Douglas and Michaels 2004; Ladd-Taylor and Umansky 1998), focusing particularly on the ways that mothers and mothering are scapegoated for a variety of social problems. Douglas and Michaels (2004) in their study of motherhood in the media remind us that hegemonic discourses remain firmly entrenched in the public mind. They analyze images of motherhood from the 1970s to the present and identify a pervasive rhetoric they term the "new momism," which represents "a set of ideals, norms, and practices, most frequently and powerfully represented in the media, that seem on the surface to celebrate motherhood, but which in reality promulgate standards of perfection that are beyond your reach" (4, 5). Just as nineteenth-century popular, political, and religious spokespersons were extolling the female virtues of piety, purity, and domesticity as making women naturally suited for child rearing, the rhetoric of the new momism "redefines all women, first and foremost, through their relationships to children" (22).

The rhetoric of "new momism" operates much like contemporary hegemonic rhetorics of familialism. First, it is a personalizing rhetoric that, in this case, frames the activity of mothering as the source of, and solution to, a host of social ills. In much the same way that <family values> rhetoric scapegoated families for a host of social ills, rhetorics of idealized motherhood scapegoat mothers as a way to let public institutions off the hook when exploring issues concerning child and family well-being. Perhaps most important, like hegemonic rhetorics of familialism, images of idealized motherhood represent a backlash against gains made in the area of women's rights. Douglas and Michaels write that the "new momism seeks to contain and, where possible, eradicate, all of the social changes brought on by feminism" (2004, 23). It is no coincidence that this rhetoric gained a particularly strong toehold in the media in the 1970s, a time when second-wave feminism was also gaining public attention.

Present-day popular notions of motherhood demonstrate the need for counter-rhetorics and actions that belie the ideals of motherhood. Politicizing motherhood and stripping the institution of its idealized trappings remain important tasks today as rhetorics that romanticize motherhood remain firmly entrenched in the minds of the public. Throughout the twentieth century, we find numerous examples of women who spoke and acted in their capacities as mothers, echoing the rhetoric and actions of women such as Ella Reeve Bloor. Such instances were not without contradiction; they were not always counterhegemonic and did not always produce long-term results (see Jetter, Orleck, and Taylor 1997). Yet, many of them provide examples of the ways that motherhood can potentially be subverted in order to call attention to its links to the public sphere.

For instance, consider the public attention gained from the efforts of mothers in Seattle, Washington, who fought for the basic rights of their own and other mentally disabled children and mobilized other people to do so. The women's experiences in organizing for their children led them from being "outraged mothers" to become "sophisticated activists utilizing a well-honed network of politicians, labor leaders, legislators, judges and the media'" (Solnit 2005).[6] Likewise, recall the efforts of Lois Gibbs and her fellow homemakers who, in the late 1970s and early 80s, organized their Niagra Falls community in order to expose the toxicity of Love Canal, which was making their children ill. In an interview, Gibbs alluded to the ethos of militant motherhood that enabled the women to succeed in their efforts. Gibbs noted that "mostly all of the organizing was done by the women in the community. And most of it was based on the protective nurturing sense that women have to protect their kids at any expense" (qtd. in Jetter 1997, 41). In both of these examples, women began to see their own experiences as mothers as linked to the experiences of other mothers; that is, they were not isolated or alone. They made direct connections between their experiences of mothering and the decision making and workings of economic and educational institutions. The persistence and prevalence of discourses that idealize motherhood call for sustained efforts, such as those described above and in earlier chapters, that link the experiences of mothering to the conditions in the workplace.

## Uses of the Personal Style and the Paradox of the Woman Orator

Hegemonic discourses framing family and motherhood were—and still are—employed to justify the notion of separate spheres and the related sexual division of labor. The related association of woman with the alleged private realm of home and family precluded the possibility that women could be actors or speakers in the public sphere. Much like mothers who worked outside the home, women who have attempted to speak or organize in public have occupied a position of paradox—that of the "woman orator." Chapter 4 noted the obstacles women faced when attempting to voice their concerns in public settings, and it explored how CP women relied on reconstitution in order to transform their audience into a group of motivated women prepared to speak and act out on their own behalf. Reconstitution was a process whereby CP activists created identification through the use of a personal style of communication. They then crafted a rhetoric of possibility through revealing accounts that envisioned social change for their listeners. Finally, through enactment, or their very presence on the public platform, CP activists became examples of what they wanted their audience to become.

The reliance of CP activists on a personal approach, as used in the initial stage of reconstitution, is characteristic of a "feminine style" of speaking. Campbell describes the feminine style as "personal in tone"; it relies "heavily on personal experience, anecdotes, and other example" and tends "to be structured inductively" (1989a, 13). It is important to note that CP activists used the feminine style not as an end in itself. Rather, they employed a personal style for expressly public ends. That is, once common ground was established through conversations focusing on personal experiences in the home (for example, dealings with husbands and children), activists led women to see the ties between their experiences and the workings of the factories where they and/or their husbands worked. From there, women were encouraged to join the CP or perhaps a local union or community organization, and they were also encouraged to talk about their experiences as women, workers, and mothers in public forums in order to instigate social change.

The use of an approach (that is, the feminine style) that emphasized the personal carried with it certain risks. As discussed above, hegemonic discourses that thwart critique of public institutions and that redirect blame to families, mothers, or individuals are themselves rhetorics that personalize. Dominant familialist and motherhood discourses place the blame for social problems such as poverty, homelessness, crime, or out-of-control children at the home doorstep or mother's lap in order to obscure or erase altogether the profound impact that broad-based and deeply entrenched economic, political, and social systems have on these issues. So, just as the uses of familialist and motherhood discourses can be double-edged, so too is the use of a personal style.

In some ways, a parallel may be drawn between the approach of 1930s CP activists and that of consciousness-raising groups formed in the 1960s and 70s, which similarly relied on the feminine style and emphasized personal experience. According to Campbell, consciousness-raising "speak[s] to women in terms of private, concrete, individual experience, because women have little, if any, publicly shared experience" (1973, 79).

Some scholars have pointed to the potential pitfalls of this form of communication, namely, the propensity to personalize all experiences without calling attention to the ways that these experiences are rooted in public patriarchal institutions. For example, Dow calls up the concern that consciousness-raising groups "were substituting talk for action and that consciousness-raising functioned more as therapy and self-help than as the basis for social transformation" (1996, 65). Cloud notes that in order for consciousness-raising to be successful, that is, in order for it to amount to more than a personal conversation or rant-session, it must "lead to the generation of public political activity and discourse aimed at transforming public structures of power" (1998a, 105).

Contemporary activists have much to learn from 1930s CP leaders who used a personal approach as a way to establish common ground and get an initial hearing. As I explained in chapter 4, these women did not stop at discussion of personal experience; rather, they launched a political program from this common ground that forged explicit links between personal experience and public institutions. Likewise, in order for contemporary activists to avoid the kind of personalization characteristic of hegemonic discourses described above, they must take care to link personal experience to the workings of broader public institutions.

## The Legacy of 1930s Activism

During the Depression, families such as that of Fanny Sepich, wife of a Pittsburgh coal miner, and Sarah Victor, an auto plant worker in Detroit, struggled to make ends meet in a time of looming insecurity. Unemployment was around 23.6 percent in 1932 and a full 75 percent of the population lived at or below the subsistence level (Foner 1980, 256). For women and minority workers of both sexes, the prospects for getting by were especially grim.

In the face of such hardships, working-class women used words and actions in creative ways to exploit the paradoxes—or reality gaps—in their lives. Reality gaps arise from the lack of concordance between prevailing, widely accepted hegemonic ideologies (for example, the public/private split or the sexual division of labor) and the reality of people's daily lives. In a contemporary context where terms such as "family" and "motherhood" continue to be employed in order to scapegoat and personalize issues rooted in public institutions, we may do well to turn to the heritage of protest left to us by working-class women of the 1930s. Women like Ella Reeve Bloor, Clara Lemlich Shavelson, as well as the lesser known Fanny Sepichs and Sarah Victors from working-class households across the country, knew that family well-being was directly affected by what went on in the workplace and thus was tied not only to healthy marriages and doting mothers but also to healthy community relationships that enabled them to join forces with their neighbors and next of kin to fight for fair wages and safe working conditions.

As present times demonstrate, uncertainty and anxiety dog the lives of the working poor regardless of the decade. In the early twenty-first century, increasing numbers of workers who before saw themselves as immune to the whims of capitalism are experiencing a heightened sense of insecurity. Outsourcing, downsizing, and the movement of entire factories overseas, where labor can be extracted even more cheaply, have all contributed to the deterioration of workplace conditions and have revealed to many what has been a truism of capitalism all along: hard work does not translate into just compensation.[7]

The actions and words of working-class women of the 1930s left us a legacy of courage and creativity that underscored community networking, speaking out, and above all, extra-discursive actions that forced the hand of owners and employers in ways that words alone could not. The tactics and rhetorical strategies used by these women—as well as their predecessors in struggles dating back to those of the mid-1800s textile-mill girls—continue to influence efforts today. The words of a Youngstown, Ohio, dressmaker carry a message as important for workers today as it was in 1931 when she said that "the only way of getting better conditions in a shop and factory and a right way of living is to organize. . . . [O]nly this way will we get demands[;] that of right of living as human beings, as workers who are making everything and don't get nothin" (Bonin 1931).

# Notes

## Introduction

1. Faue's (1991) description of community-based unionism parallels the idea of community-based activism referred to here. Community-based union emphasizes "local autonomy and community-level organization" and relies upon "personal networks, on connections with local institutions and especially with citywide labor organizations" (4). As displayed in the successful orchestration of meat and rent strikes in the early 1900s, working-class activists such as Cecilia Schwartz and Pauline Newman utilized grassroots organizing and community networking well before the CP's Popular Front of 1935–39. These activists' expertise was grounded in their firsthand experience as mothers, wives, and workers.

2. The Women's Bureau of the U.S. Department of Labor estimated that two million women were unemployed in 1933 (Foner 1980, 256–57). Grace Hutchins (1934a), author of *Women Who Work,* put the figure at four million.

3. Communication scholars have debated the status of dominant ideology critique over the past decade. Arguing that dominant ideology critique grounded in the traditional Gramscian definition of hegemony is outdated, Condit supports "critique of concord" in its place (1994, 211). McKerrow argues for a "critical rhetoric" that encompasses a "critique of domination" and a "critique of freedom" (1989, 91). Ono and Sloop advocate a "critique of vernacular discourse" that examines the language of the oppressed and the ways it "challenges the mainstream discourse" (1995, 23). These scholars vary in the degree to which their arguments challenge the significance of dominant ideology critique. Others maintain the importance of studies that focus on how dominant groups maintain their power through discourses that persuade the majority to accept the economic and political status quo (see Cloud 1996; Shugart, Waggoner, and Hallstein 2001; Triece 2001).

4. A partial listing of communication studies on women activists from the late 1700 through 1900s includes Borda 2002; Campbell 1980, 1986, 1989a; Carlson 1994; Griffin 1994; Hamlet 2000; Huxman 1996; Kendall 1974; Linkugel 1963; Mattina 1994; McClearey 1994; J. Thompson 1995; Zaeske 2002.

5. Eagleton's use of the word "standpoint" here calls up the theorization of this term, particularly by feminists (see Collins 1991; Di Stefano 1990; Harding 1993; Hartsock 1987) who have worked to get the experiences, needs, and concerns of women recognized and legitimated in a male-dominated world. Standpoint theory assumes the existence of experience/needs apart from discourse. Harding explains, "One's social situation enables and sets limits on what one can know;

some social situations—critically unexamined dominant ones—are more limiting than others in this respect, and what makes these situations more limiting is their inability to generate the most critical questions about received belief" (1993, 54–55). Collins points out that oppressed groups' "self-defined standpoints can stimulate resistance" (1991, 28). It is worth repeating here the example Collins provides in order to illustrate this point. She quotes Annie Adams, a black woman from the South, who explains how she became motivated to join the civil rights movement. Adams says, "When I first went into the mill we had segregated water fountains. . . . Same thing about the toilets. I had to clean the toilets for the inspection room and then, when I got ready to go to the bathroom, I had to go all the way to the bottom of the stairs to the cellar. So I asked my boss man, 'what's the difference? If I can go in there and clean them toilets, why can't I use them?' Finally, I started to use that toilet. I decided I wasn't going to walk a mile to go to the bathroom" (qtd. in Collins 1991, 28). Collins goes on to explain that Adams's "actions illustrate the connections among concrete experiences with oppression, developing a self-defined standpoint concerning those experiences, and the acts of resistance that can follow" (28).

6. This paragraph taps into a long-standing scholarly debate surrounding the relationship between language and social life. At issue is the usefulness of Marxist theory's base/superstructure model for describing contemporary society. On one side, postmodernist theories take a "discursive turn" whereby processes and relations of production are understood to exist in an indeterminant relationship with language, and in some cases, are reduced to language. For example, Laclau and Mouffe (1985) define concepts such as society, power, and struggle as primarily discursive and they view the relationship between economics and political ideologies as contingent or indeterminate. In contrast stand theories that maintain the base/superstructure as a practical model for explaining contemporary social life (see Hall 1996; Williams 1973).

7. Gareth Jones's (1983) work on the struggles of the English working class in the nineteenth century provides an important reminder to labor historians of the uncertain and complex nature of language, interests, and class consciousness. Yet, his work appears to accord with that of scholars of the discursive turn who emphasize language as the impetus for defining interests. Thus, his conception of political language and need is the reverse of Bitzer's. Jones writes, "The almost definitional claim of political discourse is to be a response to a pre-existing need or demand. But in fact the primary motivation is to create and then orchestrate such a demand, to change the self-identification and behaviour of those addressed. The attempted relationship is prefigurative, not reflective" (1983, 24).

8. The tension between the concepts of "woman" and "worker" was compounded when the woman was married. A married woman who worked was seen as acting improperly as a woman but also as a wife, whose concerns were not appropriately focused on her husband and children.

9. Scholars provide differing interpretations of the CP's response to what was referred to as the "woman question." What seems clear, at least, is that the party dealt with women's needs and concerns with varying amounts of attention and

enthusiasm between 1920 and 1940. See Baxandall 1993; Brown 1999; Coiner 1995; Dixler 1974; Shaffer 1979.

## Chapter 1: Establishing the Context

1. Speedups increased quotas for workers; stretch-outs put fewer workers in charge of more looms. The goal of these two practices was to get as much production as possible "in a shorter time and with reduced labor costs" (Hutchins 1934a, 119).

2. Foner (1980) and Ware (1982) provide extensive details on the plight of black women during the Depression. Ware provides statistics on black women's hours and wages in a number of occupations. Foner provides a particularly poignant story of 194 black seamstresses who were fired from their jobs at the Maid Well Garment Company in Arkansas for complaining about the fact that they received about half the wage stipulated by the NRA code (281).

3. Bernstein notes there were 1,856 work stoppages involving 1,470,000 workers in 1934. Four large, well-known strikes took place in 1934, including those by auto parts workers in Toledo, truck drivers in Minneapolis, longshoremen in San Francisco, and textile workers in New England and the South (Bernstein 1970, 217).

4. See, for instance, Kessler-Harris's *Women Have Always Worked* (1981). Foner (1979, 1980) also provides a sweeping analysis of women's work in the paid labor force.

5. There is a long and unfortunate history of male hostility toward female workers. In the late nineteenth and early twentieth centuries, male workers viewed female workers suspiciously since the hiring of women, who were paid at a lower wage, put a downward pressure on all wages. Owners and bosses deliberately pitted male and female workers against each other by using females to replace male workers. These and other practices that kept workers separated by race and ethnicity were employed in order to prevent mass class organization.

6. The Working Women's Union eventually became a female local of the Knights of Labor (Tax 1980, 46).

7. As was the case with Left organizations such as the Socialist Party and the CP, the IWW assumed that gender discrimination would disappear once capitalism was wiped out. The workings of patriarchy, both in the home and the workplace, were not addressed in any sort of systematic manner. Capitalist production was seen as the locus of oppression and of struggle.

8. Given the ideological and activist commonalities the two shared, it is a bit surprising that Bloor does not mention Jones in her memoir, *We Are Many*. Bloor does, however, mention the ongoing dispute between the IWW and the Socialist Party concerning the place of political action in the broader class struggle (Bloor 1940, 94–95).

9. The phrase "sticking capacity" was used by Melinda Scott in 1915 as she described women of the hat-making industry who stood by male comrades during a six-month struggle for workplace rights.

10. For example, see Boyer and Morais 1972; Fine 1969; Foner 1980; Kraus 1937; Lahne 1944; Lynd and Lynd 1981; Orleck 1995.

11. See Triece (2001, 177–236) on ways that working-class women activists of the early 1900s, many of them members of the Women's Trade Union League, called attention to the connections between work and home life.

12. Barrett and McIntosh offer a useful caution against making functionalist or deterministic arguments regarding the relationship between capitalism and the domestic sphere: "The construction of 'the family' as a privatized zone with rigid barriers to prevent the intrusion of the social is an ideological process rather than a given of capitalist society" (1991, 90).

13. A partial listing of such studies includes Apple and Messner 2001; Campbell 1973; Chesebro 1984; Daniels, Jensen, and Lichtenstein 1985; Erlich 1977; Keith and Zagacki 1992; Murphy 1992; J. Nelson 1985; Patton 1973; Tompkins 1976; Triece 2002.

## Chapter 2: Negotiating the Public/Private Split

1. Assuming this letter was, indeed, written by the signed "Unemployed Worker's wife," we see the extent to which official party language infused the rhetoric of "ordinary" workers. Although it is not possible to know for sure the authenticity of this and other letters appearing in CP publications such as the *Working Woman*, I believe that the letters signed as ordinary workers or wives did, in fact, represent the voices of those individuals. Having said that, we need not downplay the influence of editors and regular writers who shaped the framing and tone of the magazine's content in concordance with CP ideology. Interestingly, Staub notes that "for a time in *Labor Unity* [a CP publication], readers' voices were carefully reconstructed—selectively quoted and deliberately framed—by anonymous staff writers so that every letter without fail opened with the 'correct' politics" (1994, 115).

2. The tragic events occurring at Ludlow in April 1914 underscore the brutal extent to which life in the coal mines shaped home life. Striking mine workers who had been evicted from their homes set up tent camps for their families. On 20 April 1914, National Guard gunmen set fire to the tent village "sending families fleeing to the hills. All in all, twenty-six women and children were killed in what came to be known as the Ludlow Massacre" (Triece 2001, 228).

3. The precise role of housework within the capitalist system was a hotly debated issue within the Communist Party but will not be detailed here. Briefly, Mary Inman, a CP activist, argued in her book *In Woman's Defense* that housework was a form of productive labor similar to labor in factories. Her view was staunchly opposed by CP leadership as well as by female CP activists such as Bloor and Elizabeth Gurley Flynn. Eventually Inman left the party (see Weigand 2001).

4. Hayden (2003) does a nice job of summarizing the scholarly debate surrounding the use of maternal appeals in women's public discourses advocating social change.

5. Bloor was writing to her son, Dick.

6. Thank you to Mark Rosenzweig at the Reference Center for Marxist Studies, New York City, for permission to quote from the Elizabeth Gurley Flynn Papers.

7. The article describing this incident appeared in the CP publication *Party Or-*

*ganizer* in 1934 and was presumably written by a CPer. The extent of the CP's involvement in this strike is not clear. However, given the appearance of this article in a CP publication and given the extent to which the CP was involved in strikes large and small throughout the 1930s, we may surmise that CP activists had a hand. It is certain that the CP carried on active organizational efforts in the mining regions during the Depression.

8. After the Flint sit-down strike, many husbands prodded their wives to return to the cooking, cleaning, and caretaking in the home. This was likely the experience of many a wife and daughter who participated in strike activities under the auspices of an auxiliary. Their experiences after the fact do not negate the potentially transformative effect that auxiliary participation had on women, but they do point to the complexities that arise when gender discrimination enters into class-based struggles.

9. Mishler's study *Raising Reds* explores the role of the CP, and in particular that of the Young Pioneers, in the lives of the children of Communists. According to Mishler, the Young Pioneers emphasized the "autonomy of children from their families" with the goal of overcoming the "conservatism of family and ethnic ties" (1999, 46). The group focused on organizing children in schools and believed that schools played the same role in children's lives that factories played in the lives of adults (42, 43). The goals of the Young Pioneers may not have fully aligned with the emphasis on ethnic and family ties that played such a central role in the struggles of the women explored in this chapter. Still, this organization was instrumental in organizing the children of strikers in significant uprisings, including the Passaic textile strike in 1926 and the Gastonia textile strike in 1929. By the mid-1930s, as the CP was shifting to its Popular Front strategy and broadened ethnic and neighborhood organizing, the Young Pioneers no longer existed (63, 64).

## Chapter 3: The Paradox of the Woman Worker

1. In this chapter, I use the term "women workers" to refer to women who worked in the paid labor force. However, all women work, whether it is in the paid labor force, in the home performing unpaid domestic chores (such as cleaning, cooking, or child rearing), or both.

2. Burke explained that messages are constructed much like a drama with speakers employing some combination of the five standard elements of a drama: act (the event or thing done), agent (the person[s] who committed the act), agency (the instrument used to perform or commit the act), scene (the background or context), and purpose (the reason for committing the act).

3. Suffragists' reliance on arguments based on expediency was oftentimes accompanied by racist and classist appeals. Among the activists, Elizabeth Cady Stanton argued that giving the vote to well-off white women would "counteract the votes of the undesirable part of the electorate," that is, illiterate and minority citizens (Kraditor 1965, 53)

4. The AFL was a conservative umbrella organization for trade unions. It was known for its hostilities toward female, black, immigrant, and unskilled workers.

The AFL was often at odds with other, more radical labor organizations such as the Industrial Workers of the World and the CP.

5. According to the Flynn papers, this article appeared in the *Daily Worker*. Although an exact date is not given, the article likely appeared in 1940.

6. Whether or not the letters written to Polly Propper were authentic is not possible to discern. Authentic or not, surely readers were able to identify with the questions raised in the column and were influenced by the advice imparted.

7. A partial list of books documenting women's participation in confrontational actions within the labor movement includes Cameron 1993; Foner 1979, 1980; Jensen and Davidson 1984; Mattina 2002; Milkman 1985; Orleck 1995; Tax 1980; and Triece 2001.

8. It is not clear how extensively the CP was actually involved in this strike and the strike of laundry workers described later. Description of these events appeared in the *Daily Worker*.

9. Nowicki explains that colonizers were "red missionaries" sent into various industries in order to "do everything possible to keep jobs and organize" (1981, 72).

10. In textile mills of the Northeast, women earned considerably less than their male coworkers and often had to work the night shift so that they were available to tend to housework and child rearing during the day (Foner 1980, 199–224).

11. Barnett and Rivers (1996) approach the issue of women's paid labor from a somewhat different stance, but similarly conclude that two-income families are a mainstay of contemporary life. Specifically, they argue that women who work outside the home are healthier, happier, and make better mothers.

## Chapter 4: Challenging the Woman Orator

1. This article, which appeared in the April 1931 issue of the *Party Organizer*, was written by "A.D." It was often the case that the magazine's female contributors signed only their initials, which makes it difficult, from a historian's perspective, to establish authorship. However, it seems likely this article was written by Anna Damon, given that Damon was a significant party organizer who wrote and spoke frequently on issues pertaining to women within the party.

2. An examination of the Bloor papers archived in the Sophia Smith Collection at Smith College points to Bloor's repeated use of the Clemence example. She related the stories of Clemence's bravery in speeches predating woman's suffrage (n.d.; 1917) and in a *Working Woman* article appearing in July 1931.

3. Handbills announcing these engagements can be found in the Ella Reeve Bloor Papers, box 9, folder 1, Sophia Smith Collection, Smith College.

4. References to Flynn as a "Joan of Arc" came from the reformer Theodore Dreiser in a published magazine article and in a poem written by Adolf Wolff in 1914 (Baxandall 1987, 2).

5. For example, a speaking schedule dated 1940 shows her speaking twice daily on 24, 25, 29, and 30 October (Flynn 1940b).

6. The notation "1940?" is written on the microfilm copy of the poem, indicating the poem may have been written in 1940.

## Conclusion

1. Drawing on the work of McGee (1980), Cloud defines an ideograph as a political "god" term that shapes cultural beliefs and political decision making.

2. In what follows, I refer to "marriage promotion discourse" or "marriage rhetoric" as a reactionary rhetoric that identifies the traditional heterosexual nuclear family as the only viable familial arrangement and that views it as the central foundation upon which a stable society rests. In this sense, the rhetoric of gay and lesbian rights activists who advocate legalization of same-sex marriage is not included in this discourse; rather, theirs is considered a counterhegemonic discourse that is attempting to broaden definitions of marriage to include same-sex marriage.

3. A related discourse surrounding the "fatherhood movement" similarly personalizes social ills. According to David Blankenhorn, a key figure behind this "movement" and a colleague of Popenoe of the Council on Families in America, "Fatherlessness . . . is the leading cause of declining child well-being in our society. It is also the engine driving our most urgent social problems, from crime to adolescent pregnancy to child sexual abuse to domestic violence against women" (1995).

4. We have yet to see a full analysis of this discourse, its framings, and its hegemonic effects. As just one example of the way that marriage promotion discourse personalizes, note the comments of Judy Charlick, the director of curriculum and instruction for the Better Together project in Cleveland, Ohio. Charlick asserted that "improving couples' relationship skills is a fundamental building block, deeply related to most (maybe all) of the economic and social ills we face today" (2003).

5. See Barrett and McIntosh (1991, 21–29) and Cloud (1998b, 391) for discussion of the utopian impulse in familialist discourses.

6. Solnit is quoting from the manuscript of Susan Schwartzenberg's book *Becoming Citizens: Family Life and the Politics of Disability* (Seattle: University of Washington Press, 2005), which had not yet been published at the time Solnit wrote.

7. This truism may itself be described as a paradox. Indeed, capitalism is based upon paradox. Chris Harman describes the paradoxes or "conundrums" this way: "More wealth is being produced than ever before in history. There are inventions for increasing the output of all sorts of things, including the basic foods denied to generations of humanity. . . . Yet far from the burden of securing a livelihood getting lighter it is often getting heavier. Instead of people looking forward to living more prosperous and comfortable lives, often they can only live in fear of things getting worse. Far from poverty disappearing, it grows" (1995, 10).

# References

Abramovitz, Mimi. 1988. *Regulating the Lives of Women: Social Welfare Policy from Colonial Times to the Present.* Boston: South End Press.

American Civil Liberties Union. 1938a. Letter to Eugene Dungan. Elizabeth Gurley Flynn Papers, Tamiment 118, box 2, folder 26b, Tamiment Library/Robert F. Wagner Labor Archives, New York University Libraries.

———. 1938b. Letter to Lewis Phillips. Elizabeth Gurley Flynn Papers, Tamiment 118, box 2, folder 26b, Tamiment Library/Robert F. Wagner Labor Archives, New York University Libraries.

"An American Pogrom." 1914. *Life and Labor,* June, 171–73.

"And Mine: A True Story by a Negro Worker of the North." 1934. *Working Woman,* Oct., 10.

Apple, Angela L., and Beth A. Messner. 2001. "Paranoia and Paradox: The Apocalyptic Rhetoric of Christian Identity." *Western Journal of Communication* 65:206–28.

Aune, James A. 1994. *Rhetoric and Marxism.* Boulder, Colo.: Westview.

Barde, Gwen. 1935a. "Fashion Letter." *Working Woman,* Apr., 15.

———. 1935b. "Fashion Letter." *Working Woman,* Sept., 15.

Barker, Nydia. 1932. "Briggs Hunger March." *Party Organizer,* Jan., 3–7.

Barnett, Rosalind C., and Caryl Rivers. 1996. *She Works, He Works: How Two-Income Families Are Happier, Healthier, and Better-Off.* New York: HarperCollins.

Barrett, Michele, and Mary McIntosh. 1991. *The Anti-Social Family.* 2nd ed. London: Verso.

Barton, Ann. 1935. *Mother Bloor.* New York: Workers Library.

———. 1937. *Mother Bloor: The Spirit of 76.* New York: Workers Library.

Baxandall, Rosalyn F. 1987. *Words on Fire: The Life and Writing of Elizabeth Gurley Flynn.* New Brunswick, N.J.: Rutgers University Press.

———. 1993. "The Question Seldom Asked: Women and the CPUSA." In *New Studies in the Politics and Culture of US Communism,* ed. Michael E. Brown, Randy Martin, Frank Rosengarten, and George Snedeker, 141–62. New York: Monthly Review Press.

———. 1994. "Elizabeth Gurley Flynn." In *The American Radical,* ed. Mary Jo Buhle, Paul Buhle, and Harvey J. Kaye, 129–34. New York: Routledge.

Berkman, Edith. 1931. "Women in Lawrence Strike." *Working Woman,* Apr., 6.

———. 1933. "Undesirable." *Working Woman,* May, 12.

Bernstein, Irving. 1970. *Turbulent Years: A History of the American Worker, 1933–1941.* Boston: Houghton Mifflin.

Bitzer, Lloyd. 1968. "The Rhetorical Situation." *Philosophy and Rhetoric* 1:1–14.

Black, Edwin. 1970. "The Second Persona." *Quarterly Journal of Speech* 56:109–19.

Blakesley, David. 2002. *The Elements of Dramatism.* New York: Longman.

Blankenhorn, David. 1995. *Fatherless America: Confronting Our Most Urgent Social Problem.* New York: Basic Books.

Bloomington, Ethel. 1936a. "Movie Extras Strike Stirs Hollywood." *Daily Worker,* 5 Oct., 5.

———. 1936b. "The Women's Angle." *Daily Worker,* 29 Oct., 7.

———. 1936c. "The Women's Angle." *Daily Worker,* 4 Nov., 7.

Bloor, Ella Reeve. 1913–14. "Notes for Speech on Copper Strike, 1913–14." Ella Reeve Bloor Papers, box 9, folder 2, Sophia Smith Collection, Smith College, Northampton, Massachusetts.

———. 1917. "Address of Ella Reeve Bloor, at Madison Square Garden." Ella Reeve Bloor Papers, box 9, folder 2, Sophia Smith Collection, Smith College, Northampton, Massachusetts.

———. 1931. "Annie Clemence—The Story of a Militant Working Woman." *Working Woman,* July, 6.

———. 1932a. "'Mother' Bloor, 70, and Still Battling, Reviews Life of Struggle in the Ranks." *Daily Worker,* 8 July, 3.

———. 1932b. "Transcript of Portion of Speech by Mother Bloor." Ella Reeve Bloor Papers, box 9, folder 2, Sophia Smith Collection, Smith College, Northampton, Massachusetts.

———. 1933a. "Prepare for the Future." *Working Woman,* June, 3.

———. 1933b. "Speech to Milk Shed Conference." Ella Reeve Bloor Papers, box 9, folder 2, Sophia Smith Collection, Smith College, Northampton, Massachusetts.

———. 1933c. "Unity of Farmers and Workers." *Party Organizer,* Aug./Sept., 86–87.

———. 1935. "Mother Bloor Reports." *Equal Justice,* 11:21.

———. 1936. "Ella Bloor Tells Women Why They Should Vote Communist." *Daily Worker,* 2 Nov., 2.

———. 1937. "International Woman's Day." *Party Organizer,* Feb., 19–22.

———. 1940. *We Are Many.* New York: International.

———. n.d. "Pioneers." Ella Reeve Bloor Papers, box 9, folder 2, Sophia Smith Collection, Smith College, Northampton, Massachusetts.

Bonin, Henrietta. 1930. "Conditions Unbearable in Moyer's Pants Factory." *Working Woman,* Sept., 3.

———. 1931. "Women Work at Long Hours for Very Low Pay." *Working Woman,* Oct., 8.

Borda, Jennifer L. 2002. "The Woman Suffrage Parades of 1910–1913: Possibilities and Limitations of an Early Feminist Rhetorical Strategy." *Western Journal of Communication* 66:25–53.

Borich, F. 1934. "Miner's Wives Will Fight." *Working Woman,* Feb., 7.

"Bosses Take Advantage of the Unemployment Crisis, Slash Wage to Low Level." 1931. *Working Woman,* Dec., 2.

Bostdorff, Denise M. 1987. "Making Light of James Watt: A Burkean Approach to the Form and Attitude of Political Cartoons." *Quarterly Journal of Speech* 73:43–59.

"Bourgeois Women's Club Feed Old Food to the Waitresses." 1931. *Working Woman,* June, 3.

Boyer, Richard O., and Herbert M. Morais. 1972. *Labor's Untold Story*. New York: United Electrical, Radio, and Machine Workers of America.

"Bronx Bread Strike One of Largest in USA, for Low Price." 1931. *Working Woman*, July, 2.

Browder, Earl. 1937. Untitled tribute. In Todes and Small 1937, 17.

Brown, Kathleen A. 1996. "Ella Reeve Bloor: The Politics of the Personal in the American Communist Party." Ph.D. diss., University of Washington.

———. 1999. "The 'Savagely Fathered and Un-mothered World' of the Communist Party, USA: Feminism, Maternalism, and 'Mother Bloor.'" *Feminist Studies* 25:537–70.

"Build Women's Auxiliaries of N.M.U." 1931. *Working Woman*, Sept., 2.

Bureau of Labor Statistics. 2006. http://www.bls.gov/news.release/empsit.nro.htm. Accessed 14 July 2005.

Burke, Kenneth. 1945. *A Grammar of Motives*. Berkeley: University of California Press.

———. 1950. *A Rhetoric of Motives*. Berkeley: University of California Press.

———. 1954. *Permanence and Change*. Los Altos, Calif.: Hermes Publications.

Burlak, Ann. 1931. "Textile Women in Forefront of Fight against Worse Mill Conditions." *Working Woman*, Dec., 7.

———. 1933a. "Free Edith Berkman!" *Working Woman*, May, 12.

———. 1933b. "Textile Workers Strike against Slavery Act." *Working Woman*, Aug., 7.

———. 1934. "The Work of the Textile Unions." *Party Organizer*, May/June, 52–54.

———. 1937. "Mother Bloor's 'Girls.'" In Todes and Small, 1937, 20.

"'Buy More Clothes' Is Advice Given." 1931. *Working Woman*, Aug., 6.

Cameron, Ardis. 1993. *Radicals of the Worst Sort: Laboring Women in Lawrence, Massachusetts, 1860–1912*. Urbana: University of Illinois Press.

Camp, Helen C. 1995. *Iron in Her Soul: Elizabeth Gurley Flynn and the American Left*. Pullman: Washington State University Press.

Campbell, Karlyn Kohrs. 1973. "The Rhetoric of Women's Liberation: An Oxymoron." *Quarterly Journal of Speech* 59:74–86.

———. 1980. "Stanton's 'The Solitude of Self': A Rationale for Feminism." *Quarterly Journal of Speech* 66:304–12.

———. 1986. "Style and Content in the Rhetoric of Early Afro-American Feminists." *Quarterly Journal of Speech* 72:434–45.

———. 1989a. *Man Cannot Speak for Her: A Critical Study of Early Feminist Rhetoric*. Vol. 1. New York: Greenwood.

———. 1989b. *Man Cannot Speak for Her: A Critical Study of Early Feminist Rhetoric*. Vol. 2. New York: Greenwood.

Campbell, Karlyn Kohrs, and Kathleen H. Jamieson. 1978. "Form and Genre in Rhetorical Criticism: An Introduction." In *Form and Genre: Shaping Rhetorical Action*, ed. Karlyn Kohrs Campbell and Kathleen H. Jamieson, 9–32. Falls Church, Va.: Speech Communication Association.

Carlson, A. Cheree. 1994. "Defining Womanhood: Lucretia Coffin Mott and the Transformation of Femininity." *Western Journal of Communication* 58:85–97.

Charland, Maurice. 1987. "Constitutive Rhetoric: The Case of the Peuple Québécois." *Quarterly Journal of Speech* 73:133–50.

Charlick, Judy. 2003. "Committed to Commitment." Letter to Editor. *Cleveland Plain Dealer,* 28 Sept., sec. H, 4.

Chasin, Bessie. 1930. "The Stretch Out System." *Working Woman,* Jan., 3.

Chesebro, James W. 1984. "The Symbolic Construction of Social Realities: A Case Study in the Rhetorical Criticism of Paradox." *Communication Quarterly* 32:164–71.

"Children and Mothers Enslaved by Homework." 1931. *Working Woman,* Aug., 6.

Clarke, John. 1991. *New Times and Old Enemies: Essays on Cultural Studies and America.* London: HarperCollins Academic.

Cloud, Dana L. 1996. "Hegemony or Concordance? The Rhetoric of Tokenism in 'Oprah' Winfrey's Rags-to-Riches Biography." *Critical Studies in Mass Communication* 13:115–37.

———. 1998a. *Control and Consolation in American Culture and Politics.* Thousand Oaks, Calif: Sage.

———. 1998b. "The Rhetoric of <Family Values>: Scapegoating, Utopia, and the Privatization of Social Responsibility." *Western Journal of Communication* 62:387–419.

Coiner, Constance. 1995. *Better Red: The Writing and Resistance of Tillie Olsen and Meridel LeSueur.* New York: Oxford University Press.

———. 1996. "Literature of Resistance: The Intersection of Feminism and the Communist Left in Meridel Le Sueur and Tillie Olsen." In *Radical Revisions: Rereading 1930s Culture,* ed. Bill Mullen and Sherry L. Linkon, 144–66. Urbana: University of Illinois Press.

Colby, Merle. 1934. "Tribute from a Mere Male: Women on the Picket Line." *Working Woman,* Oct., 3–4.

Collins, Patricia H. 1991. *Black Feminist Thought: Knowledge, Consciousness, and the Politics of Empowerment.* New York: Routledge.

Coltrane, Scott. 1996. *Family Man: Fatherhood, Housework, and Gender Equity.* New York: Oxford University Press.

"Communist Rally Invaded by Veterans." 1939. Elizabeth Gurley Flynn Papers, Tamiment 118, box 2, folder 30, Tamiment Library/Robert F. Wagner Labor Archives, New York University Libraries.

"Concentration in the Chicago Stockyards." 1934. *Party Organizer,* May/June, 55–57.

Condit, Celeste M. 1994. "Hegemony in a Mass-Mediated Society: Concordance about Reproductive Technologies." *Critical Studies in Mass Communication* 11:205–30.

Conroy, Jack. 1937. "Greetings from Jack Conroy." In Todes and Small 1937, 5.

Coontz, Stephanie. 1988. *The Social Origins of Private Life: A History of American Families, 1600–1900.* London: Verso.

———. 1997. *The Way We Really Are: Coming to Terms with America's Changing Families.* New York: Basic Books.

Cooper, Jennie. 1931. "Mother of Five Jailed in Ohio for Militancy." *Working Woman,* Aug., 2.

Cott, Nancy. 1977. *The Bonds of Womanhood: "Woman's Sphere" in New England, 1780–1835*. New Haven: Yale University Press.

———. 1987. *The Grounding of Modern Feminism*. New Haven: Yale University Press.

Council on Families in America. 1995. *Marriage in America: A Report to the Nation*. http://www.americanvalues.org/html/r-marriage_in_america.html. Accessed 16 July 2006.

Cowl, Margaret. 1935. *Women and Equality*. New York: Workers Library.

———. 1936. "Neighborhood Work." *Party Organizer*, Apr., 28–30.

———. 1937a. "Party Building among Women." *Party Organizer*, June, 22–26.

———. 1937b. "We Must Win the Women." *The Communist*, June, 545–54.

———. 1974. "Women's Struggles for Equality." *Political Affairs*, May, 40–44.

"Crowd Routs a Communist Meeting Here." 1939. Unattributed newspaper clipping. Elizabeth Gurley Flynn Papers, Tamiment 118, box 2, folder 30, Tamiment Library/Robert F. Wagner Labor Archives, New York University Libraries.

Cush, Pat. 1937. "Mother Bloor in Ambridge." In Todes and Small 1937, 13.

Damon, Anna. 1932a. "The Working Woman and War." *Daily Worker*, 30 July, 6.

———. 1932b. "Women Delegates Show Splendid Spirit; Maintain Negro and White Solidarity." *Working Woman*, Jan., 1.

———. 1937. "The Tribute of Our Committee." In Todes and Small 1937, 3.

Daniels, Tom D., Richard J. Jensen, and Allen Lichtenstein. 1985. "Resolving the Paradox in Politicized Christian Fundamentalism." *Western Journal of Speech Communication* 49:248–66.

"A Day Unit for Women." 1937. *Party Organizer*, May, 16–20.

DeChaine, D. Robert. 2000. "Magic, Mimesis, and Revolutionary Praxis: Illuminating Walter Benjamin's Rhetoric of Redemption." *Western Journal of Communication* 64:285–308.

"Delegates from the New York Councils Tell Their Stories." 1931. *Working Woman*, Dec., 1.

"The Detroit Meat Strike." 1935. *Working Woman*, Nov., 12.

Diaz-Barriga, Miguel. 1998. "Beyond the Domestic and the Public: *Colonas* Participation in Urban Movements in Mexico City." In *Cultures of Politics, Politics of Cultures: Re-visioning Latin American Social Movements*, ed. Sonia E. Alvarez, Evelina Dagnino, and Arturo Escobar, 252–77. Boulder, Colo.: Westview.

Di Stefano, Christine. 1990. "Dilemmas of Difference: Feminism, Modernity, and Postmodernism." In *Feminism/Postmodernism*, ed. Linda J. Nicholson, 63–82. New York: Routledge.

Dixler, Elsa J. 1974. "The Woman Question: Women and the American Communist Party, 1929–1941." Ph.D. diss., Yale University.

"Domestic Workers Too Must Organize and Fight." 1931. *Working Woman*, Mar., 8.

"Don't Starve—Don't Stuff." 1933. *Working Woman*, June, 15.

Douglas, Susan J., and Meredith W. Michaels. 2004. *The Mommy Myth: The Idealization of Motherhood and How It Has Undermined Women*. New York: Free Press.

Dow, Bonnie J. 1996. *Prime-time Feminism: Television, Media Culture, and the Women's Movement since 1970*. Philadelphia: University of Pennsylvania Press.

Dow, Bonnie J., and Mari B. Tonn. 1993. "'Feminine Style' and Political Judgment in the Rhetoric of Ann Richards." *Quarterly Journal of Speech* 79:286–302.

Draper, Theodore. 1957. *The Roots of American Communism.* New York: Viking.

"Dress Strike Aims to End Sweatshop." 1931. *Working Woman,* Mar., 1.

Drew, Caroline. 1931. "Kentucky Coal Barons Lust for the Blood of the Coal Miners and Their Womenfolk." *Working Woman,* Oct., 6.

"Driving to Victory." 1933. *Working Woman,* Mar., 14.

Dye, Nancy S. 1975a. "Creating a Feminist Alliance: Sisterhood and Class Conflict in the New York Women's Trade Union League, 1903–1914." *Feminist Studies* 2:24–38.

———. 1975b. "Feminism or Unionism? The New York Women's Trade Union League and the Labor Movement." *Feminist Studies* 3:111–25.

———. 1980. *As Equals and as Sisters: Feminism, the Labor Movement, and the Women's Trade Union League of New York.* Columbia: University of Missouri Press.

Eagleton, Terry. 1991. *Ideology: An Introduction.* London: Verso.

Edelman, Murray. 1957. "New Deal Sensitivity to Labor Interests." In *Labor and the New Deal,* ed. Milton Derber and Edwin Young, 157–92. Madison: University of Wisconsin Press.

"Effects of Unemployment on Workers' Wives." 1930. *Working Woman,* Feb., 3.

Ellis, Christine. 1981. "People Who Cannot Be Bought." In Lynd and Lynd 1981, 9–34.

Engels, Frederick. 1890. "Letters on Historical Materialism." In *The Marx-Engels Reader,* ed. Robert C. Tucker, 760–68. New York: Norton, 1978.

Enloe, Cynthia. 1983. *Does Khaki Become You? The Militarisation of Women's Lives.* Boston: South End Press.

Erlich, Howard S. 1977. "Populist Rhetoric Reassessed: A Paradox." *Quarterly Journal of Speech* 63:140–51.

"Families in N.Y. City Verge on Real Starvation." 1931. *Working Woman,* July, 7.

Faue, Elizabeth. 1991. *Community of Suffering and Struggle: Women, Men, and the Labor Movement in Minneapolis, 1915–1945.* Chapel Hill: University of North Carolina Press.

"Fighting the High Price of Meat." 1935. *Working Woman,* June, 8.

Fine, Sydney. 1969. *Sit-down: The General Motors Strike of 1936–1937.* Ann Arbor: University of Michigan Press.

Flynn, Elizabeth G. 1915. "Men and Women." In Baxandall 1987, 100–104.

———. 1916. "Problems Organizing Women." In Baxandall 1987, 134–38.

———. 1937a. "Greetings to the Women's Charter." Elizabeth Gurley Flynn Papers, Tamiment 118, box 2, folder 4, Tamiment Library/Robert F. Wagner Labor Archives, New York University Libraries.

———. 1937b. "I Have No Regrets." *Woman Today.* Elizabeth Gurley Flynn Papers, Tamiment 118, box 2, folder 15, Tamiment Library/Robert F. Wagner Labor Archives, New York University Libraries.

———. 1938a. "May Day." Elizabeth Gurley Flynn Papers, Tamiment 118, box 2, folder 17, Tamiment Library/Robert F. Wagner Labor Archives, New York University Libraries.

———. 1938b. "Recruit the Women to Our Party." Elizabeth Gurley Flynn Papers, Tamiment 118, box 2, folder 16, Tamiment Library/Robert F. Wagner Labor Archives, New York University Libraries.

———. 1938c. "Women of Steel." Elizabeth Gurley Flynn Papers, Tamiment 118, box 2, folder 16, Tamiment Library/Robert F. Wagner Labor Archives, New York University Libraries.

———. 1939. Untitled typewritten page. Elizabeth Gurley Flynn Papers, Tamiment 118, box 2, folder 30, Tamiment Library/Robert F. Wagner Labor Archives, New York University Libraries.

———. 1940a. *I Didn't Raise My Boy to Be a Soldier for Wall Street.* New York: Workers Library.

———. 1940b. "Schedule for Elizabeth Gurley Flynn." Elizabeth Gurley Flynn Papers, Tamiment 118, box 2, folder 12, Tamiment Library/Robert F. Wagner Labor Archives, New York University Libraries.

———. 1942a. *Daughters of America: Ella Reeve Bloor, Anita Whitney.* New York: Workers Library.

———. 1942b. *Women in the War.* New York: Workers Library.

———. 1943. "Meetings on Western Trip." Elizabeth Gurley Flynn Papers, Tamiment 118, box 2, folder 12, Tamiment Library/Robert F. Wagner Labor Archives, New York University Libraries.

———. n.d. "Brain of a Woman." Elizabeth Gurley Flynn Papers, Tamiment 118, box 2, folder 113, Tamiment Library/Robert F. Wagner Labor Archives, New York University Libraries.

———. n.d. "I Am a Communist Candidate." Elizabeth Gurley Flynn Papers, Tamiment 118, box 2, folder 8, Tamiment Library/Robert F. Wagner Labor Archives, New York University Libraries.

Foner, Philip S. 1979. *Women and the American Labor Movement.* Vol. 1, *From Colonial Times to the Eve of World War I.* New York: Free Press.

———. 1980. *Women and the American Labor Movement.* Vol. 2, *From World War I to the Present.* New York: Free Press.

"Food Workers in Chain Stores Build Union." 1930. *Working Woman,* Feb., 3.

"For a Free Happy Prosperous America." 1936. Handbill. Ella Reeve Bloor Papers, box 9, folder 1, Sophia Smith Collection, Smith College, Northampton, Massachusetts.

"Free Lunches, Supplies, Shoes and Clothing Demanded." 1931. *Working Woman,* Oct., 1.

Friends of the Workers Alliance. 1937. "Extra Good News." Elizabeth Gurley Flynn Papers, Tamiment 118, box 2, folder 4, Tamiment Library/Robert F. Wagner Labor Archives, New York University Libraries.

"From a Coal Town." 1935. *Working Woman,* May, 7.

"General Electric Sweats Girl Workers." 1935. *Working Woman,* Apr., 10.

"Girls in Nat'l Electric Who Ran 30 Machines Are Now Running 60." 1931. *Working Woman,* Mar., 3.

Glenn, Evelyn N. 1985. "Racial Ethnic Women's Labor: The Intersection of Race, Gender and Class Oppression." *Review of Radical Political Economics* 17:86–108.

"'Go Elegant'—on What?" 1933. *Working Woman,* Nov., 11.

Gosse, Van. 1987. "'It's for the Kids We Are Doing This': The IWW and the Practice of Family Solidarity." Unpublished manuscript in possession of author.

———. 1991. "'To Organize in Every Neighborhood, in Every Home': The Gender Politics of American Communists between the Wars." *Radical History Review* 50:109–41.

"Govt. Sneers at Jobless Delegation." 1931. *Working Woman,* Mar., 6.

Gray, Herman. 1989. "Television, Black Americans, and the American Dream." *Critical Studies in Mass Communication* 6:376–86.

Greenwald, Maurine W. 1980. *Women, War, and Work: The Impact of World War I on Women Workers in the United States.* Westport, Conn.: Greenwood.

Griffin, Cindy L. 1994. "Rhetoricizing Alienation: Mary Wollstonecraft and the Rhetorical Construction of Women's Oppression." *Quarterly Journal of Speech* 80:293–313.

Hall, Stuart. 1996. "The Problem of Ideology: Marxism without Guarantees." In *Stuart Hall: Critical Dialogues in Cultural Studies,* ed. David Morley and Kuan-Hsing Chen, 25–46. London: Routledge.

Hamlet, Janice D. 2000. "Assessing Womanist Thought: The Rhetoric of Susan L. Taylor." *Communication Quarterly* 48:420–36.

Hammerback, John C. 1994. "José Antonio's Rhetoric of Fascism." *Southern Communication Journal* 59:181–95.

Hapke, Laura. 1995. *Daughters of the Great Depression: Women, Work, and Fiction in the American 1930s.* Athens: University of Georgia Press.

Harding, Susan. 1993. "Rethinking Standpoint Epistemology: 'What Is Strong Objectivity?'" In *Feminist Epistemologies,* ed. Linda Alcoff and Elizabeth Potter, 49–82. New York: Routledge.

"Hardly a Day without a Wage Cut on One Job or Another in Murray Body." 1931. *Working Woman,* Mar., 3.

Harman, Chris. 1995. *Economics of the Madhouse: Capitalism and the Market Today.* London: Book Marks.

Hartsock, Nancy. 1987. "Rethinking Modernism: Minority vs. Majority Theories." *Cultural Critique* 7:187–206.

Hayden, Sara. 2003. "Family Metaphors and the Nation: Promoting a Politics of Care through the Million Mom March." *Quarterly Journal of Speech* 89:196–215.

Honey, Maureen. 1984. *Creating Rosie the Riveter: Class, Gender, and Propaganda during World War II.* Amherst: University of Massachusetts Press.

"How Can I Make My Husband Understand?" 1933. *Working Woman,* June, 13.

Howe, Julia Ward. 1870. "Mothers' Day Proclamation." http://www.peace.ca /mothersdayproclamation.htm. Accessed 16 July 2006.

"How to Live on 95 Cents a Week or Less." 1931. *Working Woman,* June, 4.

Hutchins, Grace. 1934a. *Women Who Work.* New York: International.

———. 1934b. "You're Telling Me!" *Working Woman,* Oct., 11.

———. 1935. "Millions for Meat Barons; Beans for the Unemployed." *Working Woman,* June, 14.

Huxman, Susan S. 1996. "Mary Wollstonecraft, Margaret Fuller, and Angelina

Grimké: Symbolic Convergence and a Nascent Rhetorical Vision." *Communication Quarterly* 44:16–28.

"In Defense of Democracy." 1939. Handbill. Elizabeth Gurley Flynn Papers, Tamiment 118, box 2, folder 30, Tamiment Library/Robert F. Wagner Labor Archives, New York University Libraries.

"International Women's Day." 1931. *Working Woman,* Mar., 1.

"International Women's Day Finds Miners Wives in Big Strike Struggles." 1931. *Working Woman,* Mar., 2.

"I Visited Their Homes and Talked with Them." 1938. *Party Organizer,* Apr., 37–39.

Jacoby, Robin M. 1975. "The Women's Trade Union League and American Feminism." *Feminist Studies* 3:126–40.

Jablonski, Carol. 1988. "Rhetoric, Paradox, and the Movement for Women's Ordination in the Roman Catholic Church." *Quarterly Journal of Speech* 74:164–83.

Jameson, Fredric. 1979/80. "Reification and Utopia in Mass Culture." *Social Text* 1:130–48.

Jamieson, Kathleen H. 1988. *Eloquence in an Electronic Age: The Transformation of Political Speechmaking.* New York: Oxford University Press.

Janiewski, Dolores. 1983. "Flawed Victories: The Experiences of Black and White Women Workers in Durham during the 1930s." In *Decades of Discontent: The Women's Movement, 1920–1940,* ed. Lois Scharf and Joan M. Jensen, 85–109. Westport, Conn.: Greenwood.

Jensen, Joan M., and Sue Davidson, eds. 1984. *A Needle, a Bobbin, a Strike: Women Needleworkers in America.* Philadelphia: Temple University Press.

Jensen, Richard J., and John C. Hammerback. 1998. "'Your Tools Are Really the People': The Rhetoric of Robert Parris Moses." *Communication Monographs* 65:126–40.

Jetter, Alexis. 1997. "'What Is Your Wife Trying to Do—Shut Down the Chemical Industry?' The Housewives of Love Canal." Interview with Lois Gibbs. In Jetter, Orleck, and Taylor, *Politics of Motherhood,* 28–43.

Jetter, Alexis, Annelise Orleck, and Diana Taylor, eds. 1997. *The Politics of Motherhood: Activist Voices from Left to Right.* Hanover, N.H.: University Press of New England.

"Johnstown Working Women Get Their Wages Slashed." 1931. *Working Woman,* July, 3.

Jones, Gareth S. 1983. *Languages of Class: Studies in English Working-Class History, 1832–1982.* Cambridge: Cambridge University Press.

Jones, Hayes. 1936. "Women in Calumet Steel Area Organize to Aid Drive in Mills." *Daily Worker,* 9 Nov., 3.

Keith, William, and Kenneth Zagacki. 1992. "Rhetoric and Paradox in Scientific Revolutions." *Southern Communication Journal* 57:165–77.

Kendall, Kathleen E. 1974. "Frances Wright on Women's Rights: Eloquence versus Ethos." *Quarterly Journal of Speech* 60:58–69.

Kessler-Harris, Alice. 1981. *Women Have Always Worked: A Historical Overview.* Old Westbury, N.Y.: Feminist Press.

———. 1982. *Out to Work: A History of Wage-Earning Women in the United States.* New York: Oxford University Press.

Kirkwood, William G. 1992. "Narrative and the Rhetoric of Possibility." *Communication Monographs* 59:30–47.

Klehr, Harvey. 1978. *Communist Cadre: The Social Background of the American Communist Party Elite.* Stanford, Calif: Hoover Institution Publication.

Kling, S. 1935. "Miners' Wives Organize." *Working Woman,* Aug., 12.

Kraditor, Aileen S. 1965. *The Ideas of the Woman Suffrage Movement, 1890–1920.* Garden City, N.Y.: Anchor Books.

Kraus, Henry. 1937. *The Many and the Few: A Chronicle of the Dynamic Auto Workers.* Los Angeles: Plantin Press.

Laclau, Ernesto, and Chantal Mouffe. 1985. *Hegemony and Socialist Strategy: Towards a Radical Democratic Politics.* London: Verso.

Ladd-Taylor, Molly, and Lauri Umansky, eds. 1998. *"Bad" Mothers: The Politics of Blame in Twentieth-Century America.* New York: New York University Press.

Lahne, Herbert J. 1944. *The Cotton Mill Workers.* New York: Farrar and Rinehart.

Larks, Goldie. 1934. "How Women Act in Strikes." *Working Woman,* Jan., 12.

Lasch, Christopher. 1977. *Haven in a Heartless World: The Family Besieged.* New York: Basic Books.

Lasky, Marjorie P. 1985. "'Where I Was a Person': The Ladies' Auxiliary in the 1934 Minneapolis Teamsters' Strikes." In Milkman 1985, 181–205.

"Laundry Workers Win Strike." 1933. *Working Woman,* June, 11.

"Laundry Worker Tells of Speedup." 1930. *Working Woman,* June, 5.

"The Lawrence Strike." 1931. *Working Woman,* Apr., 8.

"Legion Leaders Approve Action." 1939. Unattributed newspaper clipping. Elizabeth Gurley Flynn Papers, Tamiment 118, box 2, folder 30, Tamiment Library/Robert F. Wagner Labor Archives, New York University Libraries.

"Lessons from Needle Trades." 1934. *Party Organizer,* May/June, 57–59.

"Letter to Flynn." 1940. Elizabeth Gurley Flynn Papers, Tamiment 118, box 2, folder 31, Tamiment Library/Robert F. Wagner Labor Archives, New York University Libraries.

Levine, Susan. 1983. "Labor's True Woman: Domesticity and Equal Rights in the Knights of Labor." *Journal of American History* 70:323–39.

Lewis, Cora. 1933. "We Strike and Win." *Working Woman,* Aug., 9.

Linkugel, Wil A. 1963. "The Woman Suffrage Argument of Anna Howard Shaw." *Quarterly Journal of Speech* 49:165–74.

Loader, Jayne. 1975. "Women on the Left, 1906–1941: Bibliography of Primary Sources." *The University of Michigan Papers in Women's Studies* 2, no. 1:9–82.

"Lodge 500 Welcomes Elizabeth G. Flynn." 1938. Elizabeth Gurley Flynn Papers, Tamiment 118, box 2, folder 16, Tamiment Library/Robert F. Wagner Labor Archives, New York University Libraries.

Long, Priscilla. 1985. "The Women of the Colorado Fuel and Iron Strike, 1913–14." In Milkman 1985, 52–85.

"Los Angeles Women's Councils." 1934. *Working Woman,* Aug., 7.

"Lot of Women Cotton Pickers Hard." 1931. *Working Woman,* May, 3.

"Lower Ohio Valley Section, Communist Party." 1938. Elizabeth Gurley Flynn Papers, Tamiment 118, box 2, folder 12, Tamiment Library/Robert F. Wagner Labor Archives, New York University Libraries.

"Low Wages Throws Women on Streets." 1934. *Working Woman,* Jan., 13.

Lynch, Helen. 1931. "Woman Nat'l Hunger March Delegate Tells of the Life of Jobless, Homeless Women." *Working Woman,* Dec., 5.

Lynch, Timothy P. 2001. *Strike Songs of the Depression.* Jackson: University Press of Mississippi.

Lynd, Alice, and Staughton Lynd, eds. 1981. *Rank and File: Personal Histories by Working-Class Organizers.* Princeton: Princeton University Press.

Matthaei, Julie A. 1982. *An Economic History of Women in America: Women's Work, the Sexual Division of Labor, and the Development of Capitalism.* New York: Schocken.

Mattina, Anne F. 1994. "'Rights as Well as Duties': The Rhetoric of Leonora O'Reilly." *Communication Quarterly* 42:196–205.

———. 2002. "'Don't Let Them Step on You': Gender, Class and Ethnicity in the Rhetoric of the Great Strikes, 1909–1913." Paper presented at the 2002 National Communication Association Annual Conference, New Orleans.

Mattingly, Carol. 2002. "Telling Evidence: Rethinking What Counts in Rhetoric." *Rhetoric Society Quarterly* 32:99–108.

McClearey, Kevin E. 1994. "'A Tremendous Awakening': Margaret H. Sanger's Speech at Fabian Hall." *Western Journal of Communication* 58:182–200.

McGee, Michael. 1975. "In Search of 'The People': A Rhetorical Alternative." *Quarterly Journal of Speech* 61:235–49.

———. 1980. "The 'Ideograph': A Link between Rhetoric and Ideology." *Quarterly Journal of Speech* 66:113–33.

McKerrow, Raymie. 1989. "Critical Rhetoric: Theory and Praxis." *Communication Monographs* 56:91–111.

"Men Say They Are Legionnaires." 1939. *Des Moines Register.* 8 Sept. Elizabeth Gurley Flynn Papers, Tamiment 118, box 2, folder 30, Tamiment Library/Robert F. Wagner Labor Archives, New York University Libraries.

"Milk for Our Babies." 1935. *Working Woman,* June, 8–9.

Milkman, Ruth. 1976. "Women's Work and Economic Crisis: Some Lessons of the Great Depression." *The Review of Radical Political Economics* 8:73–94.

———, ed. 1985. *Women, Work and Protest: A Century of Women's Labor History.* London: Routledge and Kegan Paul.

"Mills Shut Down!—No Jobs—No Pay." 1933. *Working Woman,* May, 4.

"Miner's Wife Tells of Hunger in Penn." 1931. *Working Woman,* July, 8.

Mishler, Paul C. 1999. *Raising Reds: The Young Pioneers, Radical Summer Camps, and Communist Political Culture in the United States.* New York: Columbia University Press.

Mitchell, Agnes. 1931. "Babies in Mine Region Had to Live on Coffee." *Working Woman,* Aug., 2.

Morrison, Louise. 1931. "Chicago Workers Win Bread Strike." *Working Woman,* Apr., 2.

"Mother of Four in Mine Region Writes." 1931. *Working Woman,* Sept., 4.

Mullen, Bill, and Sherry L. Linkon, eds. 1996. *Radical Revisions: Rereading 1930s Culture.* Urbana: University of Illinois Press.

Murphy, John M. 1992. "Epideictic and Deliberative Strategies in Opposition to

War: The Paradox of Honor and Expediency." *Communication Studies* 43:65–78.

"My Life: A True Story by a Negro Worker of the South." 1934. *Working Woman,* Oct., 10.

National Center for Children in Poverty. 2006. http://www.nccp.org/pub_lic06 .html. Accessed 14 July 2006.

"Nat. Textile Union Leads 10,000 in Lawrence Strike." 1931. *Working Woman,* Mar., 1.

"Negro Widow Cheated." 1933. *Working Woman,* May, 16.

"Negro Women Tell of Speed-Up in Laundries." 1930. *Working Woman,* Feb., 3.

"Negro Workers Doubly Exploited." 1930. *Working Woman,* Sept., 3.

Nekola, Charlotte, and Paula Rabinowitz, eds. 1987. *Writing Red: An Anthology of American Women Writers, 1930–1940.* New York: Feminist Press.

Nelson, Jeffrey. 1985. "Homosexuality in Hollywood Films: A Contemporary Paradox." *Critical Studies in Mass Communication* 2:54–64.

Nelson, Rose. 1935a. "Our Next Task." *Working Woman,* Sept., 9.

———. 1935b. "We Strike for Cheap Meat." *Working Woman,* July, 3.

New York State Committee Socialist Party. 1918. Letter. Ella Reeve Bloor Papers, box 9, folder 1, Sophia Smith Collection, Smith College, Northampton, Massachusetts.

"Nine Mass Meetings." n.d. Handbill. Ella Reeve Bloor Papers, box 9, folder 1, Sophia Smith Collection, Smith College, Northampton, Massachusetts.

"No Jobs—No Relief." 1933. *Working Woman,* May, 14.

"Northwest Canneries Work Women Workers Hard; Pay Is Low and Work Seasonal." 1931. *Working Woman,* July, 3.

Nowicki, Stella. 1981. "Back of the Yards." In Lynd and Lynd 1981, 67–88.

Ocken, Sophia. 1937. "A Mother and Child Unit." *Party Organizer,* July, 35–37.

"Ohio Children in Hunger March." 1932. *Daily Worker,* 1 Aug., 2.

Olmsted, Audrey Perryman. 1971. "Agitator on the Left: The Speechmaking of Elizabeth Gurley Flynn, 1904–1964." Ph.D. diss., Indiana University.

Ono, Kent A., and John M. Sloop. 1995. "The Critique of Vernacular Discourse." *Communication Monographs* 62:19–46.

O'Reilly, Leonora. 1904. Untitled Speech to Shirtwaist Makers at Clinton Hall. Leonora O'Reilly Papers, microfilm, reel 9, Schlesinger Library, Radcliffe Institute for Advanced Study, Cambridge, Massachusetts.

———. 1911a. "Looking over the Fields." *American Suffragette.* Leonora O'Reilly Papers, microfilm, reel 9, Schlesinger Library, Radcliffe Institute for Advanced Study, Cambridge, Massachusetts.

———. 1911b. Untitled. *Life and Labor,* Aug., 227.

"Organize the Farm Women." 1934. *Party Organizer,* May/June, 59–60.

Orleck, Annelise. 1995. *Common Sense and a Little Fire: Women and Working-Class Politics in the United States, 1900–1965.* Chapel Hill: University of North Carolina Press.

Ottanelli, Fraser M. 1991. *The Communist Party of the United States: From the Depression to World War II.* New Brunswick, N.J.: Rutgers University Press.

Patton, John H. 1973. "The Eagleton Phenomenon in the 1972 Presidential Campaign: A Case Study in the Rhetoric of Paradox." *Central States Speech Journal* 24:278–87.

Pear, Robert, and David D. Kirkpatrick. 2004. "Bush Plans $1.5 Billion Drive for Promotion of Marriage." *New York Times,* 14 Jan.

"Penna. Shirt Girls Get Wage Cuts and Many Are Jobless." 1931. *Working Woman,* May, 3.

Perry, A. 1937. "Building Women's Trade Union Auxiliaries." *Party Organizer,* Jan., 10–12.

Pervin, Bella. 1934. "Women Leagues Help Philadelphia Milk Drivers Strike." *Working Woman,* Jan., 6.

Pierce, Marie Harrison. 1936. "Some Problems in Our Women's Work." *Party Organizer,* Oct., 16–19.

*Pittsburgh Workers School.* 1938. Booklet. Elizabeth Gurley Flynn Papers, Tamiment 118, box 2, folder 16, Tamiment Library/Robert F. Wagner Labor Archives, New York University Libraries.

"Plymouth Is Still America." 1939. Handbill. Elizabeth Gurley Flynn Papers, Tamiment 118, box 2, folder 30, Tamiment Library/Robert F. Wagner Labor Archives, New York University Libraries.

Poulakos, John. 1984. "Rhetoric, the Sophists, and the Possible." *Communication Monographs* 51:215–26.

Price, J. 1936. "Hunger, Suffering by Appointment." *Daily Worker,* 19 Oct., 7.

"Public Hearings in Detroit, Flint and Other Cities Show Extent and Depth of Misery." 1931. *Working Woman,* Dec., 8.

Rabinowitz, Paula. 1991. *Labor and Desire: Women's Revolutionary Fiction in Depression America.* Chapel Hill: University of North Carolina Press.

"Rally to Win the War." 1942. Handbill. Ella Reeve Bloor Papers, box 9, folder 1, Sophia Smith Collection, Smith College, Northampton, Massachusetts.

Rand, Barbara. 1931. "Womenfolk in Mine Area Handle Their Pressing Problems." *Working Woman,* Sept., 2.

Reeve, Carl. 1937. "Mother Bloor's Children." In Todes and Small 1937, 6, 28.

Reish, F. 1933. "We Win Lower Rent." *Working Woman,* Mar., 15.

Rich, Dora. 1934. "Mothers, Shall Our Babies Have Milk?" *Working Woman,* July, 12.

Robinson, Henry. 1931. "Public Hearing Testimony Reveals Much City Suffering." *Working Woman,* Dec., 2.

Sallee, Mary. 1933. "Sweatshops Strike." *Working Woman,* Aug., 14.

Sanders, Sonya. 1938. "Story of a Woman's Day Unit." *Party Organizer,* Mar., 39–40.

"Scab Goes Nudist." 1936. *Daily Worker,* 27 Oct., 2.

Scharf, Lois. 1980. *To Work and to Wed: Female Employment, Feminism, and the Great Depression.* Westport, Conn.: Greenwood.

———. 1984. "The Great Uprising in Cleveland: When Sisterhood Failed." In Jensen and Davidson 1984, 146–66.

Schneider, Helen. 1936. "Chains and a Towel for Milady's Hands." *Daily Worker,* 30 Oct., 7.

Schwager, Esther. 1933. "We Help Them Strike." *Working Woman,* June, 7.

Scott, Melinda. 1915. Untitled manuscript. Leonora O'Reilly Papers, microfilm, reel 3, Schlesinger Library, Radcliffe Institute for Advanced Study, Cambridge, Massachusetts.

"Seattle Jobless Girls Forced to Seek Shelter, Food in City Prisons." 1931. *Working Woman,* May, 3.

Sepich, Fanny. 1931. "Miners' Children Forced to Go to School Barefoot." *Working Woman,* Aug., 2.

Shaffer, Robert. 1979. "Women and the Communist Party, USA, 1930–1940." *Socialist Review* 8:73–118.

Shavelson, Clara. 1935. "The Results of the 'Meat Strike.'" *Working Woman,* Aug., 7.

"Shoe Workers Strike." 1930. *Working Woman,* Jan., 3.

"Short Bread Strike in Phila. Is Won against Bosses." 1931. *Working Woman,* July, 2.

Shugart, Helene A., Catherine E. Waggoner, and D. Lynn O'Brien Hallstein. 2001. "Mediating Third-Wave Feminism: Appropriation as Postmodern Media Practice." *Critical Studies in Media Communication* 18:194–210.

Simons, Herbert W. 1972. "Persuasion in Social Conflicts: A Critique of Prevailing Conceptions and a Framework for Future Research." *Speech Monographs* 39:227–47.

"6 Girl Pickets Bring Out 300 at Ohio Plant." 1936. *Daily Worker,* 19 Oct., 3.

"Slaved at Paris Garter, Now Thrown Out on Streets to Starve." 1931. *Working Woman,* June, 3.

Small, Sasha. 1934. "Life *à la* Ladies Home Journal." *Working Woman,* July, 10.

———. 1935. "Woman's Place in the United States Today—Is It in the Home?" *Working Woman,* Apr., 3.

Smith, Carrie. 1933. "We Strike and Win." *Working Woman,* Aug., 8.

Smith, Mary. 1930. "Women in the Mining Struggle." *Working Woman,* Sept., 3.

Solnit, Rebecca. 2005. "The Housewife Theory of History." *Orion,* May–June, online http://www.alternet.org/story/22186. Accessed 28 July 2005.

"Special Attention to Problems of Women Workers." 1933. *Party Organizer,* Feb., 65–68.

"Special Course on 4 Saturday Afternoons." 1937. Handbill. Elizabeth Gurley Flynn Papers, Tamiment 118, box 2, folder 4, Tamiment Library/Robert F. Wagner Labor Archives, New York University Libraries.

Stachel, Jack. 1937. Untitled tribute. In Todes and Small 1937, 17–18.

Stanton, Elizabeth C. 1892. "The Solitude of Self." In Campbell, *Man Cannot Speak for Her,* vol. 2, 371–84.

Staub, Michael. 1994. *Voices of Persuasion: Politics of Representation in 1930s America.* Cambridge: Cambridge University Press.

"Steel Drive Is Spurred by Women." 1936. *Daily Worker,* 23 Oct., 3.

Stevens, Ethel. 1937. "Building a Women's Steel Unit in the Strike Area." *Party Organizer,* Sept., 14–16.

"Story of the Militant Labor Movement." 1938. Handbill. Elizabeth Gurley Flynn Papers, Tamiment 118, box 2, folder 16, Tamiment Library/Robert F. Wagner Labor Archives, New York University Libraries.

Strom, Sharon H. 1983. "Challenging 'Woman's Place': Feminism, the Left, and Industrial Unionism in the 1930s." *Feminist Studies* 9:359–86.

Sugar, Maurice. 1980. *The Ford Hunger March.* Berkeley, Calif.: Meiklejohn Civil Liberties Institute.

Tax, Meredith. 1980. *The Rising of the Women: Feminist Solidarity and Class Conflict, 1880–1917.* New York: Monthly Review Press.

"They Got the Shoes!" 1933. *Working Woman,* May, 15.

Thompson, Julie M. 1995. "Incarcerated Souls: Women as Individuals in Margaret Fuller's Woman in the Nineteenth Century." *Communication Quarterly* 43:53–63.

Thompson, Louise. 1937. "Negro Women in Our Party." *Party Organizer,* 25–27.

Todes, Charlotte. 1931. "Mother Bloor—A Fighter of the Working Class for Many Years." *Working Woman,* July, 6.

Todes, Charlotte, and Sasha Small, eds. 1937. *Mother Bloor Seventy-fifth Birthday Souvenir Book.* New York: Mother Bloor Celebration Committee.

"Toledo Jobless Seize Groceries." 1932. *Daily Worker,* 14 Sept., 1.

Tompkins, Phillip K. 1976. "On 'Paradoxes' in the Rhetoric of the New England Transcendentalists." *Quarterly Journal of Speech* 62:40–48.

Tonn, Mari B. 1995. "Elizabeth Gurley Flynn's *Sabotage:* 'Scene' as Both Controlling and Catalyzing Acts." *Southern Communication Journal* 61: 59–75.

———. 1996. "Militant Motherhood: Labor's Mary Harris 'Mother' Jones." *Quarterly Journal of Speech* 82:1–21.

Trast, Jenny. 1937. "Women's Clubs in the United Front." *Party Organizer,* May, 21–24.

Triece, Mary E. 1999. "The Practical True Woman: Reconciling Women and Work in Popular Mail-order Magazines, 1900–1920." *Critical Studies in Mass Communication* 16:42–62.

———. 2000. "Rhetoric and Social Change: Women's Struggles for Economic and Political Equality, 1900–1917." *Women's Studies in Communication* 23:238–60.

———. 2001. *Protest and Popular Culture: Women in the U.S. Labor Movement, 1894–1917.* Boulder, Colo.: Westview.

———. 2002. "Framing Miss-conduct: The Rhetoric of Paradox in the Struggle of Cleveland Conductorets during World War I." *Women's Studies in Communication* 25:197–222.

———. 2003. "Appealing to the 'Intelligent Worker': Rhetorical Reconstitution and the Influence of Firsthand Experience in the Rhetoric of Leonora O'Reilly." *Rhetoric Society Quarterly* 33:5–24.

Turner, Lowell, and Richard W. Hurd. 2001. "Building Social Movement Unionism: The Transformation of the American Labor Movement." In *Rekindling the Movement: Labor's Quest for Relevance in the Twenty-first Century,* ed. Lowell Turner, Harry C. Katz, and Richard W. Hurd, 9–26. Ithaca, N.Y.: ILR Press.

"Unemployed Women Raise Voices." 1934. *Working Woman,* Feb., 6.

"A Unit of Steel Women." 1937. *Party Organizer,* July, 22–23.

Van Veen, Sadie. 1931a. "Negro Women and the Elections." *Working Woman,* Sept., 7.

———. 1931b. "Women Show Determination to Fight Evictions; For Cash Relief from the Government." *Working Woman*, Dec., 6.

———. 1931c. "Women's Issues in the New York Elections; Relief to Jobless Is the Main Issue." *Working Woman*, Oct., 8.

———. 1934. "Mrs. Roosevelt's 'Sweet' Promises." *Working Woman*, Jan., 3.

Victor, Sarah. 1930. "Slavery in Auto Plant." *Working Woman*, June, 3.

Vorse, Mary Heaton. 1969. *Labor's New Millions*. New York: Modern Age Books.

Ware, B. L., and Wil A. Linkugel. 1973. "They Spoke in Defense of Themselves: On the Generic Criticism of Apologia." *Quarterly Journal of Speech* 59:273–83.

Ware, Susan. 1982. *American Women in the 1930s: Holding Their Own*. Boston: Twayne.

Warren, Elizabeth, and Amelia W. Tyagi. 2003. *The Two-Income Trap: Why Middle-Class Mothers and Fathers Are Going Broke*. New York: Basic Books.

"Watch Your Manners." 1936. *Daily Worker*, 19 Oct., 7.

Watson, Martha. 1999. *Lives of Their Own: Rhetorical Dimensions in Autobiographies of Women Activists*. Columbia, S.C.: University of South Carolina Press.

"Weary 'Marchers' Reach the Capital." 1931. *New York Times*, 7 Dec., 1.

Weigand, Kate. 2001. *Red Feminism: American Communism and the Making of Women's Liberation*. Baltimore: Johns Hopkins University Press.

Weiler, N. Sue. 1984. "The Uprising in Chicago: The Men's Garment Workers Strike, 1910–1911." In Jensen and Davidson 1984, 114–45.

Wells, Agnes. 1931. "From a Working Woman." *New Masses*, Apr., 2.

Welter, Barbara. 1966. "The Cult of True Womanhood: 1820–1860." *American Quarterly* 18:151–74.

"We Need Women Fighters for Unemployment Relief." 1931. *Working Woman*, Mar., 6.

"Western Electric Speed-Up—Lay Off." 1930. *Working Woman*, June, 3.

Whedbee, Karen. 2001. "Perspective by Incongruity in Norman Thomas's 'Some Wrong Roads to Peace.'" *Western Journal of Communication* 65:45–64.

Williams, Raymond. 1973. "Base and Superstructure in Marxist Cultural Theory." *New Left Review* 82:3–16.

———. 1977. *Marxism and Literature*. New York: Oxford University Press.

*With Babies and Banners*. 1978. New York: New Day Films.

"Woman Domestic Worker Given Garbage to Eat." 1931. *Working Woman*, May, 3.

"Women Auxiliaries Aid." 1931. *Working Woman*, Aug., 1.

"Women Especially." 1918. Handbill. Ella Reeve Bloor Papers, box 9, folder 1, Sophia Smith Collection, Smith College, Northampton, Massachusetts.

"Women Halt Train." 1936. *Daily Worker*, 21 Oct., 3.

"Women Help Lead Picketing of Struck Mines." 1931. *Working Woman*, July, 8.

"Women in Michigan Auto Cities Tell of Need for Jobless Insurance." 1931. *Working Woman*, Dec., 8.

Women's Commission, Central Committee. 1937. "Mother Bloor's Seventy-fifth Birthday." *The Communist*, July, 672–74.

Women's Commission, Communist Party New York State. 1938. Letter. Elizabeth Gurley Flynn Papers, Tamiment 118, box 2, folder 16, Tamiment Library/Robert F. Wagner Labor Archives, New York University Libraries.

"Women's Work in the Shops." 1930. *Party Organizer,* Feb., 12–14.

"Women Workers Being Poisoned; Pay Low; Speed-up Growing." 1930. *Working Woman,* Feb., 3.

Wood, Julia T., and Charles Conrad. 1983. "Paradox in the Experiences of Professional Women." *Western Journal of Speech Communication* 47:305–22.

"Work among Women." 1931. *Party Organizer,* Sept./Oct., 30.

"Work among Women in the Mining Fields." 1934. *Party Organizer,* Apr., 23–25.

"Working Women Fighting Hard against Wage Cuts, High Costs, Other Miseries." 1931. *Working Woman,* May, 1.

"Working Women Wage Winning Fight on High Costs Meat, Bread." 1931. *Working Woman,* June, 4.

"Work Side by Side with Men, Fight Side by Side with Them." 1931. *Working Woman,* Mar., 1.

"Young People's Forum." 1937. Handbill. Elizabeth Gurley Flynn Papers, Tamiment 118, box 2, folder 4, Tamiment Library/Robert F. Wagner Labor Archives, New York University Libraries.

Zaeske, Susan. 2002. "Signatures of Citizenship: The Rhetoric of Women's Antislavery Petitions." *Quarterly Journal of Speech* 88:147–69.

Zaretsky, Eli. 1976. *Capitalism, the Family and Personal Life.* Great Britain: Pluto Press.

# Index

**MARY E. TRIECE** is the author of *Protest and Popular Culture: Women in the U.S. Labor Movement.* Her articles have appeared in journals such as *Rhetoric Society Quarterly, Women's Studies in Communication,* and *Critical Studies in Mass Communication.* She is on the faculty of the School of Communication at the University of Akron.

The University of Illinois Press
is a founding member of the
Association of American University Presses.

---

Composed in 9/13 ITC Stone Serif
with ITC Stone Sans display
by Type One, LLC
for the University of Illinois Press
Designed by Paula Newcomb
Manufactured by Thomson-Shore, Inc.

University of Illinois Press
1325 South Oak Street
Champaign, IL 61820-6903
www.press.uillinois.edu